The Dryad Book of
BOBBIN LACE

Frontispiece
Sara Lett of Olney making lace at the beginning of the twentieth century. Note the lacemaker's lamp, pillow and stand, bobbin-winder and very large parchment pattern

The Dryad Book of BOBBIN LACE

Raie Clare

DRYAD PRESS LTD   LONDON

To my husband John

ACKNOWLEDGMENT

I want to record my thanks to all those who
helped, without whom I could not have
completed the work, and especially the
following: my husband John; Julie de Vonald;
Marion Aaron; Mary Bradbury; Pat Coopland;
Lyn Davy; Irene Hotchin; Elaine Lyall; Agnes
Morgan (my mother); Eileen Smithson; Enid
Taylor; and the photographer John Black.

ISBN 0 8521 9710 1

Typeset by Keyspools Ltd, Golborne, Lancs.
and printed in Great Britain by
Anchor Brendon Ltd
Tiptree, Essex
for the publishers
Dryad Press Ltd
8 Cavendish Square
London W1M 0AJ

Contents

Introduction

Bobbin lace-making has been practised in Britain since the Huguenots settled here in the mid-sixteenth century, although Richard III is known to have worn lace at his coronation in 1485. This lace, however, is thought to have had foreign origins. Other types of lace such as netting and needlepoint are much older.

Bobbin lace might look complicated, but basically there are only two simple movements to learn (which can be mastered in five minutes), and a small number of extra techniques to grasp at a later stage. The stitches are common to all types of bobbin lace. The technique is very similar to weaving except each thread is attached separately to a bobbin. This gives the characteristic appearance to a lace pillow and provides infinite flexibility in the movement and placing of bobbins. It is this flexibility which gives scope to the endless variations of patterns and effects. It is also this which, for some students, causes problems when first learning lace-making.

A typical lace edging consists of a headside, which is usually scalloped, and a footside, which is usually plain and straight. The area between the two sides, unless very narrow, is filled with extra pattern details. The background is filled in with 'ground', which is a mesh background worked in many different variations. An insertion, being sewn on *both* sides, has a footside on both sides.

In this country lace is worked with the straight footside on the right and the headside on the left, whereas on the Continent and in the USA the opposite applies.

These types of lace are technically known as trolly lace which means that the same number of pairs of bobbins remains in the lace throughout the piece. Three features appear consistently in trolly lace, they are: a) the lace has a close mesh background; b) it is worked on a diagonal line, a small section at a time; c) the number of bobbins remains the same throughout the working of the lace (with later exceptions for advanced lace-makers).

Bedfordshire lace, which is covered in Chapter 2, is a guipure lace. It has an open background behind the main pattern areas, which are linked with bars. It is therefore quicker to work (having larger holes in the lace), very light and pretty, but not quite so strong because of the gaps instead of a solid ground. You must choose your size of thread with these factors in mind.

The fourth type of lace covered in this book is often called Russian lace as it is made extensively in that country and in Eastern Europe. It is basically a 'tape lace', consisting of a narrow braid which is worked with a great variety of design, but always within the discipline of the narrow meandering band. Where the bands come alongside each other, they are linked together. This type of lace is easy to do (the easiest in fact) but can be rather boring and repetitive.

The final type of lace, featured in the last five patterns is usually known as Honiton. I prefer to call it 'sectional lace', or 'pictorial lace', the latter because it is usually in the form of a picture (though not in Pattern 1, Chapter 4), the former because it is made in separate sections and not all in one piece as are the other four laces. There were also other types of lace made in the Honiton area. In a European context it is important to note that Honiton is only one of many laces made in sections, as will be discovered when you work through the fourth chapter, which has adaptations of designs from Milan and Valenciennes.

This book assumes no previous knowledge of making pillow lace. It is a complete beginner's guide to lace-making, explaining all the necessary stitches and techniques in detail. Chapter 1 covers torchon lace because, whilst not the easiest lace to learn, it is ideal for the beginner as, once understood, it provides the key to all other types of lace. Thus, once Chapter 1 is mastered, the student may follow with any of the other chapters. Stitch-by-stitch instructions are given for the first four patterns, and then for each new technique as it is encountered. The chapter includes 14 patterns for a variety of different articles, with an enlarged working diagram and an illustration of the finished lace for each one. The final two pieces, which are test pieces for pure pleasure, do not include illustrations as I am sure you will be able to do them without further help, so long as you work exactly one quarter of the mat at a time, starting at the corner. I suggest that you mark in guidelines on your pattern so that you can pick out the quarters.

1 *Preparation*

THREAD-SIZING CHART

I devised this chart some 15 years ago and the patterns have always worked out correctly, so it can be relied on.

You will need some stiff acetate film; washed X-ray plates are ideal. On to the film make an accurate copy of this thread guide, by tracing over the writing and pricking in the dots.

To use the guide, place it over the pattern or lace you wish to copy, so that you can see one section at a time, and check whether that section is pricked at exactly the same distance apart as the pattern or lace you are looking at; it must be identical in every direction before you accept it as the correct one.

Then look at the relevant linen thread size written underneath it on the chart, and that will be the correct size of linen thread. If you wish to use a different thread (e.g. cotton), flick through the list of thread requirements at the beginning of each new pattern in this book and you will soon find listed an alternative thread of the same size as the linen; I list many alternatives for this reason. It is pointless to include a graduated list of thread sizes, since they are so frequently discontinued and new threads introduced; this comparison with the old threads is the safest way, as they are standard sizes.

To compare threads, it is helpful both to look at them (obviously), but also to run them through your fingers: this is often more accurate than doing it by eye.

USING THE PATTERNS

These patterns are designed so that the lace can easily be made as a continuous length if required.

It will be found that the end of the pricking exactly dovetails into the beginning. Thus, to work a continuous length on the pillow, it is suggested that you prick the pattern by fixing it on to your pricking card and pricking through each hole as accurately as possible. Next, cut off the lower section as indicated by the dotted line. This 'floating section' can then be used both at the beginning and end of the pattern in the following way:

Make a pad to go under the floating section. You can either stick several layers of felt together like a contour map of a hill, each layer being smaller than the one beneath, or you can use $\frac{1}{2}$in thick foam or rubberised underfelt, cutting all the edges in a slanting fashion so that you end up with gently bevelled edges. The pad should be about 4in long.

Pin down the main section of pricked card on to the pillow and work it. When nearing the bottom of this section, pin the floating section into place at the bottom, putting the pad under it, sliding any extra length under the end of the main section. Continue making lace until every pin-hole in the floating section has been used, then remove any pins remaining in the main section.

Next, fold the lower end of the worker-cloth back over the bobbins like a bag and pin the bobbins into small sections within the cloth in order to keep them tidily in the correct position. The floating section can now be prised gently away from the pillow and carefully eased into its new position, jig-sawed into place at the top of the pricking. All this time, the bobbins in the improvised bag must be supported so that they do not pull down from the unattached lace. Push the section down onto the pillow and the tips of

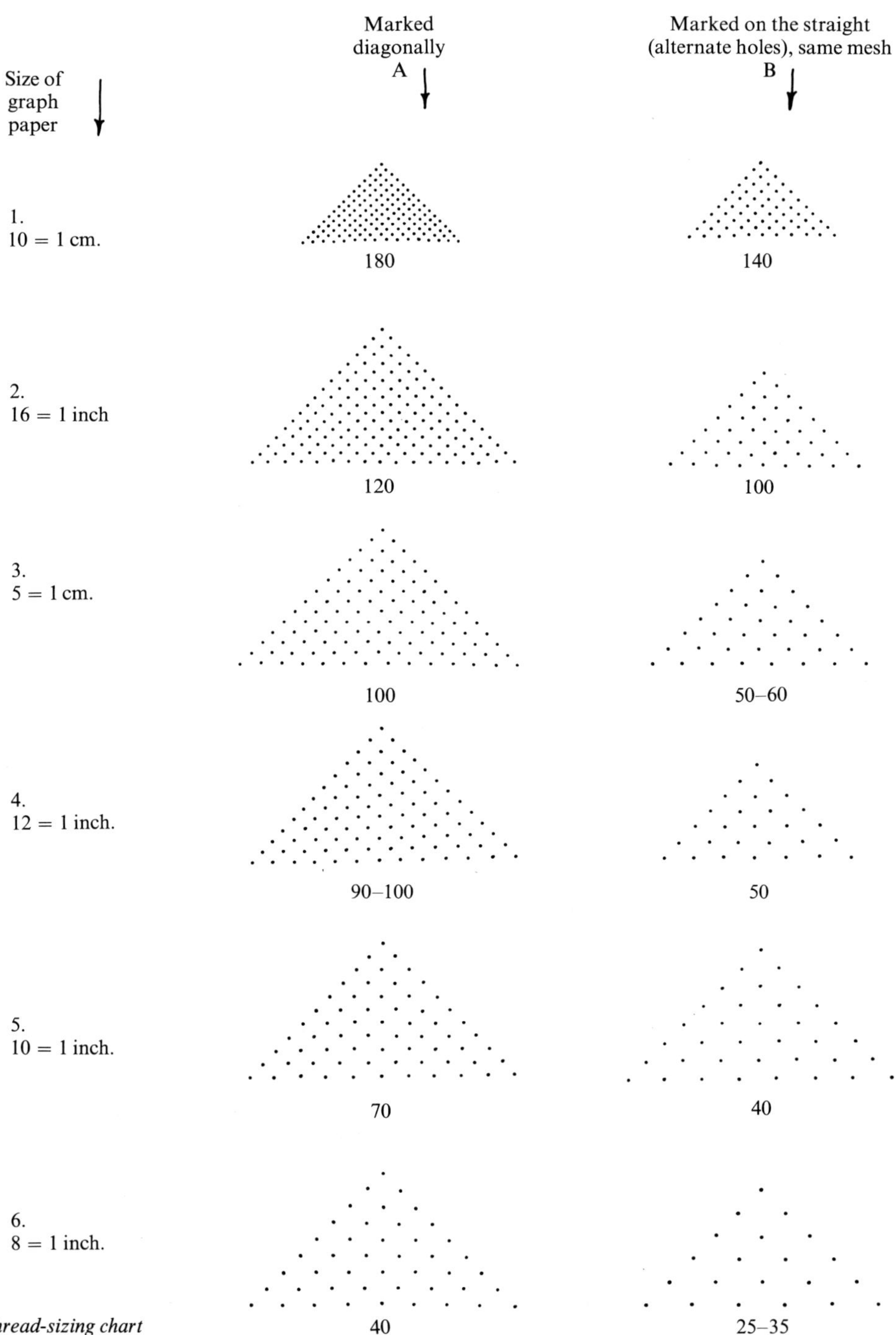

Fig 1 *Thread-sizing chart*

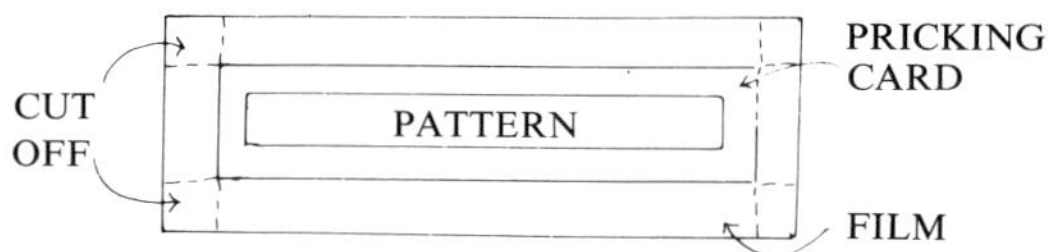

Fig 2 *Aid to pricking card*

pins sticking through the pad will fix the section into its new place. Some of the pins may need lifting up a little and replacing if they are at too much of an angle, but they will not need to be lifted right out of the pricking and the lace. You can now release the bobbins from their 'bag', replace the worker-cloth and continue working. Note: The 'worker-cloth' is the cloth which a lace-maker lays over the lower part of the pricking, on which bobbins lie as she works.

If you wish to avoid the trouble (and possible mistakes) involved in marking the lines on your pricking card, there is a simple remedy. Cut out the pattern and lay it on your pricking card. Cut the card $\frac{1}{4}$in larger all round than the pattern. To ensure accurate placement fix the pattern to the pricking card by a smear of paste on the back or a strip of sticky tape at the top and bottom.

Next you need some coloured transparent sticky-backed film: blue is best. Cut out a piece $\frac{3}{4}$in larger all round than the pricking card. Before removing the backing, lay the card on the film and cut out the four corner sections indicated in Fig 2. Now remove the backing and stick the film on carefully to avoid wrinkles, folding the surplus edges over to the back to fix it securely. It may be easier to lay the pattern on the film rather than vice versa.

If you cannot obtain coloured transparent film, then you can use clear sticky-backed film (or wide sticky-backed tape) as long as you paint over the pattern first with water-colour paint. If you leave it white, working on it will be confusing and difficult, as the threads will not show up.

Having done all this, you are now ready to prick the pattern as usual.

The numbers at the top of patterns indicate the pinholes where pairs of bobbins are to be hung as you start working. For example, where a 2 is written above a pinhole, you hang on two pairs of bobbins round that pin. Each line on the working diagrams indicates *a pair* of threads.

ABBREVIATIONS

LH: left-hand
RH: right-hand
st(s): stitch(es)
hc st(s): honeycomb stitch(es)
$\frac{1}{2}$st: half stitch
WS: whole stitch
pr(s): pair(s)

NOTES FOR BEGINNERS

Materials

a pillow
10 pairs of bobbins with spangles
a pricker and needle
pricking card
a pricking board
DMC Cordonnet cotton thread no. 50
a packet of medium brass or stainless steel pins
scissors

Lace-making is not as difficult as it looks. It is always surprising, at first, to learn that all pillow lace is made with a very small number of different stitches, the three main variations of which will be taught in Pattern 1.

Once you have learned these basic stitches the chief difficulty will be to learn which bobbins to use. Confronted with 20 or so bobbins this may seem daunting. However, when you find that bobbins are used in pairs, the number is halved immediately. Once you have mastered the basic logic, you will quickly understand how to work the patterns.

TWO TYPES OF LACE PILLOW

Typical lace pillow

Materials

chipboard, 18in square, $\frac{1}{2}$in thick
2 pieces of calico 20in square (each)
plain dark material (e.g. casement or gaberdine) in dark green, blue or brown, 26in square. (You could probably manage using half the width of a 48in fabric.)
straw or hay or wood wool, elastic or string

a) Turn up and sew a $\frac{1}{2}$in single hem on one side of each calico square, for the open end.

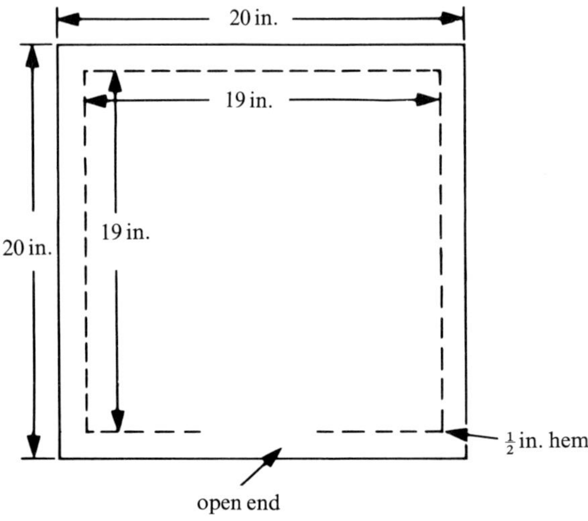

Fig 3 *Making lace pillow*

b) Seam the other three sides together with ½in turnings. You now have a 19in square bag, as in Fig 3.

c) Turn right side out and slip the board into the bag.

d) Now sew up 6in at each end of the open side, thus leaving a large gap in the middle.

e) Through this gap, stuff the top side with straw or hay or wood wool *as hard as possible*. (If you use straw, ensure that it is cut up first.) Bang with a rolling pin (or similar) and stuff again. Keep doing this until you can't stuff in another straw. This is quite tough work but it is essential to keep on until it is rock-hard.

f) Sew up remainder of open end. This is difficult and I sew it up roughly first, then I can do it tightly the second time.

g) Make a slip cover of the dark material, making a hem all round, with a gap through which you thread elastic or string and draw up tightly on the pillow.

Sectional lace pillow

This is particularly useful for painlessly moving up the lace and turning corners.

From a sheet of expanded polystyrene or similar material, approximately 1in thick, cut one piece 17in × 17in; two pieces 5½in × 17in; three pieces 5½in × 5½in.

Cover all pieces with dark plain cloth (stick or stitch).

Stick B to left-hand side of A.

Arrange D, E and F down the centre of A so that they fit snugly (loose not stuck).

Stick C to A to hold D, E and F firmly between B and C.

Using a sectional lace pillow

Pin the top of the pricking on to the middle section E overlapping on to the bottom section F. Work the pricking down the middle section E until you come to the join with bottom section F.

Remove the top section D. Push the middle and bottom sections E and F up, and D becomes the bottom section.

A small additional 'floating' section of the pricking, about 3in long, is used to 'leap-frog' onto the next section when you reach the end of the main pricking.

Continue to make lace using the 'main' and 'floating' pricking, moving the three sections of the pillow as described above.

Spangling

If the bobbins have no spangles, hang seven glass beads on to the end of each bobbin by passing a 3in (8cm) long piece of brass or copper wire through the hole in the end of the bobbins. A single strand of wire untwisted from a rabbit snare or picture-hanging wire is ideal.

Hang three beads on each side of the bobbin, then a seventh bead (usually more ornamental and slightly bigger) on to the wire on one side. Link the ends of the wire and bend back ⅛in (0.4cm) on each side, cutting off the surplus. Press down this small piece against the wire with pliers so that there is not a rough edge to catch on the pillow or other bobbins. It is often possible to push this linked end into the hole of the centre bead to get a perfectly neat finish.

Winding bobbins

Wind six pairs of bobbins with no. 50 DMC Cordonnet cotton thread by holding the spangle end to the left, then wind about 1 yard of thread on to the thin neck by winding *away* from you. This direction is important or the bobbins will slip undone when working. Do not cut off the thread yet. Make a hitch as in Fig 5 by making a loop in the thread with the free end *behind* the thread coming from the bobbin. Then place the top of this loop over the head of the bobbin and

Fig 4 *Making a sectional lace pillow*

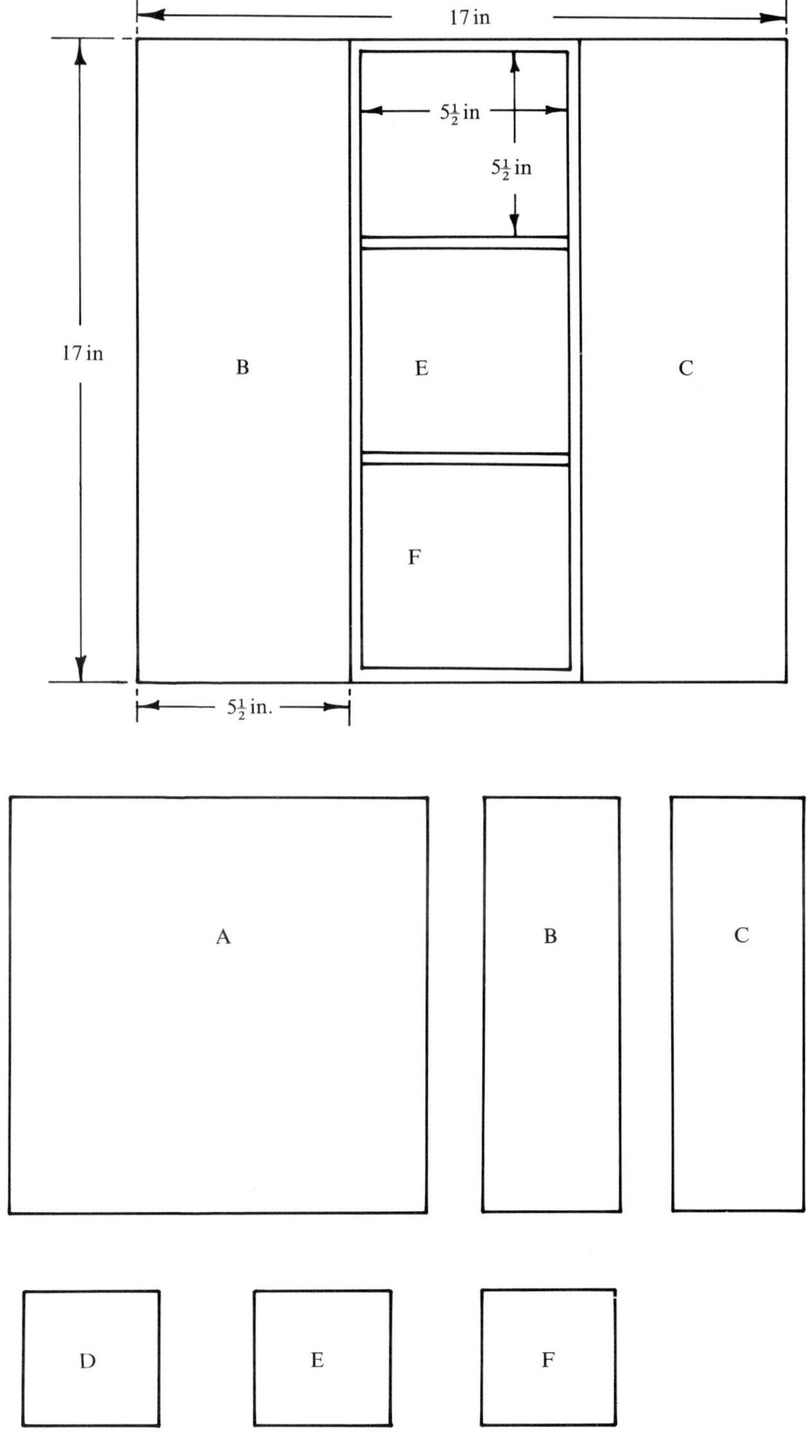

wind the loop three times round the head from front to back (in the same direction as the previous winding round the neck) before drawing up the free end of the thread. The resulting hitch will hold the thread so long as there is tension from the weight of the bobbin on the pillow. (This means that it may sometimes slip undone and need to be re-hitched while the bobbin is lying waiting to be used on the pillow.)

As you work and the thread becomes used up, you can quickly lengthen it by twisting the bobbin so that its head is towards you and spangle end away from you and the angle between the thread and the bobbin is less than 90 degrees. At this stage you can untwist the bobbin the required amount and the thread will unwind without undoing the hitch. When you drop the bobbin to its correct position, the hitch will again hold without slipping. You should keep about a 3in (7.5cm) length of thread between bobbin and pins. This distance should be about the same on all your bobbins. There should not be some long threads and some short ones or some may fall into the wrong place without your noticing it, thus making the work wrong.

You should still not have cut the thread from the ball. At this stage you pull off about 1 more yard of thread from the ball and cut it, then start winding this cut end on to a second bobbin until the bobbins are about 8in (20cm) apart. Now make a hitch on the second bobbin in the same way as the first and the pair will be ready for use.

After working the first two samples, for which you don't need very much thread, you should *fill* your bobbins with thread before you start each new piece of lace, winding thread on to the bobbin until the small neck, filled with thread, is roughly the same diameter as the rest of the shank.

Pricking the pattern
Do this by placing the pattern on top of your pricking card and cutting out a piece of pricking card about the same size as the pattern or a little bigger. (See the section about the transparent sticky-backed film in the general instructions, though this is not necessary for the first very simple pattern.)

You will need a pricking board. Fibre-board or cork are ideal, but polystyrene can be used for a time, although it soon starts crumbling. If nothing else is available, you can use your pillow or the arm of a chair temporarily. The pricking board should ideally be 12in (30cm) square, but a smaller piece will do at first.

Using drawing-pins, pin down the pattern on top of the pricking card firmly on to the board. Holding your pricker vertically (*not* in a slanting direction like a pen), prick accurately through each marked pinhole on the pattern. If you have a pricker, you should fix into it a needle which will make a hole in the card into which you can *just* (with difficulty) push the pins you are going to use. The holes must not be so large that the pins fit loosely. If you have no pricker yet, you can temporarily use a glass-headed pin or a wall-map marker-pin.

When you have pricked all the holes, lift both card and pattern *together* off the board by keeping the drawing-pins still through both. Hold them up to the light and check carefully for a regular pattern of holes, to ensure at this stage that you have not missed pricking any of the holes. Still keeping in the drawing-pins, it is wise also to turn over the card and inspect the back, where it is usually obvious if any holes have been missed. If they have, replace the pattern and card on to the board and prick the missing holes. Only when you are sure that the pricking is complete should you separate it from the pattern.

Mark the pricking by copying the lines from the pattern. (Again see the section about sticky-backed film for more complicated patterns.)

Fix the pricking on to your pillow, placing the top of the pricking as near to the top of the pillow as possible. But *not* so near that it slopes downhill away from you to any marked extent. It *will* do this if:
a) your pillow is more domed than it should be or
b) you fix it too near the top of the pillow.
Note If your pillow *is* too domed it will be because the original cover is too large, allowing too much straw to be pushed in. Do not try to cure it by taking out some of the straw. The only cure is to start again and make the cover smaller but to stuff in as much straw as you possibly can. It is impossible to stuff it too tightly. On the contrary the first pillow a student makes is usually too loosely stuffed. It should be rock-hard.

You have now finished the preparation and are ready to begin.

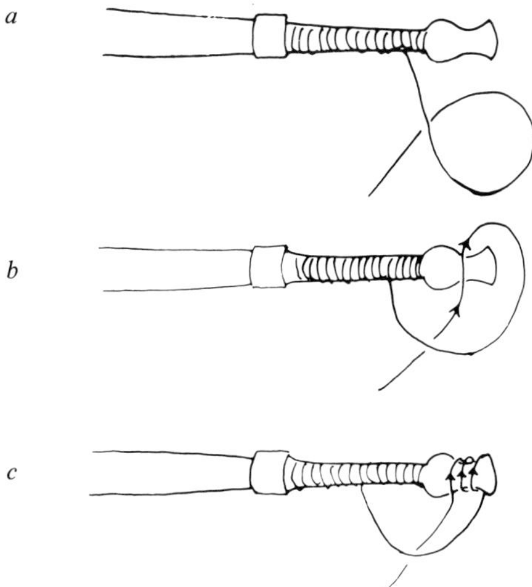

Fig 5 *Making hitch for thread on bobbin*

REPLACING THREADS

Although it is unlikely that you will need this information so soon, I have described below what to do should you run out of or break a thread when working a large piece of lace. To join in a new thread:

1. Wind a full bobbin and use the old and new threads together for an inch or two, after which you cut off the almost finished thread and continue with the full bobbin. You can tempor-arily keep the two pairs together with a rubber band.

2. In many patterns there is a 'squashed in' section, e.g. between two heads, where the threads are pressed tightly together. In such a situation you can lay back the nearly-finished thread and pin a new full bobbin well behind the line of working, bringing it forward to its correct place to continue working. Darn in the ends when the lace is finished, if necessary.

3. Always look ahead. If a worker is likely to run out you may swap it with the next-door passive bobbin by crossing the bobbins an extra time at a suitable place (left over right). By careful pulling up at the end of the row this change is invisible.

4. If a thread breaks near the lace you must make a weaver's knot. There must be a length of at least $\frac{1}{2}$in (12mm), if there is not, you will have to undo some of the lace to give you a workable thread. Loop the thread round the finger and draw the loop (not the end) through the circle of thread, a slip knot. Draw this gently into a circle of about $\frac{1}{4}$in. Push the short, broken end of thread into this loop. You now have to make a quick jerk to transfer the knot from the first loop to the short, straight end. This, if you can tat, is easy but, if not, you may find your first efforts frustrating if your thread keeps pulling out. You can't cheat here; you must pull the new thread firmly to check that the knot has transferred. If not, you must make the knot again. It is simple, with practice.

2 Torchon Lace

INTRODUCTION

Torchon lace is generally considered to be the easiest and quickest to work of all the bobbin laces, probably because of the balanced geometry of its shape and because there are few stitches to master. It is an ideal starting place for would-be lace-makers to embark on the craft as it gives students a good general idea of the basic techniques involved in bobbin lace-making. Even a layman, at a glance, would find it reasonably comprehensible.

PATTERN 1   BRAID SAMPLER

Materials

6 pairs of bobbins
DMC Cordonnet cotton thread no. 50
(It is not worth using an expensive linen thread for a first sampler.)

Hang on one pair of bobbins at each pinhole A, B, C, D, E and F (see Fig 6a). Mark the bobbins hanging on pin F by fixing a thread or a safety pin on to each of their spangles. These are your workers. The other five pairs are passives. In the first two sections of braid, namely whole-stitch (which can also be called cloth-stitch or full-stitch) and twisted whole-stitch, the worked threads from these five pairs will always continue straight down the pillow, whilst the worker threads cross from pinhole to pinhole, as indicated by the zig-zag marking on the pattern. So keep an eye on the marked bobbins to make sure they remain as workers.

Whole-stitch braid

Whole stitch is worked as in Fig 6b, using two pairs of bobbins at a time. In the instructions for the stitches the numbers refer to the position of the bobbins *at that moment*. For example once 2 has been passed over 3, it becomes 3, whilst the former 3 becomes 2.

*Work WS from right to left, using the pairs from F and E first. Then lay aside the RH pair and work with the pair from D. Lay aside the RH pair and work with the pair from C and so on through the five passives. Then twist the workers twice (i.e. right over left twice), stick pin at G with worker threads behind it and worker bobbins to the left of it.

Work WS, left to right, through the five pairs. Then twist the workers twice, stick pin at H with worker threads behind it and worker bobbins to the right of it.*

Continue from * to * until you are very familiar with the stitch.

Twisted whole-stitch braid

With workers on the right, after you have stuck the pin, make a WS between workers and next pair on the left, then twist the RH bobbin over the LH bobbin of each pair (see Fig 6c). Discard RH pair and continue taking workers to the left through each pair, working this same WS followed by a twist with each pair. At the end of row, twist workers once only, making a total of two twists. Then stick the pin and work back to the right with the twists as before, and only one extra twist before you stick the RH pin, as you did on the left.

This stitch is referred to in these patterns as WS, twist.

You will notice that, in this sequence of stitches, you are, in fact, repeating step 1 and step 2. It is for this reason that the third stitch that you

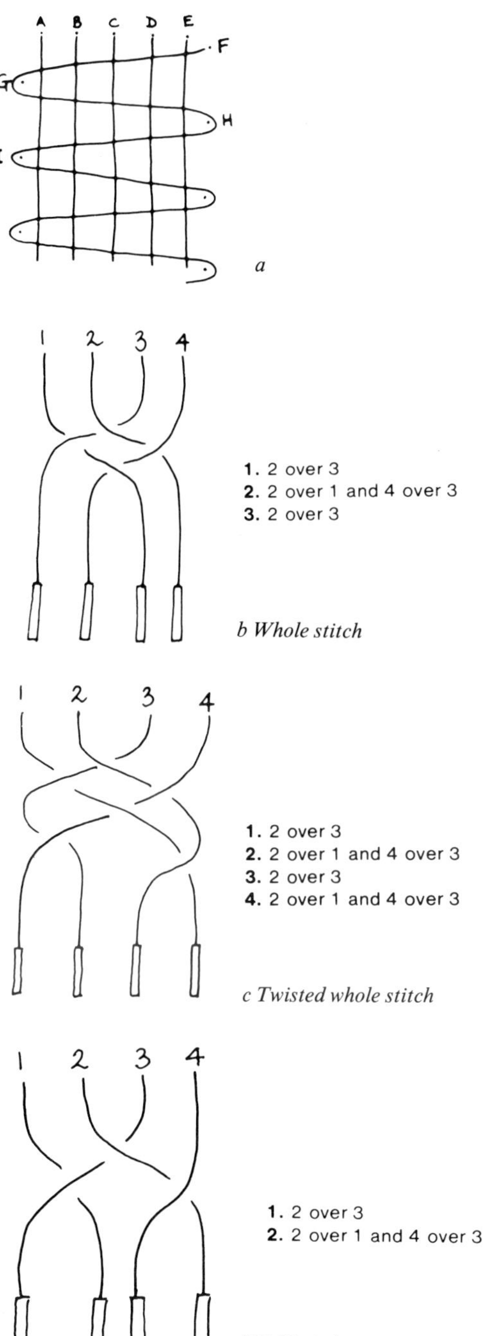

Fig 6

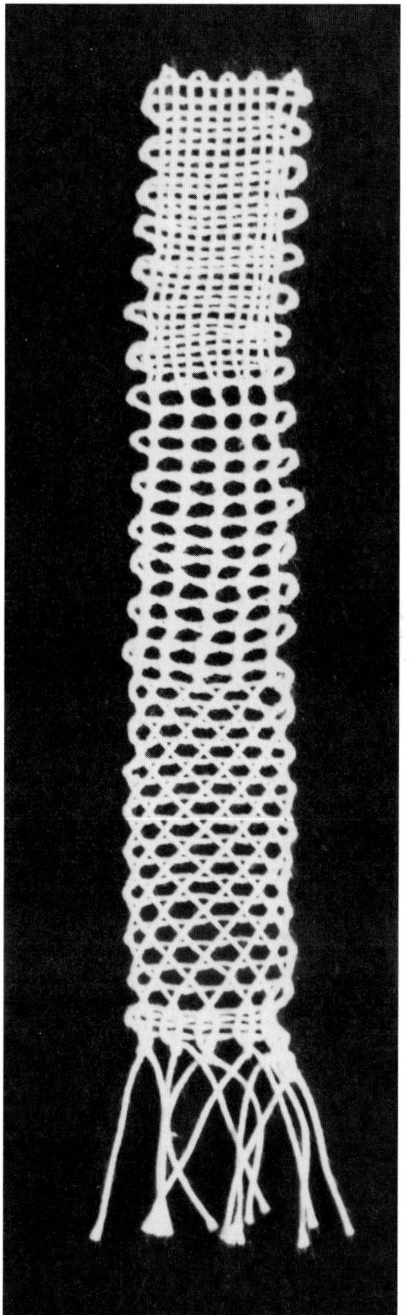

Fig 7 *Finished braid sampler*

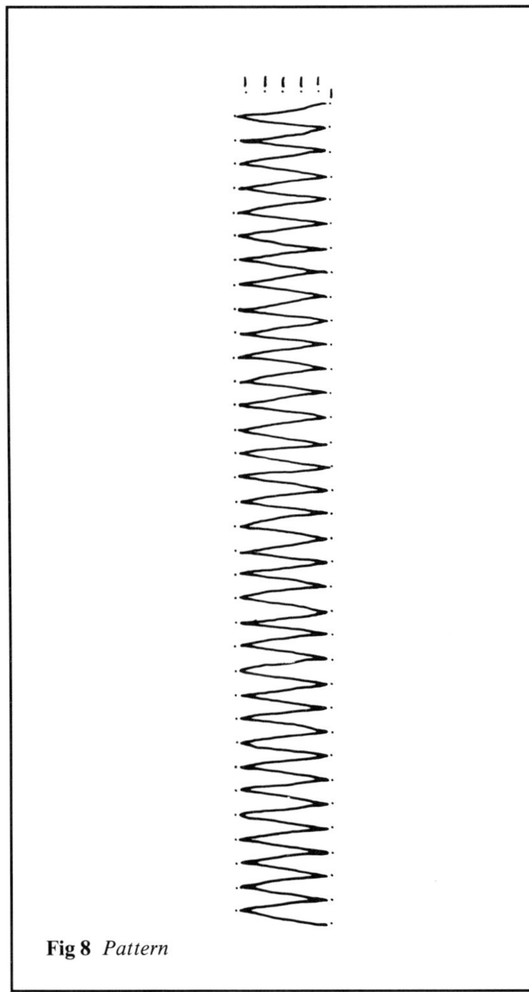

Fig 8 *Pattern*

are about to learn is called half-stitch, as it is just half of a twisted whole-stitch. In some patterns you are told to make two ½sts. This, of course, is identical to WS, twist.

Half-stitch braid

Start with workers on the RH side, having just stuck the pin. Remove marker thread from extreme RH bobbin but leave it on the LH bobbin of this pair. In this braid only the leading bobbin remains as a worker, the other one of the pair dropping behind after each stitch. The passives also will no longer continue on their former route straight down the lace, but will travel crosswise. It is like making a piece of material on the bias. The braid therefore

stretches but this practice piece is only a means to an end and not a piece of usable lace in itself.

With RH two pairs work ½st, as in Fig 6d. *Leave RH pair and work another ½st with next pair on left*. Continue from * to * through all five pairs. At pinhole twist workers once only, making a total of two twists, since the last part of the stitch is a twist. Then stick pin to right of workers, as usual. This makes the same marked bobbin become the leader again and so it should continue throughout. You now use LH pair (workers) to make a ½st with next pair on right. Discard LH pair and work ½st with next pair on right. Continue thus to pin, where you twist workers *once* then work back as before.

When proficient at all these three stitches, finish by enclosing a pin at one edge with WS. Now tie each pair in a reef-knot close up to the work and cut off the ends with a ½in (1.25cm) end.

PATTERN 2 TORCHON EDGE

Materials

7 pairs of bobbins
DMC Cordonnet cotton thread no. 50

This pattern is worked in diagonal rows from right to left only, and not back again, as you did in the braid.

If, as I suggest, you use these first two pieces for practice only, it will not be necessary to rewind the bobbins for Pattern 2, but merely to tie them in bundles of four and pin them on to the back of the pillow, with the bobbins hanging down towards you.

Hang two pairs of bobbins on pinhole A, one pair splayed outside the other pair. Make WS, twist, with these pairs, then twist the RH pair twice more. (This makes a strong twisted edge.) Lay aside this RH pair. Hang two pairs of bobbins on pinhole B, *side by side*, and use the RH of these pairs to work WS, twist, with the LH pair from the previous stitch, then lay aside the RH pair. Work ½st between the LH pair hanging from B and the LH pair from the previous stitch. Take a pin in your right hand and slide it up carefully between these two pairs into pinhole B, at the last moment removing the pin already there with your left hand. Enclose the pin with ½st between the same pairs.

The RH of the two original pairs from B will

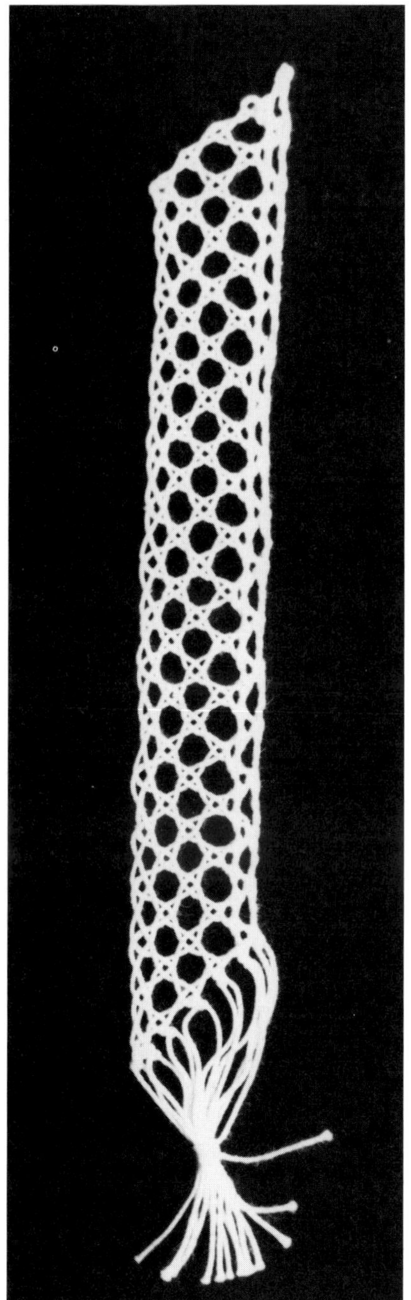

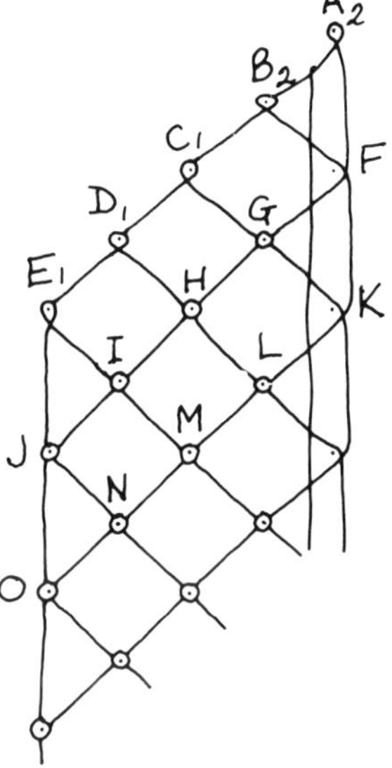

Fig 10 *Working diagram, torchon edge*

Fig 11 Pattern

have slid off into the gap between A and B. This is correct, as that pair of passives runs straight down the footside inside the edge, as can be seen in both the diagram and the sample.

Hang one pair of bobbins on pin C and *work $\frac{1}{2}$st between it and the LH pair from the previous stitch. Carefully slide up a pin between these two pairs into pinhole C, removing the pin already there with your left hand. Enclose it with $\frac{1}{2}$st between these same two pairs*.

Hang one pair of bobbins on pin D and repeat from * to *.

Hang one pair of bobbins on pin E and repeat from * to *.

The lace is now set up with all the pairs of bobbins hung on. The remaining rows are all identical to each other.

†Work a *footside* thus:

With third pair from right and second pair from right, work WS, twist. Leave LH pair and work WS, twist, between edge two pairs. Give edge pair an extra two twists and stick pin F to left of both of these pairs. Leave edge pair and work WS, twist, with second and third pairs from right, thus enclosing pin. After each of these twisted whole stitches you need to draw the bobbins firmly apart to get a good stitch†.

‡Discard RH pair and, with next pair to left (i.e. between fourth and third pairs from right), work a $\frac{1}{2}$st, stick pin G between the two pairs and enclose it with a $\frac{1}{2}$st between same two pairs. Lay RH pair to the right and take in next pair on the left (i.e. fifth and fourth pairs from right). Work $\frac{1}{2}$st, stick pin between them at H and enclose with $\frac{1}{2}$st between same two pairs. Work pins I and J in the same manner‡.

Now lay the LH four pairs well to the left of pillow and return to the third pair from right to work the footside as before (between † and †) at hole K. Then work pinholes L to O as before (between ‡ and ‡).

Repeat the following rows in a similar manner until you are completely familiar with the routine, since this forms the basis of the footside and ground in most torchon patterns. It is suggested that you use this lace simply as a sampler. Therefore, when you have done all you intend to, knot each of the pairs as they hang round the pin and cut off the ends about half an inch away.

You are now ready for the first real pattern having practised the separate components. This is the torchon fan, which has been taught to beginners, certainly for 100 years and probably a great deal longer.

PATTERN 3   TRADITIONAL TORCHON FAN

Materials

10 pairs of bobbins
Swedish linen thread no. 50
or DMC Cordonnet cotton thread no. 50

The holes are worked in alphabetical order. One pattern is complete when you have worked Y and you then begin again at A^1.

Like most torchon patterns, this is worked in sections. You cannot go right across the lace at one time. First you work the triangle bounded by holes A, D and J. You require six pairs of bobbins for this section and it is worked like the torchon edge pattern (no. 2). The only difference is that, in that pattern, each diagonal row had five holes, whereas, in this pattern, the first row has four holes (hence one less pair of bobbins) and succeeding rows have three, two and one holes respectively. Each row is worked with one pair of bobbins less than the previous row. To accomplish this, the LH pair is laid aside to the left as you finish the row. It is wise to put a glass-headed pin in front of it to remind you not to use it again in the triangle.

Start the next row by returning to the third pair from the right, as in the torchon edge pattern.

Here are the exact details of each stitch:
Start by hanging two pairs of bobbins on pinhole A, one pair splayed outside the other pair. Make WS, twist, with these pairs, then twist the RH pair twice more. Lay aside this RH pair. Hang two pairs of bobbins on pinhole B, *side by side*, and use the RH of these pairs to work WS, twist, with the LH pair from the previous stitch, then lay aside the RH pair. Work $\frac{1}{2}$st between the LH pair hanging from B and the LH pair from the previous stitch. Take a pin in your right hand and slide it up carefully between these two pairs into pinhole B, at the last moment removing the pin already there, with your left hand. Enclose the pin with $\frac{1}{2}$st between the same pairs.

The RH of the two original pairs from B will have slid off into the gap between A and B, which is correct.

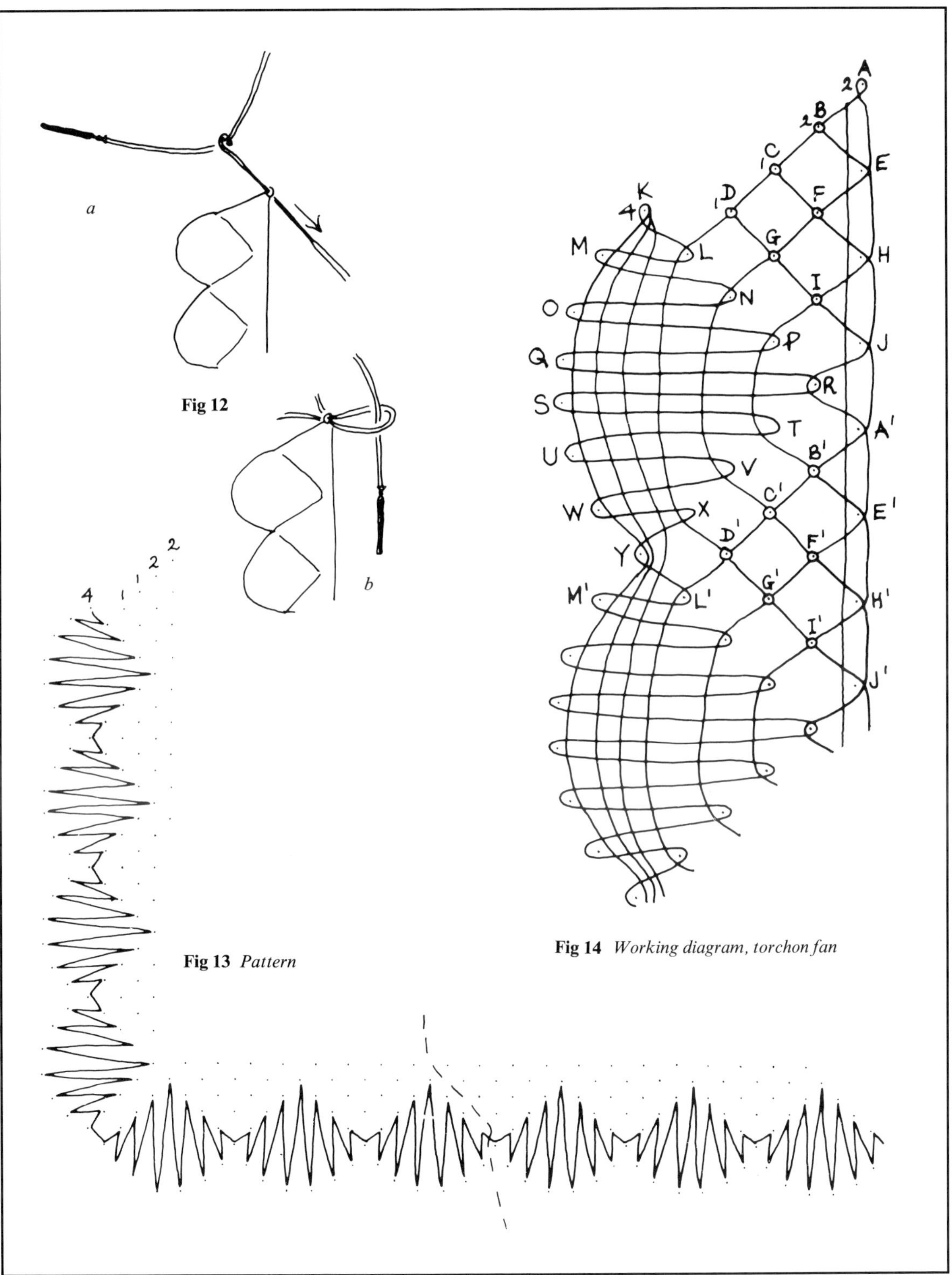

Fig 12

Fig 13 *Pattern*

Fig 14 *Working diagram, torchon fan*

Hang one pair of bobbins on pin C and *work ½st between it and the LH pair from the previous stitch. Carefully slide up a pin between these two pairs into pinhole C, removing the pin already there with your left hand. Enclose it with ½st between these two pairs*.

Hang one pair of bobbins on pin D and repeat from * to *.

§After this stitch lay aside the LH pair well to the left and hold it back with a glass-headed pin to remind you not to use it again in the triangle. Lay the next two pairs over to the left temporarily as you return to the third pair from the right to start the footside thus:

†With third pair from right and second pair from right, work WS, twist. Leave LH pair and work WS, twist, between edge two pairs. Give edge pair an extra two twists after this stitch and stick pin E to left of both these pairs. Leave edge pair and work WS, twist, with second and third pairs from right, thus enclosing pin. After each of these twisted whole-stitches you need to draw the bobbins firmly apart to get a good stitch†.

Discard RH pair and, with next pair to left (i.e. between fourth and third pairs from right), work a ½st, stick pin F between the two pairs and enclose it with a ½st between same two pairs. Lay RH pair to the right and take in next pair on the left (i.e. fifth and fourth pairs from right). Work ½st, stick pin between them at G and enclose with ½st between same two pairs.

After this stitch lay aside the LH pair well to the left with the other pair behind the glass-headed pin. It will not be used again in the triangle. Lay the next pair temporarily over to the left as you return to the third pair from the right and work the footside at pin H, as before († to †).

Discard RH pair and, with next pair to left (i.e. between fourth and third pairs from right), work a ½st, stick pin I between the two pairs and enclose it with a ½st between same two pairs.

After this stitch lay aside the LH pair well to the left with the other two pairs behind the glass-headed pin and work the footside at pin J, as before († to †). Now lay all six pairs well over to the right.

Having completed the triangle of torchon ground and footside, you now turn your attention to the headside and work the fan.

Hang four pairs of bobbins side by side on pin K. The LH pair will be the worker pair for the fan and will remain so until it changes place with the outer pair of passives at the corner. It is, therefore, a good idea to mark them by hanging a thread on each of the two spangles. Just tie it on with a knot or fix a safety-pin on each. These can then be changed over at the corner to the fresh workers. When you are more experienced at lace-making, it will be quite unnecessary to mark bobbins in this way, but at this stage it is useful to be able to recognise the workers instantly. This is to ensure that you do not leave them out of the fan at holes R, T, V or X by mistake, instead of the passives.

Using the LH pair as workers, work to the right through the other three pairs hanging from pin K in WS. Now, in order to make the fan grow wider, you take in an extra pair at each of the holes L, N, P and R. You therefore work through the pair left hanging from D, which will be the LH pair of the group of bobbins from the triangle. (When the instructions say 'work through', it is assumed that you will do so in WS, since the entire fan is worked in WS.) Stick a pin at L, with workers (twisted twice) to the right of it. Work back to the left through the four pairs and stick a pin at M, with workers, twisted twice, to the left of it. Work back through the four pairs and one more pair left hanging from G, then stick a pin at N, with the workers to the right of it, having been twisted twice. Work back to the left through the five pairs and stick a pin at O with workers, twisted twice, to the left of it. Work to the right through five pairs and one more pair left hanging from I, then stick a pin at P, with the workers (twisted twice) to the right of it. Work back to the left through the six pairs and stick a pin at Q with workers, twisted twice, to the left of it. Work to the right through six pairs and one more pair (which were the footside workers from J), then stick a pin at R, with the workers (twisted twice) to the right of it.

You have now reached the halfway point and from now on the fan grows smaller so you must leave out a pair at each of the holes R, T, V and X. This means that, having just taken a pair in at pin R, you must drop it off again after the pin. It is important to remember that you do not just leave out the RH pair after sticking the pin. If you were to do this you would have left the workers behind, and they were specially marked to avoid precisely this error. What you must do is to *enclose the pin* with a WS and then lay aside the RH pair, giving it a twist as you lay it down. (Remember that 'twist' always means placing the RH bobbin over to the left of the LH bobbin.) The workers then continue through six more pairs to the left, then stick pin at S with workers, twisted twice, to the left of it.

Work to the right through six pairs and stick pin at T with the workers (twisted twice) to the right of it. Enclose the pin with WS and, after the stitch, lay aside the RH pair, twisting it once as you lay it down. It is as well to stick a glass-headed pin in front of these pairs as you leave them out to remind you not to use them on the next row. The workers pass through five more pairs to the left and stick pin at U with the workers, twisted twice, to the left of it.

Work to the right through five pairs, stick pin at V with workers, twisted twice, to the right of it, then enclose the pin. After this stitch lay aside the RH pair, twisting it once as you lay it down. The workers work back through four more pairs to the left, then stick pin at W with workers, twisted twice, to the left of it.

Work to the right through four pairs then stick pin at X with workers, twisted twice, to the right of it. Enclose the pin with WS and after the stitch, lay aside the RH pair, twisting it once as you lay it down. This is the last of the four pairs left out of the fan, which will in due course be taken into the torchon ground triangle. The workers pass through the remaining three pairs of passives in the fan (to the left) then the final pin of the fan, pin Y, is stuck with the workers, twisted twice, to the left of it. The fan is now complete and you will know where to find your workers when you start the next fan.

Lay the four LH pairs well over to the left, since they are not used in the torchon ground triangle. You can hold them back with a glass-headed pin to keep them separate from the rest of the bobbins. Lay the next three pairs temporarily over to the left and start the footside at A[1] with the third and second pairs from the right, as in the instructions † to †.

Discard RH pair and, with next pair to the left (i.e. between fourth and third pairs from right), work a $\frac{1}{2}$st, stick pin B[1] between the two pairs and enclose it with a $\frac{1}{2}$st between same two pairs. Lay RH pair to the right and take in next pair on the

left (i.e. fifth and fourth pairs from right). Work $\frac{1}{2}$st, stick pin between them at C[1] and enclose with $\frac{1}{2}$st between same two pairs. Lay RH pair to the right and take in next pair on left (i.e. sixth and fifth pairs from right). Work $\frac{1}{2}$st, stick pin at D[1] and enclose with $\frac{1}{2}$st between same two pairs.

Follow the instructions for the remainder of the torchon ground triangle and the fan, as given above, from § onwards.

The corner

You will be familiar with the pattern by the time you reach the corner. It should, therefore, hold no problems for you if you remember:

1. At the corner one section of triangular ground is omitted. You therefore work a second fan as soon as you have completed the fan immediately before the corner.
2. The only difference in this fan is that the pinhole which ends the first fan, Y in Fig 14, normally coincides with the beginning of the next fan. At the corner there is an extra hole, one to end the fan before the corner and another to start the next fan after the corner. To work these, end the first fan with your workers to the left, as usual. On this occasion twist both pairs (workers and outer passives) once before sticking the pin, followed by WS, twist, to enclose the pin. Place the next pin between the same two pairs (i.e. the starting pin for the second fan). Twist the next two pairs to the right once. Now turn your pillow round through 90 degrees, think yourself into the new direction and start the fan in the usual way, using the pair to the left of the pin as workers (exchanging the marking devices, which will now be on the new outer passives) and working through four pairs of passives to the right, before sticking the pin (equivalent to pin L in Fig 14.)
3. Make sure you have twisted all the four pairs left out of the previous fan, so that all the pairs coming across the corner are twisted.
4. It is wise to mark on your pricking a diagonal line down the centre of the corner between the two fans to make absolutely sure that you do not prematurely work any of the pinholes that come after the corner. It is a common mistake for students to work an extra footside hole too soon, which will make the pattern inaccurate. You *must not start* any holes of the triangular ground section that come after the corner until the fan after the corner is complete.

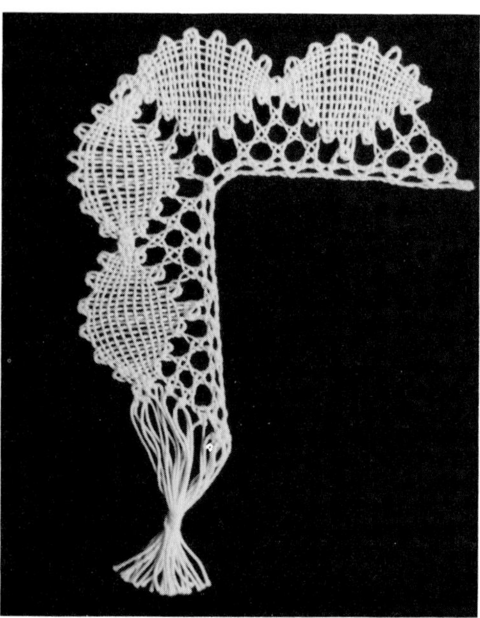

Fig 15 *Finished torchon fan corner*

To finish off

If you wish to make a complete handkerchief edging, move up the pattern in the way described in the general notes and complete four equal sides. Ensure that the fourth side has the correct number of heads to equate with the other sides.

To join the end to the beginning you must make 'sewings'. Pin down the beginning of the lace on to the appropriate part of the pattern and push the pins down to their heads. Start with the inner, footside, hole A. Make sure your footside workers are at this edge. They and the edge pair must be sewn into hole A. Remove pin A, then take one of these pairs first and, using a very fine crochet hook, draw a loop of the threads through the hole in the lace, where pin A has been, as in diagram A. Carefully thread the other bobbin of the pair through the loop as in diagram B and draw up both pairs, first replacing pin A. Repeat with the second edge pair through the same hole (which is a bit fiddly). After drawing up the threads you can either tie a reef-knot and a half and cut the thread ends off closely or you can leave the ends hanging and, after you have finished all the sewings, very carefully darn in the ends a little way in either direction in as invisible a manner as possible. This latter is the better alternative.

Continue to make sewings with each pair of threads into the starting hole of that equivalent pair of threads until all ten pairs are sewn in, followed by the knots or the darning in.

PATTERN 4   CHOKER

Materials

8 pairs of bobbins
Swedish linen thread no. 90
½yd (0.5m) narrow ribbon ⅜in (0.9cm) wide
½in (1.5cm) Velcro

This pattern is not a true torchon pattern, but I have included it as it makes a fairly painless transition at this point, between Patterns 3 and 5 and besides it is a favourite pattern with students.

There are four holes at the top of the pricking, A, B, C and D in the diagram, on to each of which you hang two pairs of bobbins. Hang them with one pair straddled outside the other pair. Make WS, twist, with each pair.

*Using the second and third pairs from the right, make WS, twist, (no pin) and leave them.

Using the second and third pairs from the left, make WS, twist, (no pin) and leave them.

Return to the two centre pairs (fourth from right and fourth from left). Work WS, twist, with these pairs, stick pin between them in centre hole, E, and enclose it with WS, twist twice. These are the worker pairs. You can mark them if you wish with threads knotted on to the spangles (or safety-pins) as they will remain workers throughout.

With the RH of these pairs work to the right through three pairs in WS, twist. Twist the workers (RH pair) an extra time and stick pin F to the left of them. Work back through three pairs in WS, twist, and stick pin G with workers to the left of it and give them an extra twist.

Return to the LH workers (fourth from left) and work through three pairs to the left in WS, twist, stick pin H with workers to the left, giving the workers an extra twist. Work back through the three passive pairs in WS, twist, and stick pin at I with workers to the right of it, giving the workers an extra twist.

With the two centre pairs (the workers) make WS, twist twice (no pin) after which the former RH worker pair becomes the LH worker pair and vice versa.

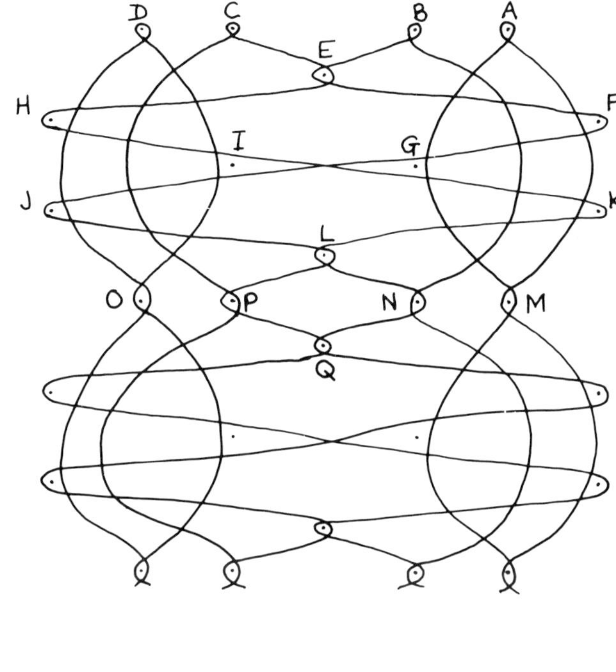

Fig 16 *Working diagram, choker*

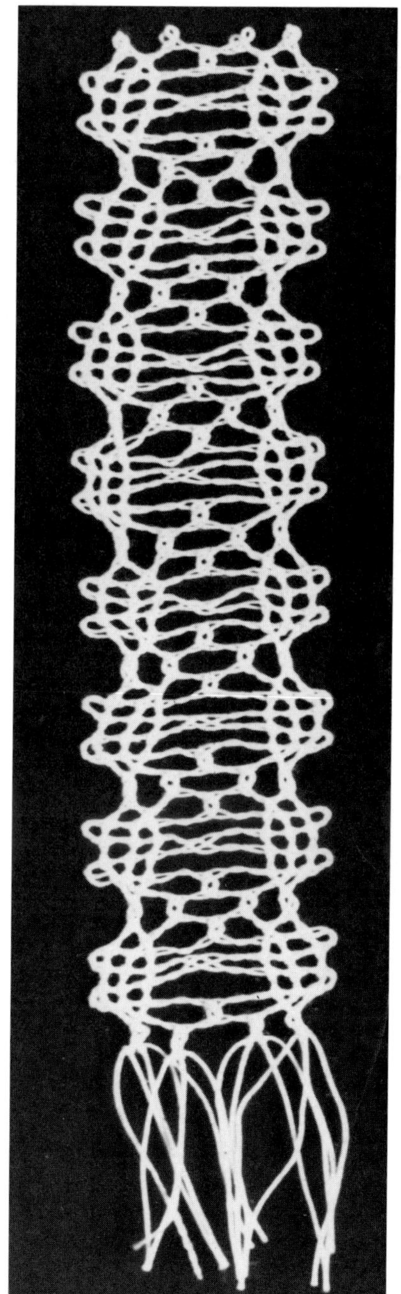

Fig 17 *Close-up of choker during working*

Finish the LH head by passing the LH centre pair through three passive pairs to the left in WS, twist. Stick pin J with workers to the left of it and give workers an extra twist.

Work back through three pairs in WS, twist, and leave workers at left centre, giving them an extra twist. Return to the RH side.

With the RH centre pair (fourth from right) work WS, twist, through three pairs to the right. Stick pin K with workers behind it to the right. Give workers an extra twist and return in WS, twist, through three pairs to the centre, where you give workers an extra twist.

Work WS, twist, between the two centre pairs, stick pin L between them and enclose it with WS, twist.

Draw the RH passives up to a good shape. Work WS, twist, between second and third pairs from the right (no pin).

Work WS, twist, between first and second pairs on the right, stick pin M between them and enclose it with WS, twist.

25

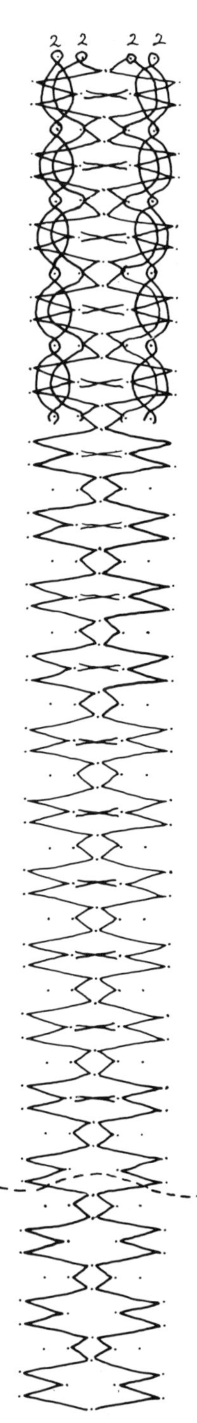

Work WS, twist, between third and fourth pairs on the right, stick pin N between them and enclose it with WS, twist.

Draw the LH passives up to a good shape. Work WS, twist, between second and third pairs from the left (no pin).

Work WS, twist, between first and second pairs on the left, stick pin O between them and enclose it with WS, twist.

Work WS, twist, between third and fourth pairs on the left, stick pin P between them and enclose it with WS, twist.

You have now completed one pattern. Repeat from * with hole Q equivalent to hole E.

When you have completed a sufficient length to go round your neck (about $14\frac{1}{2}$in), tie the threads in pairs in a reef knot and cut off the ends about $\frac{1}{4}$in long. Take a piece of ribbon $\frac{3}{8}$in or 0.9cm wide and thread it through the lace, *over* the bar between the holes I and G in Fig 16 and *under* the diamond-shaped section LPQN in Fig 16 and continue in this manner throughout the length of the lace. (Velvet ribbon is very effective).

Cut off a piece of Velcro, $\frac{3}{8}$in long. Mount one half at the beginning of the choker, the other at the end. When mounting the Velcro, sew the lace on at the same time. This sewing at the beginning and end is all the sewing the lace needs. When sewing the end of lace, sandwich the raw thread ends between Velcro and ribbon for a perfect result.

PATTERN 5   ROUND MAT

Materials

11 pairs of bobbins
Swedish linen thread no. 90

Start this pattern at the footside, as indicated in Fig 22. The diagram also indicates where new pairs are to be hung on. Two pairs are hung on at the first hole on the right and worked in WS, twist. The inside edge pair does not have three twists, as is more usual, because the inner holes are so close together. Next, hang two pairs temporarily on a pin placed in the previous edge hole to that on which you started. With the LH pair from the previous stitch work WS, twist, with each of these two pairs. At the next pin on the left, indicated in Fig 22, hang on a new pair,

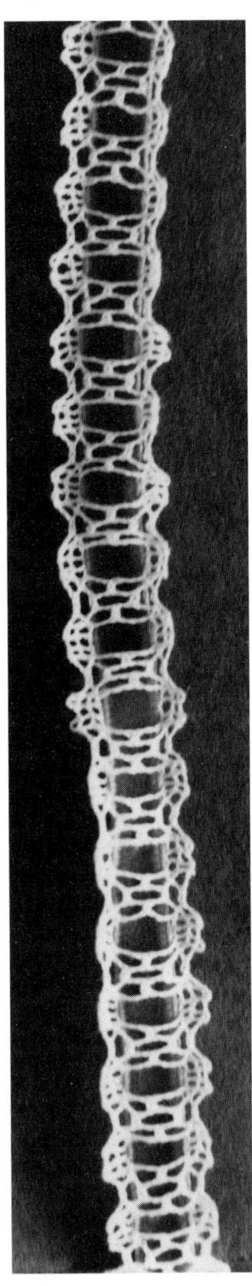

Fig 18 *Completed choker*

Fig 19 *Pattern*

work through it in your chosen stitch (see following alternatives), twist the workers twice, replace pin with workers to the left of it and work back towards the footside. Take out the temporary pin and draw up the loop of thread gently until no loop remains.

Alternative ways of working triangles.
These are photographed in order from the top in the sample, with the first triangle repeated at the end.
1. WS with each pair but one twist of workers only (not passives) before seventh and eighth pairs of passives from the right (i.e. last two pairs taken in) and from then on, twisting workers in the gap between the sixth and seventh pairs and between the seventh and eighth pairs whilst these are in the point of the triangle.
*The three RH pairs of passives are worked in

Fig 20 *Pattern*

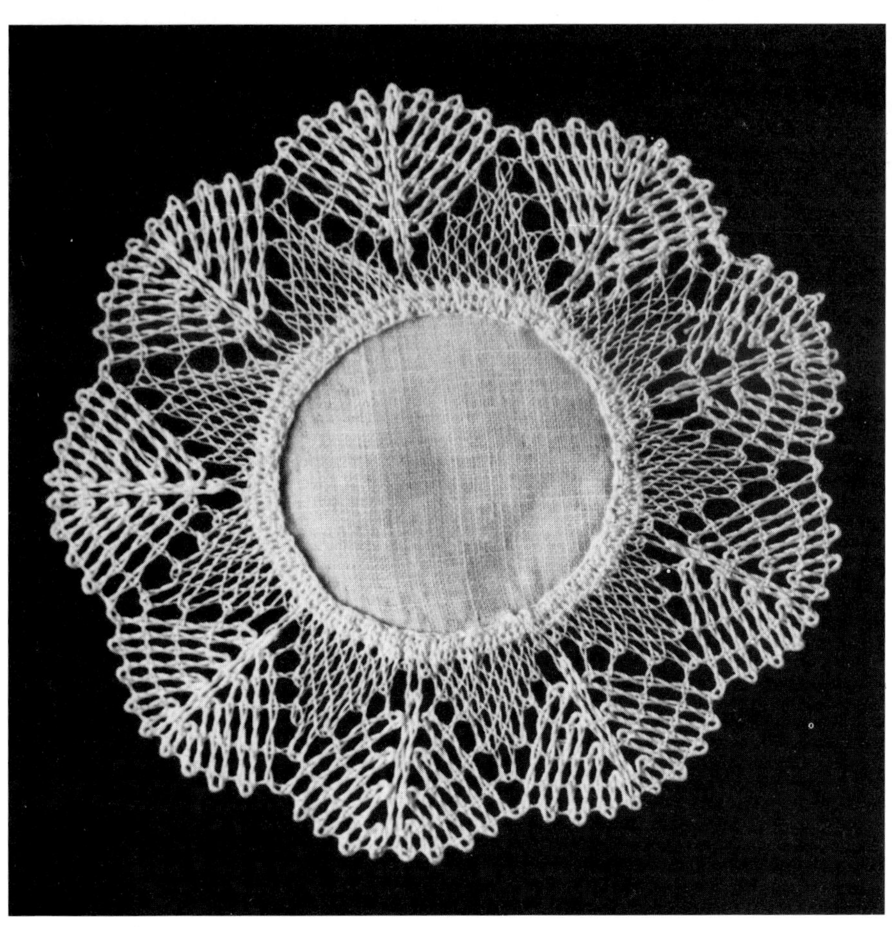

Fig 21 *Completed mat, made up*

WS, twist, throughout. Coming towards the right, the workers need to be twisted before working the WS, twist, with the third pair from the right in order to keep a twist in that gap in each direction. The pin on the inner circle is always placed to the left of the two RH pairs after their WS, twist. The inner of the two pairs is then used as the worker pair when working back to the left*.

2. WS, twist, before and after the nine pinholes on the LH, pointed side, $\frac{1}{2}$st all the rest of the time except when working with the three RH pairs of passives, which are worked as from * to * in the previous instructions.

3. Half-stitch all the way except when working with the three RH pairs of passives which are worked as from * to * in the first instructions.

4. Half-stitch all the way except:

a) WS, twist, *outside* each of the nine pinholes on the LH, pointed side: i.e. as pairs are taken in, the

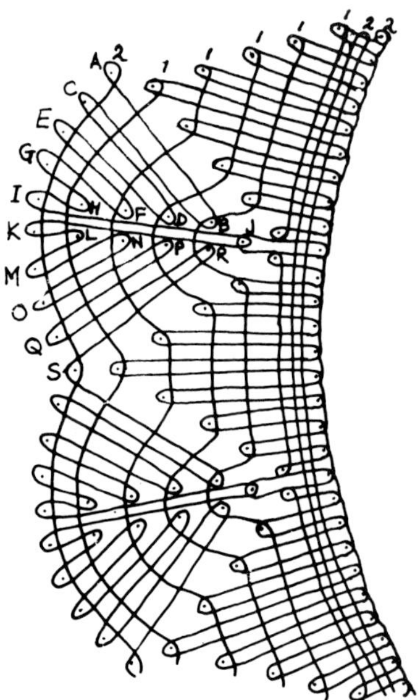

Fig 22 *Working diagram, round mat*

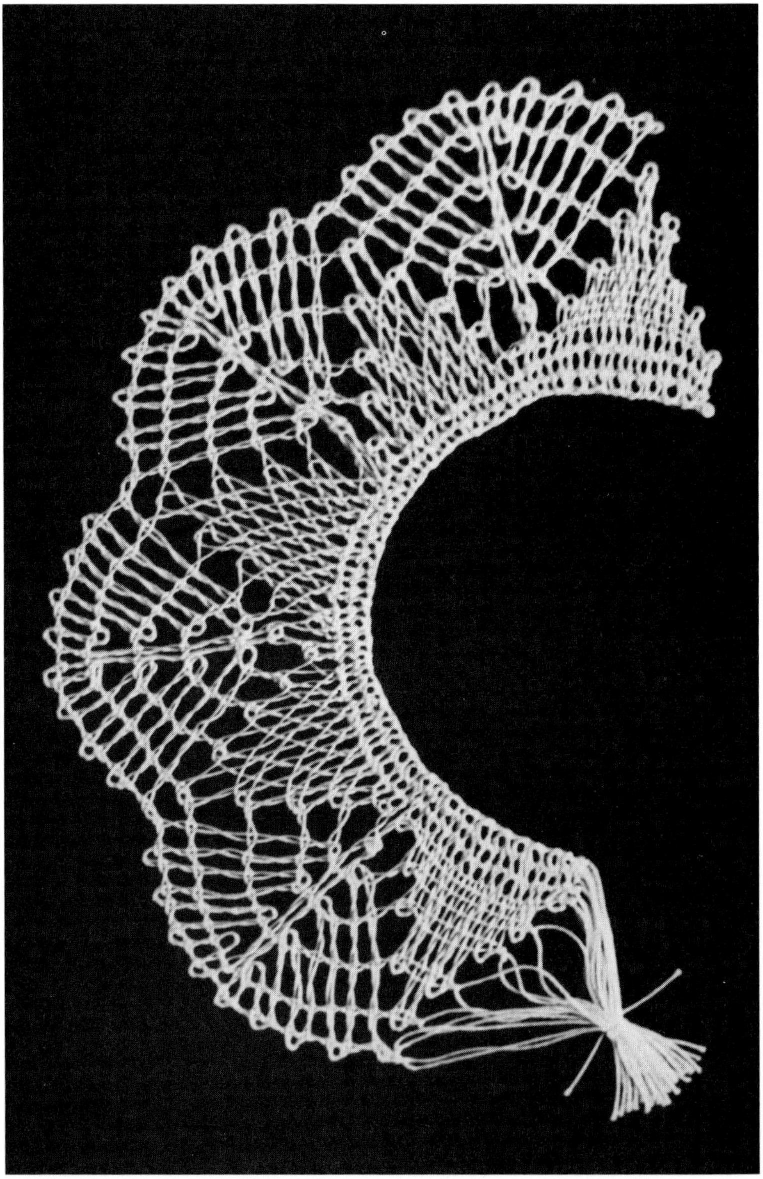

Fig 23 *Enlargement of mat for student to see working*

stitch is *before* the pin, then, as pairs are left out, the stitch is *after* the pin. At the point, the WS, twist, is both before and after the pin.
b) When working with the three RH pairs of passives, work as from * to * in the first instructions.

The shell edge is worked as follows:
Hang on the last two pairs at A with one pair splayed outside the other. The pair to the left of the pin will be the workers throughout. Work them through five pairs to the right, doing WS, twist, with each pair. Stick pin at B (with an extra twist of worker pair) then back to C, still doing WS, twist, with all the five pairs. At C, give an extra twist to the workers and stick the pin. Return by passing the workers through four pairs to the right and then sticking pin at D (giving the workers an extra twist at each pinhole throughout the shell edge) then back to E, work through three pairs to F and back to G, through two pairs to H and back to I.

Work from I to J by passing through *six* pairs (one extra to those which were used in going from A to B). Stick pin at J and work back through six pairs to K.

From K to L work through two pairs and back to M. Work through three pairs to N and back to O. Work through four pairs to P and back to Q. Work through five pairs to R and back to S. Leave the workers here after enclosing the pin with WS, twist.

You then return to the foot and work the next triangle, after which the next shell is worked, starting with the second pair from the left. These were the workers of the previous shell. As they have already worked the first stitch of the shell they will only work through *four* pairs before sticking the pin at B and continuing as before.

When you are fairly near the end you will be working towards the beginning of the pattern where your pins will obviously get in the way of your bobbins. As long as you leave in all the first line of pins and the edge pins (both inner and outer) you can remove the other pins near the beginning, as long as you always keep at least four complete pattern repeats under pins. Return to the pins near the start which you have had to leave in. Push them right down to their heads. Now you need a slider. These are of clear, stiff plastic like the 'windows' in some display boxes. Used X-ray film which has been washed is ideal if you can obtain it. Cut your slider so that it measures about $3\frac{1}{2}$in $\times$ $2\frac{1}{2}$in (9cm $\times$ 6.5cm). You now cover up the pinheads with the slider so that the threads do not catch on the pins. The lower edge of the slider is tucked under the top edge of your worker cloth.

To finish off, make sewings into the appropriate holes then darn in the ends or tie knots. Sew the round piece of lace on to a piece of fine lawn.

PATTERN 6   BOOKMARK

Materials

18 pairs of bobbins
Swedish linen thread no. 90

Hang on the pairs as indicated in Fig 25, two pairs at each pinhole along the top. Do not twist them. Start by working WS with the two pairs round the LH pin. After this stitch, the RH pair is the worker pair which works through all the remaining pairs to the right in WS. Twist the worker pair twice after the last stitch, take out the last (right-hand) pin and replace it with the pin in front and to the left of the worker pair. This latter pair now works three more rows of WS through all the other pairs. Spread out the pairs into a tidy position as you work.

When you work the next, torchon ground, section, you will be working straight instead of diagonally as usual. The difference is that you use two pairs at each hole (naturally) but then lay *both* pairs aside and use two more pairs for the next hole. To ensure that you use the correct bobbins, start somewhere in the middle and make the stitch with pairs from adjoining pin-holes. If you then work both to right and to left, using two new pairs for each hole you will be right. Fig 25 shows exactly where the pairs go.

In the small torchon ground section you work the normal torchon footside, starting with the second and third pairs from the right. WS, twist, with the inner passive pair and WS, twist, with the edge pair, then twist the edge pair twice more, place the pin to the left of both of these last pairs, leave the RH pair, and enclose the pin with the second and third pairs from the right in WS, twist. Reverse this procedure on the LH side.

The triangular sections are worked in cloth stitch (i.e. WS). At the point of each triangle, I have twisted every passive pair once before

Fig 24 *Finished bookmark*   Fig 25 *Working diagram*   Fig 26 *Pattern*

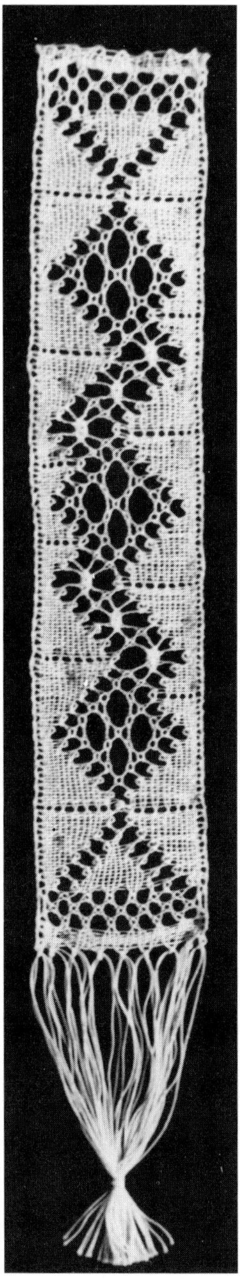

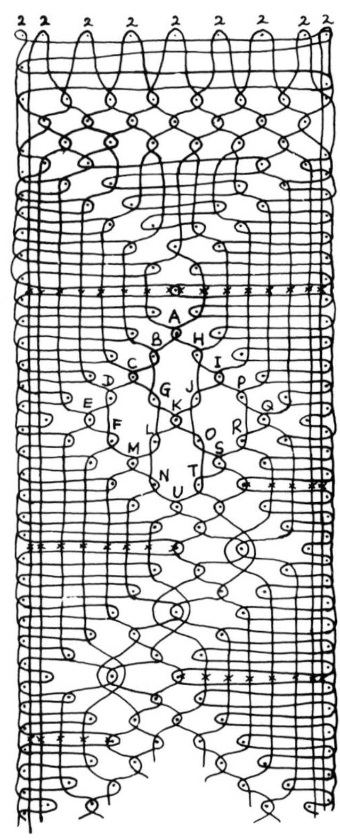

returning through them. You can vary this as you wish, perhaps by twisting in only the first and last triangles, perhaps by twisting in only the large triangles.

Once you are in the cloth stitch section, the edge on each side is made simply by working in WS up to the last passive pair. Then twist the workers once and work WS, twist, with the edge pair. Twist the outer pair twice more, stick the pin with two pairs outside it and then use the inner pair to continue working the triangle in WS.

The honeycomb section is worked as follows: Having completed the triangles on each side, you will have five pairs of bobbins hanging from each side. Referring to Fig 25, using the two centre pairs (one from each side), work $\frac{1}{2}$st, twist, pin, $\frac{1}{2}$st, twist, at A. With the LH pair and the next pair on the left work the same stitches at B. Continue down the line, working C, D and E, each time laying aside the RH pair and taking in a new pair on the left. The stitch throughout the honeycomb is $\frac{1}{2}$st, twist, pin, $\frac{1}{2}$st, twist.

The row you have just completed is called the long row. You now work the short row. Here, because there are less pinholes, you work less stitches. Thus, instead of taking a pair from the previous stitch on to the next pin to work round that, as in the long row, you now leave *both* the pairs after enclosing the pin and use fresh pairs for the next pin.

Thus for F you use the RH pair from E and the pair hanging from D. For G you use the pairs hanging from C and B. For H you use the pair hanging from A and take in a new pair from the right.

You are now back on to a long row. The first hole, I, is worked with the RH pair from H and a new pair taken in from the right. J is worked with the LH pair from I and the pair left hanging from H. Continue carrying the LH pair to the next hole on the left, as in the previous long row.

After M, lay aside the LH pair and use the RH pair from M and the pair hanging from L to work the pin N. Work O with the pairs hanging from K and J. Work P with the pair hanging from I and a new pair taken in from the right. Work Q with the RH pair from P and the last of the five pairs taken in from the right. Work down the long row as before. The honeycomb section is now complete.

There should be no difficulty with the spiders. Any sections of the spiders which are not surrounded by the cloth stitch triangles are instead 'framed' by torchon ground stitch ($\frac{1}{2}$st, pin, $\frac{1}{2}$st). This is shown clearly in Figs 24 and 25. To work each spider you use two pairs hanging diagonally from the left and two pairs hanging diagonally from the right. Each of these pairs will be twisted once already. Give them all two more twists. *With the centre two pairs work WS, with the two LH pairs work WS, with the two RH pairs work WS, with the centre two pairs work WS*. Stick centre pin of spider with two pairs on each side and draw up the pairs neatly. Repeat from * to *, draw up the pairs and twist all four legs three times each.

When the lace is finished stick in the final row of pins so that each pair of bobbins has a pin between them. Take each of these two pairs in turn and tie a reef-knot between them round their own pin and close up to it. Cut off the threads to leave a tail.

Finally, mount the bookmark on to a ribbon slightly wider than the lace. If it is a nylon ribbon the raw ends of the ribbon can be just touched down on to an electric or solid-fuel hotplate. This will seal the ends and stop them from fraying. The most satisfactory way of sewing on the lace is to use an 'invisible' thread and take a very small stab stitch through the lace and ribbon, then back through the ribbon. Then make a long running stitch along the ribbon under the edge of the lace, then come up through the lace and down again through lace and ribbon, a tiny stitch and back up to make a long stitch along the ribbon under the lace. In this way the sewing hardly shows at all.

PATTERN 7   Vs AND LOZENGES INSERTION

Materials

16 pairs of bobbins
Swedish linen thread no. 70
or DMC Cordonnet cotton thread no. 100

This insertion is unusual because the two sides are not symmetrical. It is therefore more suitable for setting into a vertical surface, like a blouse, petticoat or christening dress rather than a horizontal surface such as a table-cloth or tray-

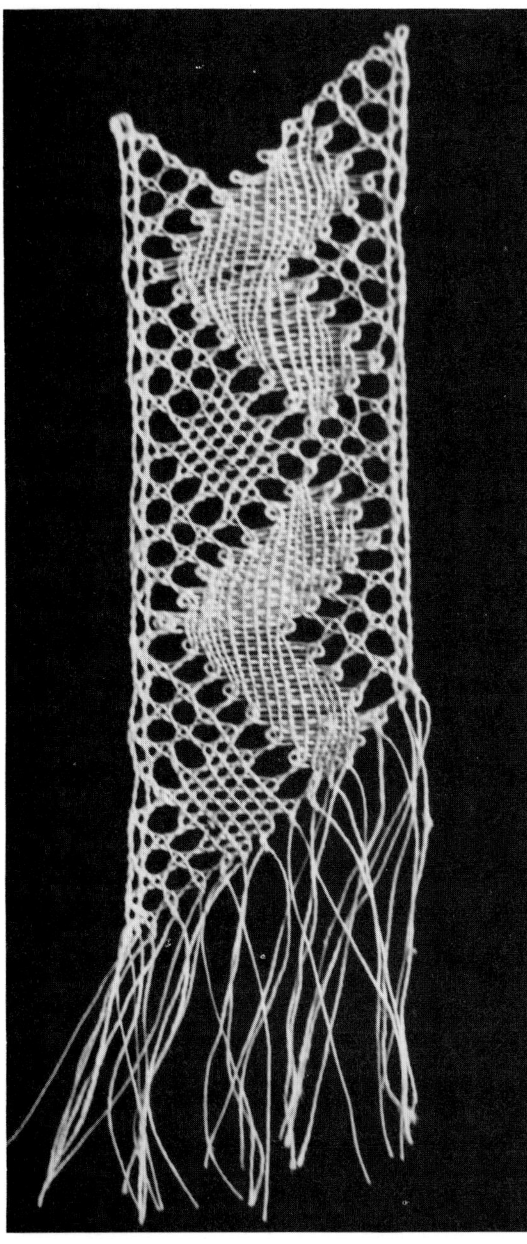

Fig 27 *Finished Vs and lozenges*

cloth. The sample shows the variations from which you can choose, of working the Vs in either WS or $\frac{1}{2}$st and similarly the lozenges. The small triangles of torchon ground on each side can be worked in $\frac{1}{2}$st, pin, $\frac{1}{2}$st, as in the sample; or $\frac{1}{2}$st, twist, pin, $\frac{1}{2}$st, twist; or WS, twist, pin, WS, twist.

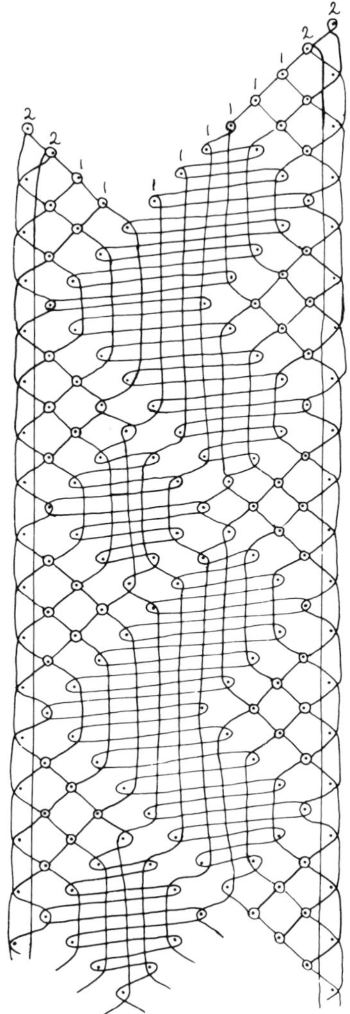

Fig 28 *Working diagram*

Other possible variations are:
1. To alternate the Vs, one $\frac{1}{2}$st then one WS and similarly the lozenges.
2. Where you are working a WS V, you can twist all the passive pairs once when you arrive at the point of the V, to make an ornamental line.
3. You can similarly twist the passives of the lozenge at the widest point.
4. You can twist the workers of the lozenge once in the middle of every row to make a line in the other direction.
5. You could work the first half of each V in WS and the second half in $\frac{1}{2}$st to give a 3-D, shaded effect.

PATTERN 8   HANDKERCHIEF CORNER

Materials

20 pairs of bobbins
Swedish linen thread no. 50
or DMC Cordonnet cotton thread no. 50

There are a few points to notice in this pattern:
1. The footside is worked at a different angle from the rest. Therefore, in order to allow the threads to hang correctly while working, twist your pillow so that the *footside* is coming towards you at a right angle when working the footside. When working all the rest of the corner, twist the pillow through 45 degrees so that the *headside* is coming towards you at a right angle. If you omit to do this you may well find yourself starting the rose or the spider with the wrong pairs and getting in a muddle. (See also point 5.) These directions are marked in Fig 31 with big arrows.
2. It is advisable to draw a line straight through the exact centre, like the line on the pattern. You can then ensure that you complete every single pinhole of the first half plus the three pinholes on this centre line before you proceed round the semi-circular headside.
3. *Before* the half-way line you add on a pair at every inner pinhole of the double row of holes at the footside edge (except the very first hole where two pairs are added). To add a pair, hang it from a nearby hole temporarily, make a WS through this pair by the workers when they have come from the edge through the other passive pair in WS, twist, towards the inner footside hole. Then stick the pin in this hole with the workers (twisted twice) to the left. Work through the newly-added pair again in WS, twist, then the workers continue to the edge as usual and the new pair has the extra temporary pin removed. The threads are drawn snugly up to the inner footside hole and this new pair is then ready to be taken in at the corresponding hole of the fan, lozenge or rose ground, as indicated in the diagram (Fig 31).
4. Instructions for working rose ground (see enlarged rose beside the main diagram [Fig 31]):
a) Holes 1, 2, 7 and 8 are the 'before and after' holes, worked in $\frac{1}{2}$st, pin, $\frac{1}{2}$st.
b) Holes 3, 4, 5 and 6 are the rose proper, worked in $\frac{1}{2}$st, twist, pin, $\frac{1}{2}$st, twist.

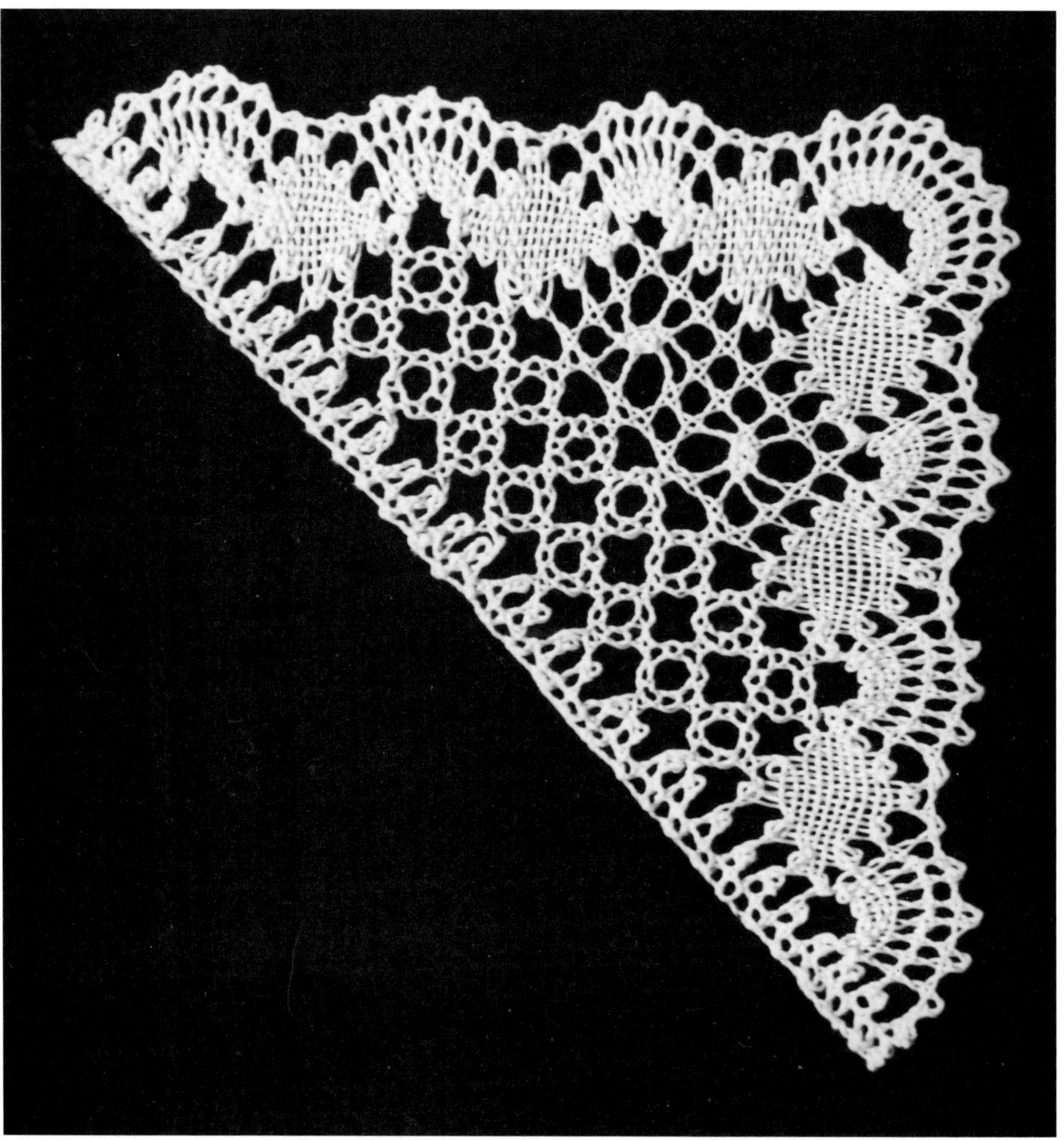

c) Most patterns do not have pinholes 1, 2, 7 and 8 marked for pricking. It is, however, much better to prick these holes, as a far better rose results every time. If the holes *are* pricked, you work $\frac{1}{2}$st, pin, $\frac{1}{2}$st at each hole. If they are *not* marked, you work WS, twist, at the place where the hole would be. You will realise that, with the pins removed, each of these alternatives gives identical results. However, with the pins there to keep the rose in shape as work progresses, you will find you can consistently achieve better roses.

d) Without the extra hole marked, it is all too easy for the inexperienced to forget to work the 'before and after' stitches, in which case the rose is spoilt.

e) For those who find diagrams muddling, here is a stitch by stitch account of how to work a rose.

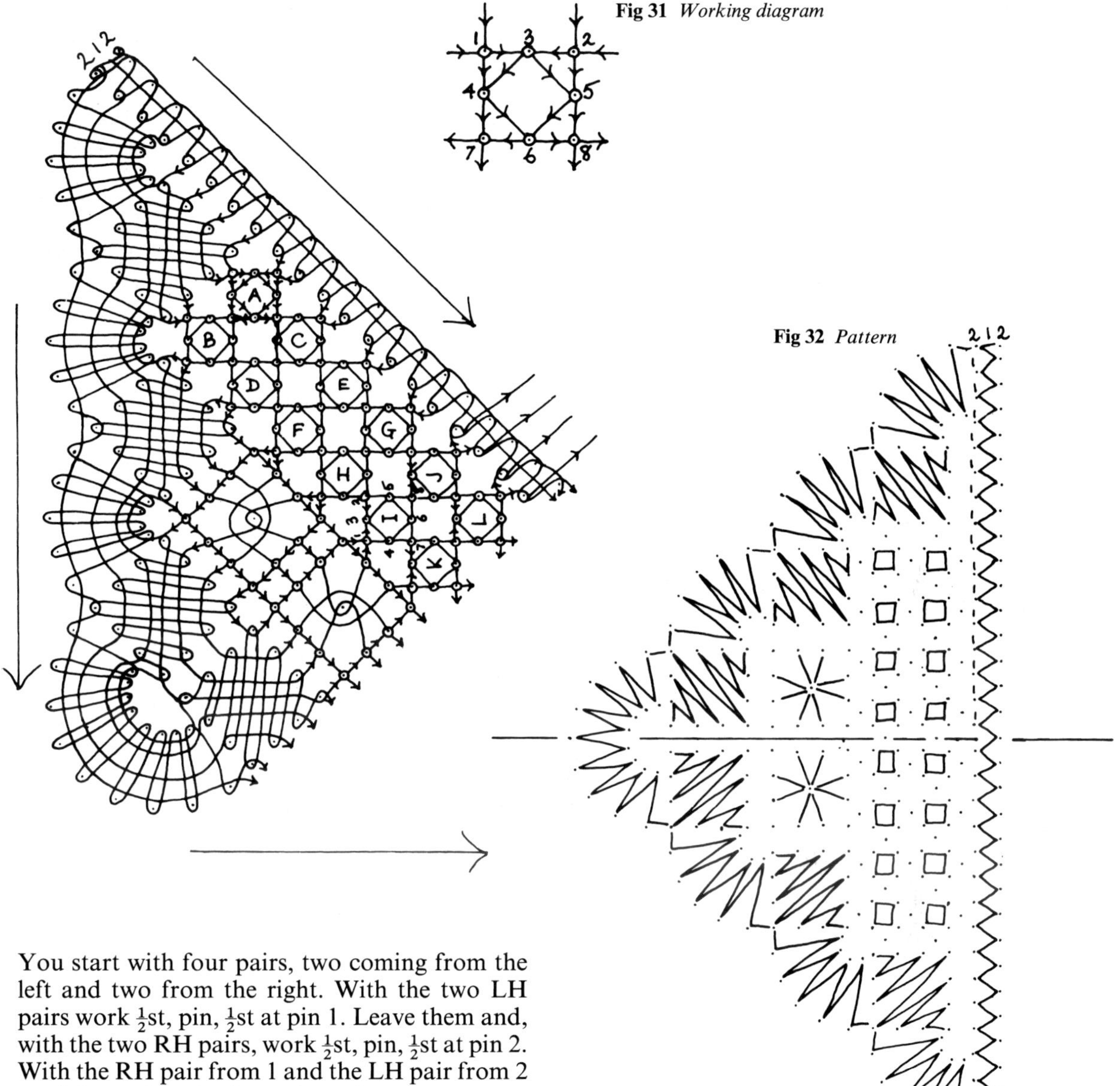

Fig 31 *Working diagram*

Fig 32 *Pattern*

You start with four pairs, two coming from the left and two from the right. With the two LH pairs work $\frac{1}{2}$st, pin, $\frac{1}{2}$st at pin 1. Leave them and, with the two RH pairs, work $\frac{1}{2}$st, pin, $\frac{1}{2}$st at pin 2. With the RH pair from 1 and the LH pair from 2 work $\frac{1}{2}$st, twist, pin, $\frac{1}{2}$st, twist at 3.

With the LH pair from 1 and the LH pair from 3, work $\frac{1}{2}$st, twist, pin, $\frac{1}{2}$st, twist at 4.

With the RH pair from 2 and the RH pair from 3, work $\frac{1}{2}$st, twist, pin, $\frac{1}{2}$st, twist at 5.

With the RH pair from 4 and the LH pair from 5, work $\frac{1}{2}$st, twist, pin, $\frac{1}{2}$st, twist at 6.

With the LH pair from 6 and the LH pair from 4, work $\frac{1}{2}$st, pin, $\frac{1}{2}$st, at 7.

With the RH pair from 6 and the RH pair from 5, work $\frac{1}{2}$st, pin, $\frac{1}{2}$st at 8. This completes the rose.

f) If you refer to Fig 31 you will see that, after rose A, you work rose B, using pinhole 7 from A (the 'after' stitch) as the approach stitch to B, pinhole 2 in the rose diagram.

You use the RH pair from the point of the lozenge and last remaining pair hanging from the right of the lozenge to work pinhole 1 of rose B. After this rose, returning to rose C, you use pinhole 8 of rose A as the approach stitch to rose C, the equivalent of pinhole 1 in the rose diagram.

5. At the halfway line, turn your pillow round through 90 degrees so that the unworked head-side pricking is coming towards you at a right angle. Turn the diagram (Fig 31) round similarly, as the markings after the corner are in the new direction, as indicated by the large arrow at the side.

6. **After** the half-way line, when you have finished the semi-circular head, work the lozenge then, working towards the footside, work the spider, then the four roses I, J, K and L, then take out four pairs to the edge (for which instructions follow) before returning to the top-left headside and working a block towards the footside, etc.

7. To take out a pair (at every pinhole of the footside after the half-way line), proceed as follows. Hang safety-pins on to the spangles of the pair of bobbins to be left out (the furthest back pair to the right each time when that section of work is completed, other than the three footside pairs). At the pinhole, one in from the edge, work WS, twist, between footside workers and this pair, with an extra twist to the LH pair, stick pin between the pairs and enclose it with another WS, twist, between the same two pairs. Now carry the extra pair down to the foot thus: using the two LH pairs as one pair work WS, twist, with the second pair from the right. In other words, counting 1, 2, 3, 4 from the left as when learning WS, 'bobbins' no. 1 and no. 2 are each a *pair* of bobbins, worked as a single thread. Next, with the double pair, which is now second from the right, work WS with the edge pair in similar manner. The pair with safety-pins is now on the right and is left there and eventually cut off with a 3in end, to be oversewn with the edge later when the corner is sewn to the handkerchief. When sewing it on, I lay this first pair of threads along the edge up to the starting point, where I trim it off, then all the remaining pairs I trim to a ¼in long, so that each lies along the edge, reaching the previously left-out pair. Thus, when over-sewing, there is an even thickness of two threads down the length of the footside and all the threads are firmly secured. After leaving out the pair with the safety-pins the next pair (from the back on the right) is the edge pair and this pair is twisted three times while the next pair in is

twisted once. The pin is stuck as usual to the left of these two pairs and is enclosed with the second and third pairs from the right, working WS, twist.

Repeat the procedure with the next pair waiting to be left out, transferring the safety-pins to them. The use of the safety-pins is to ensure that the correct pair is left out at the edge, and not the workers by mistake.

Cut off all the bobbins leaving 3in ends of thread on the work and remove the pins.

When sewing the edge to the lace the neatest way is to run the finished threads along the edge for a short distance, catching the finished-off threads in with the hem.

PATTERN 9   TORCHON ZIG-ZAG

Materials

15 pairs of bobbins
Swedish linen thread no. 70
or DMC Cordonnet cotton thread no. 100

This pattern is included for extra practice and should present few problems. I find it helpful to put a small circle round the pinholes at the top and bottom of the zig-zag, where the stitch is to change from WS to ½st.

The only variation is at the corner, where you work as follows: at A work the edge stitch as usual (WS, twist three times on the left and twist once with the RH pair).

Then work WS, twist, with the second and third pair from the right. This is the only extra stitch.

Now turn your pillow round through a right angle and start the next side at B by working WS between the edge two pairs, followed by three twists of the edge pair and one twist of the inner pair, as usual. The rest of the pattern should be obvious from the diagram (Fig 35).

Fig 33 *Close-up of torchon zig-zag*

Fig 34 *Completed torchon zig-zag*

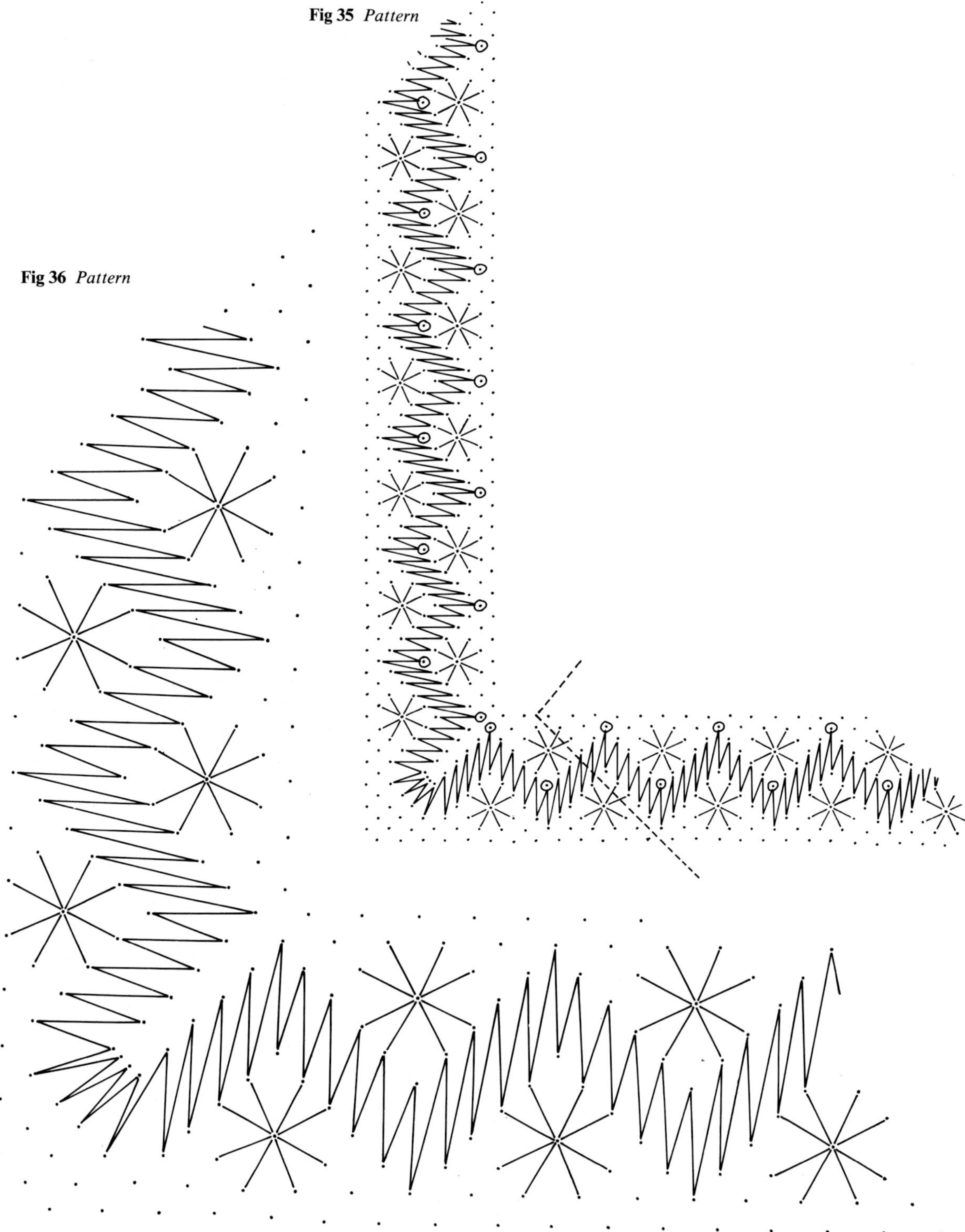

Fig 35 *Pattern*

Fig 36 *Pattern*

PATTERN 10 BOOKMARK WITH PAIRS OF SPIDERS

Materials

14 pairs of bobbins wound with
Barbour or Campbell's 100 linen
or Bockens 90/2 or DMC Retors d'Alsace 30

Start by working the point: hang on two pairs at
A and work WS, twist. Leave the RH pair aside.
*Hang another pair on to a pin at B and work ½st,
then place a pin between these two pairs, removing the original pin B, then enclose the pin with
another ½st*. Repeat from * to * at C.

Go back to pin A and, using the RH pair from
pin A and *hanging on a new pair at pin D, work
½st, then place a pin between these two pairs,
removing the original pin D, then enclose with
another ½st*. Repeat from * to * at next hole, E.

Lay aside these pairs and go to pin F. Work
pins F, G, H and I in torchon ground stitch (i.e.
½st, pin, ½st).

Work the LH spider thus: hang on pairs at J
and K (as at B and C). Twist the legs J and K
twice more (i.e. three twists altogether) and twist
G and I twice more. †Work a spider by working a
WS between the two centre pairs of the four
spider legs then work WS between the two LH
pairs, then another WS between the two RH
pairs, and finally a WS between the two centre
pairs†. Stick the centre pin of spider with two
pairs to the right and two pairs to the left.
Complete the spider by repeating from † to †.
Twist the four spider legs three times each.

Return to the RH spider, laying aside to the
left all four LH spider legs. The LH legs from H
and I must have three twists altogether. Hang on
pairs at L and M, as you did at B and C. Twist the
two RH legs twice more at L and M and work the
spider as from † to †. Stick the pin in the centre,
as before, and finish the spider, as from † to †.

Work the central four torchon ground stitches
(½st, pin, ½st) at holes N, O, P and Q.

Now work the LH fan. Hang on two pairs
from pin at R and work through them in WS with
the pair from K. Replace pin to the left of the
newly-hung-on pairs and work WS, twist. Continue the fan by working through the next two
pairs, then twisting workers twice, turn and
work back to the edge, where you twist the
workers. Then work WS, twist, between the two

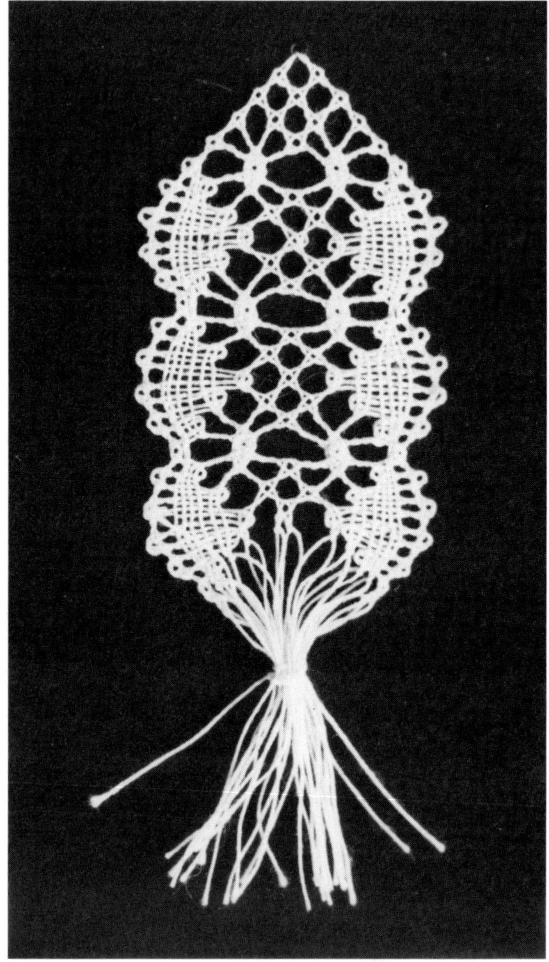

Fig 37 *Finished bookmark with pairs of spiders*

edge pairs; place a pin between them, and repeat
WS, twist. Apart from these edge stitches, the
rest of the fan is worked in WS, twisting the
worker pair twice each time as you stick the inner
pin.

Now work the RH fan. Hang on two pairs
from pin at S and work through them in WS with
the pair from S. Replace pin S to the right of the
newly-hung-on pairs and work WS, twist. Continue the fan by working through the other two
pairs, then twisting the workers twice, turn
and work back to the edge, where you twist
the workers. Then work WS, twist, between the
two edge pairs, place a pin between them, and
repeat WS, twist. At holes T, U and V you take in

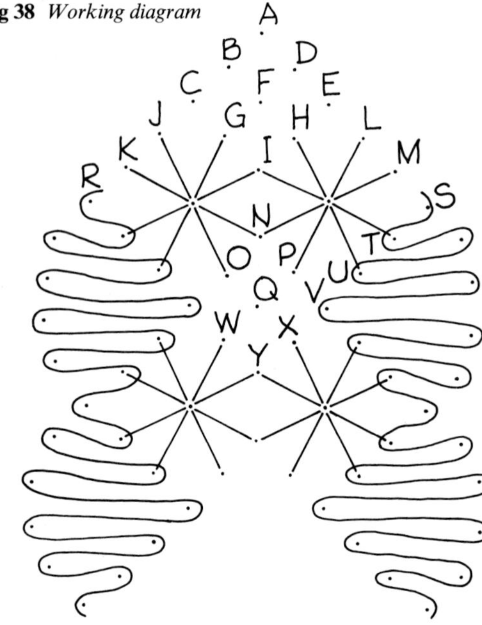

Fig 38 *Working diagram*

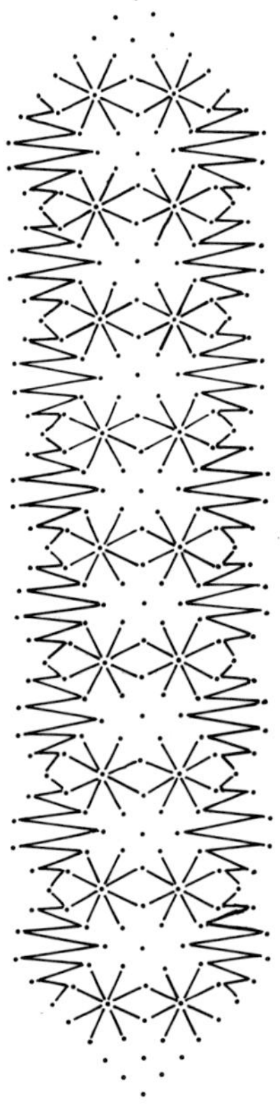

Fig 39 *Pattern*

an extra pair each time, and then you drop them off again, one pair at a time.

Next work torchon ground stitch at holes W, X and Y, in that order.

You are now ready to start the third and fourth spiders, so from now on the pattern repeats.

PATTERN 11   BOOKMARK WITH GIMP

Materials

18 pairs of bobbins wound with
Barbour or Campbell's 100 linen
or Bockens 90/2 or DMC Retors d'Alsace 30
and 4 gimp bobbins wound with DMC Coton
Perle 8

Hang on two pairs at A and work WS, twist. Leave the RH pair aside. *Hang another pair on to a pin at B and work ½st, then place a pin between these two pairs, removing the original pin B, next enclose the pin with another ½st*. Repeat from * to * at C and the following five holes.

At the final hole, D, work WS, twist, between the two edge pairs, stick a pin between them at D, then enclose it with WS, twist. (At the edge hole on each side, as you come to it, repeat this WS, twist, pin, WS, twist, right down the edge.)

Return to the RH pair left hanging from A, and hang a pair on to a pin at E, continuing to repeat from * to *, as before, up to the last hole on the diagonal line. As at D, you now work WS, twist, between the two edge pairs, stick a pin between them at F, then enclose it with WS, twist. Continue to work the edge stitch in this way right down the edge.

Work a series of torchon ground stitches from G to H and I to J.

Hang the LH gimp pair round a pin at K. Lay aside the LH gimp. The pair hanging from H is going to pass through the RH gimp. †Give it an extra twist, then lay the gimp thread (from left to right) *under* the first thread and *over* the second thread of the pair from H. Twist the workers once more†.

The pair hanging from L is going to pass through the LH gimp. Give it an extra twist, then lay the gimp thread (from right to left) *over* the

40

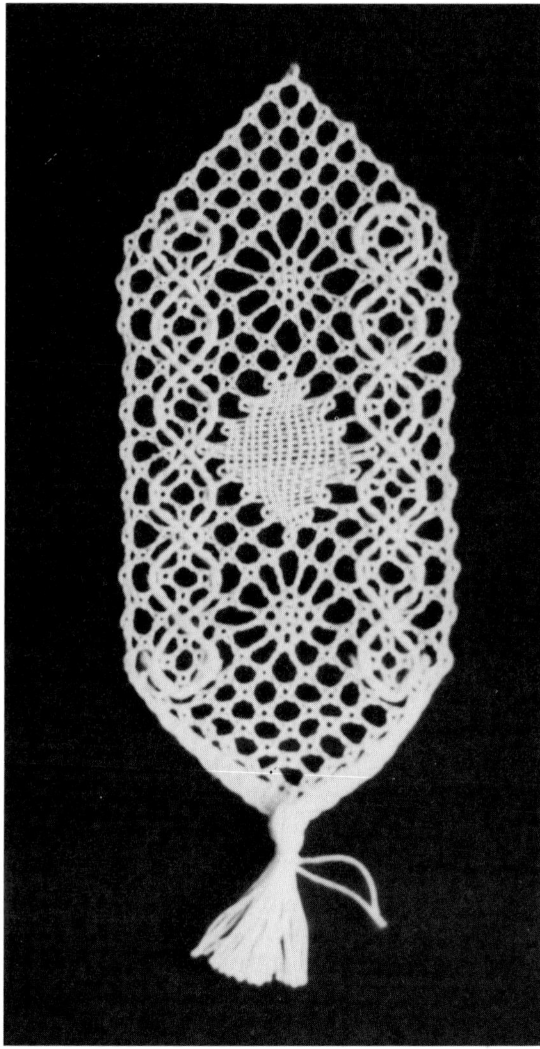

Fig 40 *Finished bookmark with gimp*

Fig 41 *Working diagram*

first worker thread and *under* the next. Twist the workers once more.

The two pairs to work pin K are now in position inside the gimp. Work hc st between them, i.e. $\frac{1}{2}$st, twist, pin, $\frac{1}{2}$st, twist, taking out and replacing the support pin at K in the correct position.

Bring the pair from J through the RH gimp. Repeat from † to † if you need reminding how to do it.

Work a hc st at M, then take the RH of these two pairs out of the gimp. Don't forget that this gimp is now travelling from right to left through the worker pair, so it goes *over* the first worker thread and *under* the next. Twist the workers once more (right over left).

Now bring a pair from N through the gimp to work a hc st at O. The gimp is going from right to left, remember, so it goes over and under (plus an

Fig 42 *Pattern*

extra twist).

The LH pair after this stitch is taken out of the gimp. The gimp is now going from left to right, so it goes *under* the first thread and *over* the second, plus an extra twist.

Finish the honeycomb ring with a hc st before and after the last pin.

Now pass the LH gimp through the LH pair from P (from left to right), and the RH gimp through the RH pair from P (from right to left).

Cross the gimps, left over right. (Actually, it does not matter whether you put left over right or right over left, but it is important to keep to the same throughout.)

With the help of the diagram (Fig 41), the rest of this pattern should present no problems. I worked the spiders in $\frac{1}{2}$st instead of the more normal WS, but you can choose or you can alternate them.

1. At first the passing through of the gimps seems very muddling, but you cannot make a mistake if you remember this. When passing the gimp through, the thread that goes *over* is the one that has just passed *over* its partner and the thread that goes *under* is the one which has just passed *under* its partner. So you don't need to keep trying to work out whether the gimp is travelling to left or right (which can be surprisingly muddling). This rule is infallible and, once you have grasped it, you have mastered gimps for life. Incidentally, the extra twist before passing the gimp through is because one twist is lost as you pass the gimp through.

2. This pattern could cause occasional problems if you were to work the pinholes in the wrong order. There is again an infallible rule, which *always* works; work the *furthest-back* pinhole in any one section first. Basically, once you have got going, you will be working along a diagonal line slanting down from right to left (which is the normal way of working a trolly lace). You will work a section at a time, starting at the hole which is furthest back. This should keep you right, particularly at the edges with the gimps, where you may sometimes find yourself working an edge hole which is in front of an empty pinhole; you will know this is wrong.

3. When you come to the end and wish to finish off the gimps, cross them over as you normally would, then lay each one backwards, in the same channel, without twisting the threads until both pairs have passed through in each direction. You need to think ahead here in order to get all four pairs through the gimp. You may need to undo a few stitches in order to free the threads. Now twist the four pairs from the honeycomb ring, as you normally would after passing the gimps through.

4. To finish, start at the top left pair, work through the next eight pairs in WS. Return to the top left pair and work through the next seven pairs in WS, then the next six pairs, and so on until you have gone through all the pairs. Now go to the top right pair and work through the next eight pairs in WS. Return to the top right pair and work through the next seven pairs in WS, then the next six pairs and so on until you have gone through all the pairs. Now draw the two centre pairs together (i.e. ninth pair from left

and ninth pair from right) and work WS between them, then make a reef-knot between these two pairs. Next draw the eighth pair from left and eighth pair from right together and make a reef-knot between them. Continue this through all the pairs. When all are knotted, take the last two pairs used and, taking one pair to the left and the other to the right, encircle the bundle with these two pairs and tie the back two threads in a reef-knot round the bundle and then the front two threads in a reef-knot round the bundle. Cut off all threads level to form a tassel.

Fig 43 *Finished diamond bookmark*

PATTERN 12   DIAMOND BOOKMARK

Materials

18 pairs of bobbins
Swedish linen thread no. 70
or DMC Cordonnet cotton thread no. 100

Fig 44 *Working diagram*

Fig 45 *Pattern*

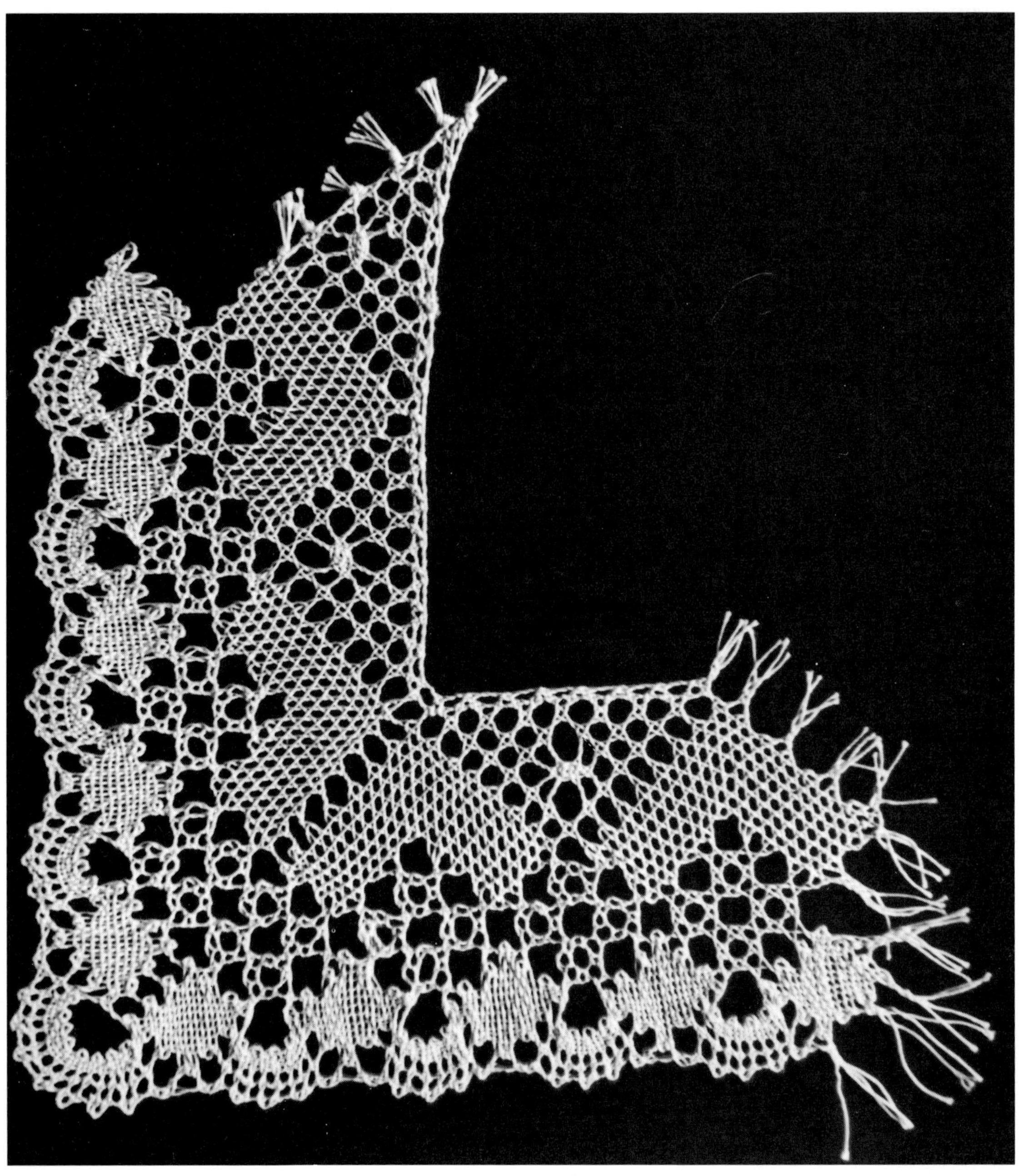

Fig 46 *Finished "All Fours" lace*

PATTERN 13 'ALL FOURS'

Materials

23 pairs of bobbins
Swedish linen thread no. 40
or DMC Cordonnet cotton thread no. 50

Fig 47 *Pattern*

PATTERN 14   STAR MAT

Materials

56 pairs of bobbins
Swedish linen thread no. 70
or DMC Cordonnet cotton thread no. 100

Fig 48 *Pattern*

3 Bedfordshire Lace

INTRODUCTION

Bedfordshire lace has always been called Maltese lace by its olden-day practitioners, a few of whom are still working at the craft of lace-making, which has been handed down through the generations in a 400-year unbroken tradition in Buckinghamshire and Bedfordshire. This style of lace was, in fact, introduced into Bedfordshire after a local person saw the lace from Malta on display at the Great Exhibition of 1851.

It is the ninepin edge which hallmarks the lace as Bedfordshire. Also the old Bedfordshire and Buckinghamshire workers always made their plaits (now called leaves) square-ended, whereas in Malta they are pointed at the ends, resembling leaves and petals. Nowadays, we usually make our leaves pointed, as they are more attractive this way. Lace from Malta is characterised by the shiny, cream-coloured thread, the inclusion of the Maltese cross in the design and quantities of beautifully worked leaves in the design.

Basic instructions

In order to avoid repetition in the patterns, I have written here the basic instructions for Bedfordshire techniques, to which you can easily refer when using the patterns. For other basic lace-making techniques, reference should be made to Chapter 1.

Legs (also known as plaits, brides, bars or straps)
These are the bars which link the footside with the headside in place of a groundwork. They are simply made by performing a number of $\frac{1}{2}$sts consecutively with two pairs of bobbins. Draw

up after three or four stitches at the most. The most even legs can be made by holding the bobbins up in the air and working that way, as you can then keep a good tension on your bobbins all the time.

Leaves (also known as plaits, petals, tallies and leadworks)
The traditional names for legs (above) and leaves are legs and plaits; I learned these from the old Buckinghamshire workers in the 1940s, so they are the names I still use. I will, however, refer to plaits as *leaves* in order to avoid confusion, since some modern lace-makers refer to legs as plaits.

To make a leaf you use two pairs (see Fig 49). If you want a pointed leaf, start with a WS, then, using the thread which did the last part of the stitch (2 over 3), pass it under the fourth thread then back over it, under the middle; over, round and under the LH thread, over the middle thread, then under the RH thread again. Draw the threads up carefully, keeping the weaver thread taut but not too tight and splaying out the two outside threads to the desired shape. Repeat

Fig 49 *"Leaf"*

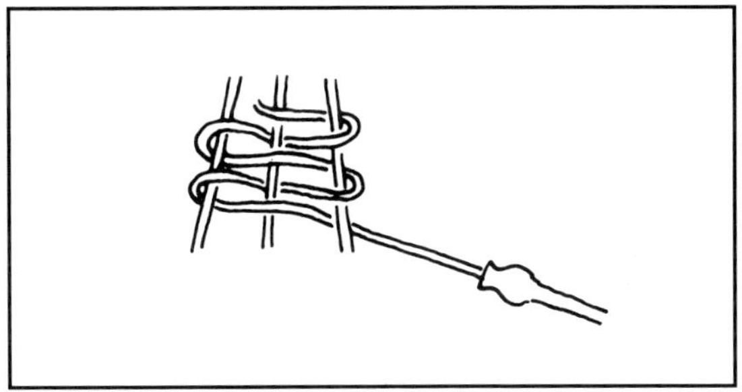

these two rows, drawing up every time the weaver arrives at the RH side. Shape the leaf out, then very gradually in again. It needs a lot of practice, as, at first, you will tend to get little loops at the edge at the point where the leaf decreases in size.

Many workers prefer to hold their bobbins up in their hands to make leaves, as they have more control than with the bobbins down on their pillow.

To make a square-ended leaf (e.g. a tally), start by twisting both pairs twice (or three times with very fine thread), then use the second thread from the left as weaver (over the third, under the fourth, etc.). Finish by twisting each pair two or three times, as before.

Picots
(i) Double (for edge) (see Fig 50). The usual one, on the LH side, is made, normally in a leg, with the pair on the outside (i.e. the LH pair). The pair will have one twist, following the leg. Twist twice more, then lay the pin on top of the outside thread, point to the left, twist the thread once round the pin and stick the pin into the appropriate hole. Take the other bobbin of the pair and wind its thread once round the pin clockwise, twist the pair three times, then draw both threads up tightly. The loops should now be twisted together round the pin.

To make a double picot on the RH side (Fig 51), again use the outside pair of the leg (the RH pair), give it two extra twists, then lay the pin *under* the outside thread, point to the left, and twist the point towards you, round the thread and back to its original position, then stick it in the appropriate hole. Take the other bobbin of the pair and wind its thread once round the pin anti-clockwise, twist three times, then draw both threads up tightly. Do not draw the threads up tightly until this last stage or they will not twist together round the pin.

(ii) Single picot (see Fig 52). Use these on legs inside the work and not on the edge. Twist the outside pair nearest the picot hole once. Pick up the bobbins in your left hand with your index finger between them and turn them over (right over left) so that the tips of your fingers point upwards. Place a pin under the RH thread and hold it up then hold that right hand still while you twist your left hand back again so that the palm is

downwards, twisting the threads *under* the raised pin. Bring the pin and its loop of thread towards you and down between the bobbins, then put the point of the pin up under the LH thread to come out between the two threads, bringing a loop of thread with it. Take this loop out to left or right, depending on where the pinhole is.

Where there are two picots, one each side of the leg, as in the radiating legs of the motifs in Pattern 7, work one picot as above then a $\frac{1}{2}$st between the two pairs, then a second picot the other side.

In Bedfordshire lace pairs of threads go in and out of the different sections in various directions. Four threads at a time are used for legs or leaves to secure one section of lace to another and to provide more or less threads for a section of pattern which is growing larger or smaller. If the designer does not want the pairs of threads in a particular section either to increase or decrease, yet needs to attach it to the next section of lace, there are two common methods of achieving this: cucumbers and kisses. (The quaint terminology is one of the joys of Bedfordshire lace.)

Cucumbers
These are in fact sideways-on tallies. Instead of the narrow side being the width and the longer side the length, the reverse is true. They are worked with the worker pairs from two adjacent sections. A short, wide tally is worked, with perhaps about eight or ten rows in all, then the workers return to their places. Each pair is twisted either two or three times (depending on the space available) both before and after the tally.

Kiss
(i) Workers cross. This is worked using the worker pairs from two adjacent sections. As each worker arrives at the corresponding pin, the pin is stuck. The worker pair is twisted a suitable number of times to fit the space, often three times. The two worker pairs work a WS, twist, following which each pair returns to the other pair's section to be the worker pair and enter the section after the pin which has just been stuck. (Sometimes there is a pinhole between the two sections, at which the two workers will work $\frac{1}{2}$st,

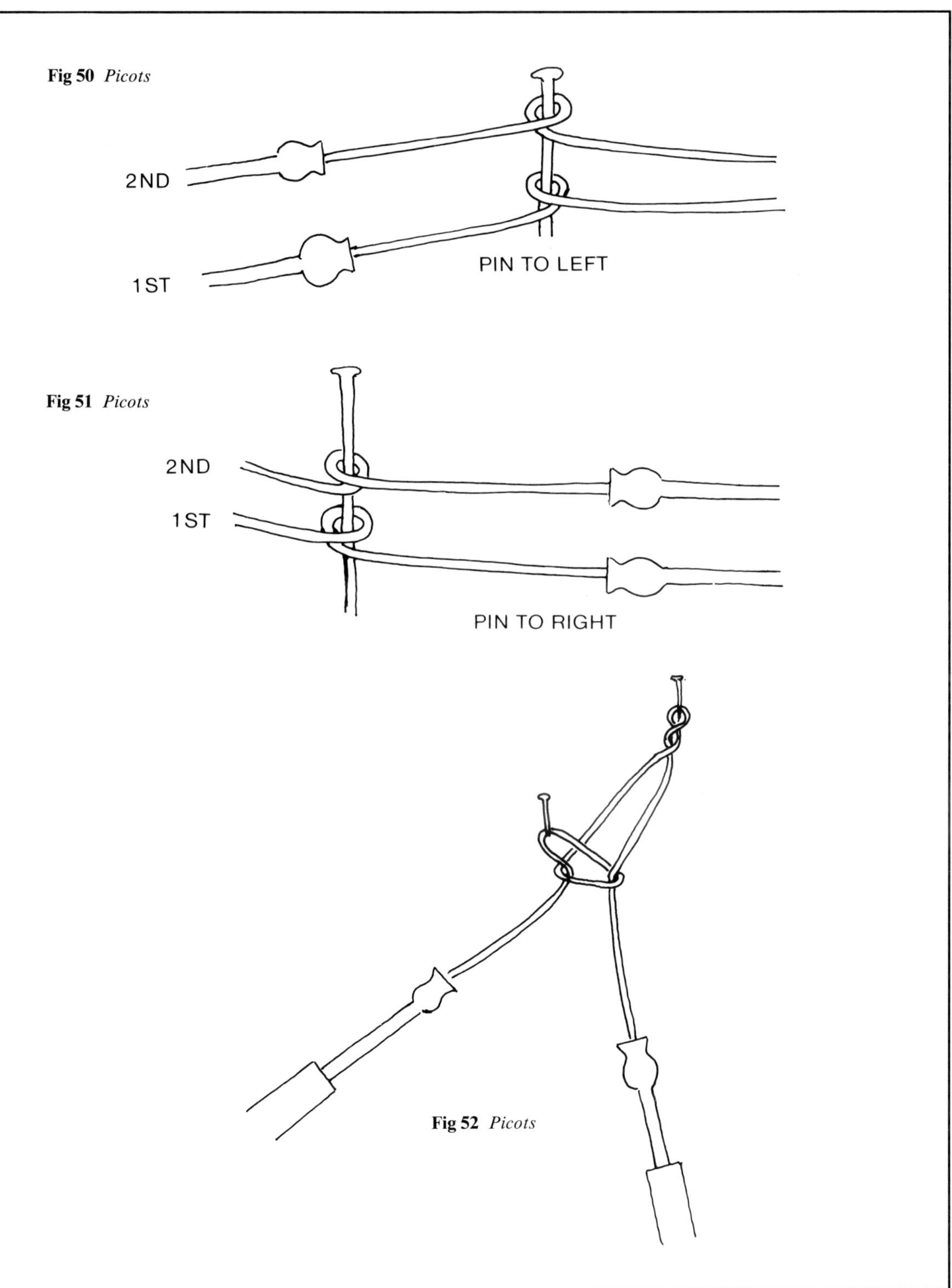

Fig 50 Picots
2ND
1ST
PIN TO LEFT
Fig 51 Picots
2ND
1ST
PIN TO RIGHT
Fig 52 Picots

pin, $\frac{1}{2}$st, which is exactly the same in result as WS, twist.)

(ii) One pair crosses to an adjacent section and returns, doing a sewing to itself. This kiss is used when only one pair can be spared and there is not another worker pair available in the next section, as in the Town Trot pattern. The worker pair is twisted about five times after the pin has been stuck; it is then taken into the adjacent section and released again. It then twists about twice. Make a sewing by drawing a loop from one of the threads of this pair behind the other twisted threads. Thread the other bobbin of the pair through the loop, draw it up, and twist the pair twice. Return it to the section where it started.

Windmill

This is the stitch used when four pairs cross at one point. Use each pair as if it were a single bobbin and work a WS, but stick the pin between the two double pairs before the final move which is 2 over 3.

6-pair crossing

This is used, for example, in the centre of the motif (Pattern 8), where three leaves have been worked and then need to cross each other before working three more leaves with the same pairs. It is also used in the motif at M, where three legs meet.

Use each pair of bobbins as a single thread.

Pass the left centre pair under the next pair to the left.

Pass the right centre pair over the next pair to the right.

Twist the two centre pairs, right over left.

Pass the left centre pair under the next pair to the left and over the next pair to the left.

Pass the right centre pair over the next pair to the right and under the next pair to the right.

Put a pin in the centre.

Pass the left centre pair under the next pair to the left.

Pass the right centre pair over the next pair to the right.

Twist the two centre pairs, right over left.

Pass the left centre pair under the next pair to the left.

Pass the right centre pair over the next pair to the right.

Pull up carefully and do a WS with each pair then work the next section.

8-pair crossing

Use each pair of bobbins as a single thread.

Make a $\frac{1}{2}$st with the centre four pairs.

Make a $\frac{1}{2}$st with the RH four pairs.

Make a $\frac{1}{2}$st with the LH four pairs.

Repeat these three $\frac{1}{2}$sts.

Stick a pin in the centre.

Make a WS with the centre four pairs.

Of the RH four pairs, cross the centre two left over right.

Of the LH four pairs, cross the centre two left over right.

Pull up carefully and do a WS with each pair, then work the next section.

Taking in and letting out a leg or leaf from trail or footside

The obvious and simple way to do this is to work through the two extra pairs of the leg with the workers as they arrive at the pinhole where the leg is to be taken in, as you would when taking any pairs into another section. You would then twist the workers twice, stick the pin with the workers behind it, then work back through the two extra pairs, continuing on through the remaining pairs of the section and releasing the extra pairs to work their next leg.

However, a neater and better way is as follows. Work through the two extra pairs with the workers as they arrive at the pinhole where the leg is to be taken in. Stick the pin *between* the two leg pairs (i.e., there are two pairs outside the pin). Enclose the pin by working WS between the pairs on each side of the pin. Now continue the leg with the two outside pairs, whilst the inner pair after enclosing the pin becomes the new worker pair.

Adding on a new pair

Either in the early stages of a new pattern or at a corner, it is often necessary to add on one or two pairs in order to have sufficient pairs to make a leg, leaf, etc.

When you arrive at the pinhole where this pair is needed, hang a pair of bobbins on a pin stuck into any convenient empty pinhole (it will soon be removed).

Work through this new pair in WS, with your workers. Twist the workers and stick the pin as usual and work through the new pair as the workers make their way back through the pairs of this section. Immediately you have worked through the new pair, take out the temporary pin and draw up the threads carefully so that there are no loops. Work the workers at least to the next pin before you use the new pair so that it is firm and the new pair does not drag the work out of place.

If you are hanging on two pairs at the same time, follow exactly the same procedure, hanging the two pairs side by side on the temporary pin.

Taking out a pair

Towards the end of a mat or motif, or after a corner, you may have pairs that you have finished with and wish to drop off.

There are different ways of doing this, depending on the section of pattern where this occurs.
(i) If the pairs arrive at a WS section of pattern, take them into this and work them in. Either drop off corresponding pairs which are already in this section or work these pairs in for four rows or so before dropping them off. To drop them off all you do is lay the pairs to the back of the work. Cut them off now with a 10cm end if you wish. Then when the work is finished, trim the ends off very close to the work. Do not drop off more than one pair at a time or that section will change shape too suddenly.
(ii) If the pairs arrive at a more open section of pattern, legs, leaves, etc., you may need to use your ingenuity. You can, for example, 'hide' one extra pair in a leg by working two of the threads double, or hide it in a leaf by having two of the passive threads double. After working such a leg or leaf, the extra pair could be cut off. This would be equivalent to darning in the ends and a great deal quicker and neater.
(iii) When you have worked round a motif and arrive back at the section where you started, you can make 'sewings' (Chapter 1), and then tie off or darn in the ends.
(iv) In Patterns 7 and 8, where pairs go round the pattern to right and left and all meet together at the bottom centre, use your discretion as to the most suitable methods of finishing compatible with the end use of the article. For example, if you plan to mount the motif and put it under glass, it does not matter what the back looks like, nor is strength important, so long as it lasts in one piece until it has been mounted. A perfect appearance on the right side is the top priority.

You can therefore do various unconventional things. For example, you could sew groups of ends out through the back of the mount, or you could leave some groups of ends as much as 2cm long. Pinch them together and roll them round to make them stay behind the more solid bits. You will find this will often show less than cutting the ends short.

However, for Pattern 7, if it is to be used as a mat rather than mounting it, it must be strong for repeated washings. Keep it as neat as possible on the back because some future non-lace-making owner may display it either way up. Where trails or legs meet, the threads may be tied to their corresponding threads where they meet. After the knot, do not cut off short but leave a 16cm end, which you should darn in a little way when the work is complete.

Naturally, in both these patterns, you will take out pairs as described in (i) and (ii) where possible, as soon as they are finished with, leaving the smallest number possible to deal with at the end.

Reference should be made to the instructions in the Introduction on the use of coloured transparent sticky film if you wish to avoid the marking out of patterns.

PATTERN 1   NINEPIN

Materials

8 pairs of bobbins
Swedish linen thread no. 90 or 100
or DMC Cordonnet no. 50 for a stronger edge

Hang four pairs of bobbins at A, the three LH pairs being splayed one outside the other. The fourth (RH) pair is on last, separately. Hang two pairs at B side by side. With LH pair from A do WS to the right through the next four pairs.

Twist workers once and do WS through edge pair. Now twist new edge pair three times, and second pair from the right once. These are the new workers. Replace pin at B with those four threads behind it and both pairs now to the right of it.

*WS through the next two pairs to the left with the new workers. Twist twice, stick a pin at C with workers to the left of it.

Work back through two pairs, twist the

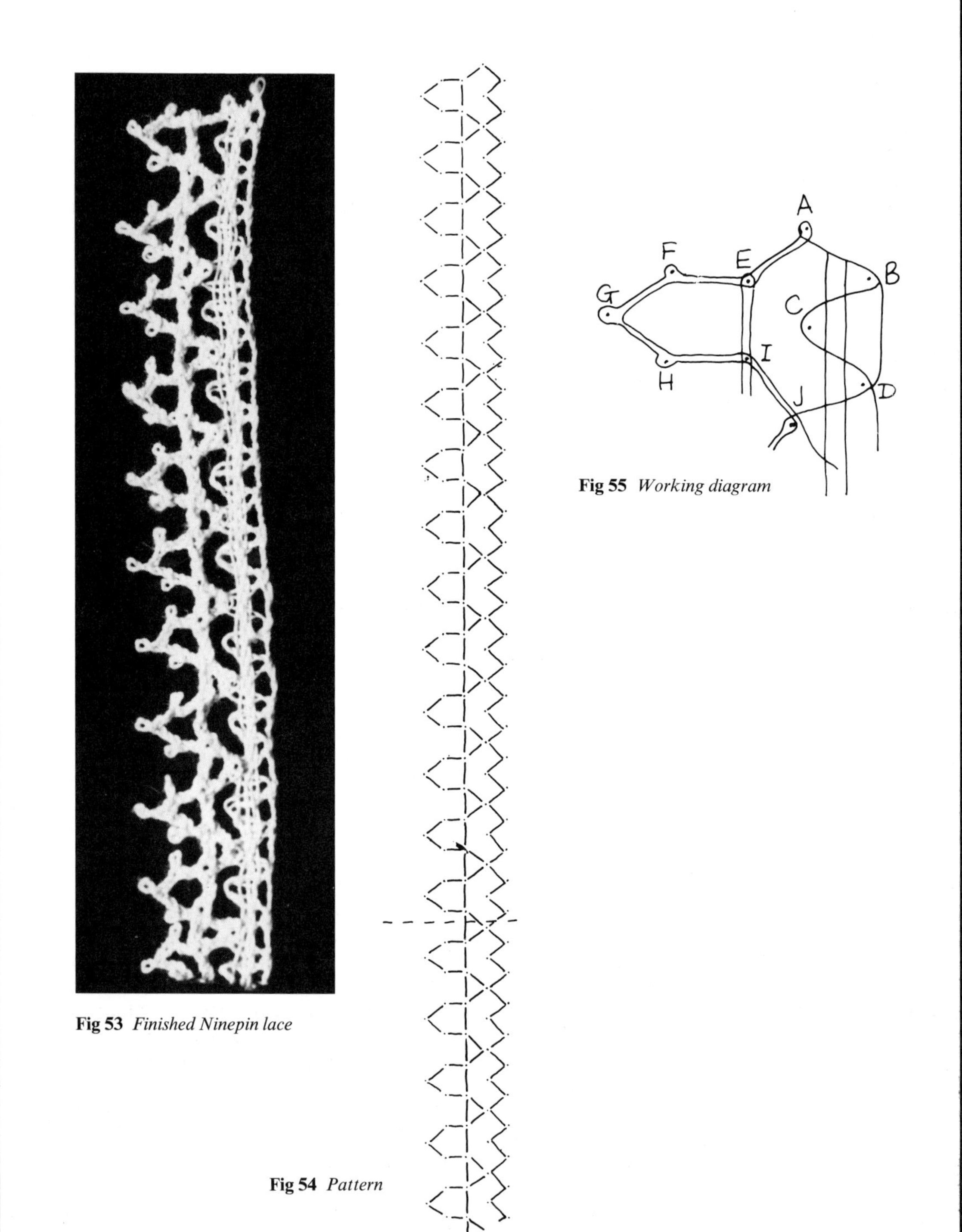

Fig 53 *Finished Ninepin lace*

Fig 54 *Pattern*

Fig 55 *Working diagram*

workers once and do WS with edge pair. Twist the new edge pair three times, the inner pair once: these are the new workers. Stick a pin at D with both pairs to the right of it and do WS to the left with new workers through the other two pairs*.

You must now leave the footside until you have worked the next head. Pin J is the catchpin which links the headside with the footside (and is a repeat of pin A).

†Work $\frac{1}{2}$st leg (i.e. about five $\frac{1}{2}$sts consecutively) with the two pairs left hanging from A at the beginning. Hang two more pairs at E, one outside the other, and make a windmill stitch with these four pairs. Count each pair as a single bobbin, doing a $\frac{1}{2}$st, then stick a pin between them (i.e. replace pin at E with two pairs to the left and two to the right). Complete a WS by crossing the second pair from the left over the third pair from the left.

Work a $\frac{1}{2}$st leg (about six $\frac{1}{2}$sts) with the two RH pairs then leave them.

Work a $\frac{1}{2}$st leg (about four $\frac{1}{2}$sts) with the two LH pairs then make a double picot at F. Make a leg to G, where you repeat the picot. Make another leg to H and another picot, then another leg to I.

Here make a windmill stitch as before, then a $\frac{1}{2}$st leg with the LH two pairs (about six stitches), then leave them. Make a $\frac{1}{2}$st leg (about five $\frac{1}{2}$sts) with the two RH pairs to reach the catchpin at J. This joins the headside and footside†.

‡At J take your footside workers (fourth pair from the right) and work a WS through these two pairs. Stick pin at J between the two passive pairs (i.e. with two pairs of bobbins to the left of the pin). Enclose the pin by working WS with the pair on each side of the pin (the former passives)‡. After this the RH pair becomes the footside worker pair and the two LH pairs make the $\frac{1}{2}$st leg as you start the repeat again from † to †. Do this next. It is more convenient from now on to work the headside before the corresponding footside.

When you have completed the head from † to †, work the footside, by using the RH pair coming from pin J as workers. Work in WS through two pairs to the right. Twist workers once, then do a WS with edge pair. Twist the inner pair once and edge pair three times and stick edge pin to the left of these two pairs. Continue from * to *. Finish the section by

repeating from ‡ to ‡, for the catchpin, followed by the headside, then the footside and so on.

(You will notice that there are nine pins from A to I, which give the pattern its name: J starts the next repeat.)

PATTERN 2   NARROW EDGING

Materials

10 pairs of bobbins
Filato di cantu thread no. 50
or Swedish linen thread no. 90 or 100

I suggest that you start this pattern as I did in the sample at pin E in Fig 57. First hang on two pairs, splayed one outside the other, at E. Work WS, twist, between them, then twist the RH pair two extra times. Hang two passive pairs temporarily on pin D, then drop them off after two or three rows. Work through these two pairs in WS with the LH pair from E. Twist the workers twice and place pin F to the left of them. Work two WS to the right through the two passives then twist the workers once. Work WS, twist, with the edge pair then twist the edge pair two extra times. Stick a pin at G with these two pairs to the right of it. Use the second pair from the right to work two WS to the left through the passives.

Now hang two pairs temporarily on the pin L, side by side. Work through them in WS with these workers, twist the workers twice and stick pin N to the right of the workers. Work back in WS through these two pairs then remove pin L and draw up the threads neatly. Make a leg (about six $\frac{1}{2}$sts) with these two LH pairs to reach to P and leave them.

Return to the workers (fourth pair from the right) and make two WS to the right through the two passive pairs. Twist the workers once, work WS, twist, with the edge pair, twist the edge pair two extra times and stick pin O to the left of these pairs. Remove temporary pin D and draw up the threads neatly, then leave the footside and return to the leg hanging from N to P.

Hang two pairs (one splayed outside the other) temporarily at pin M to the left of the leg from N to P. Using these four pairs, make a windmill and stick a pin at P, then remove pin M and draw up the threads neatly. Make a leg to V with the two

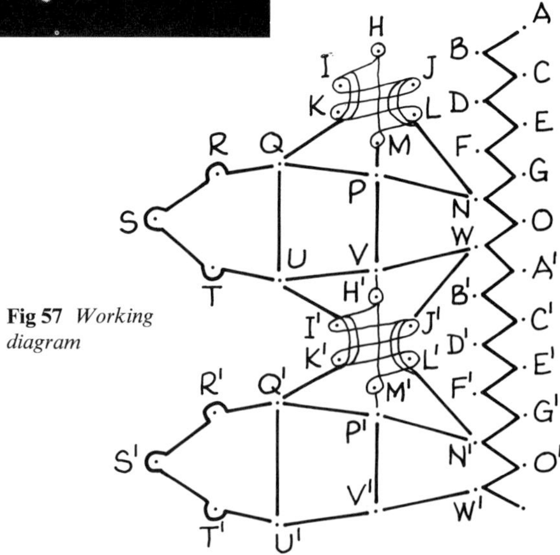

Fig 56 *Finished narrow edging lace*

RH pairs (about four ½sts) and leave them.

With the two LH pairs make a leg to Q (about four ½sts). Hang two pairs side by side temporarily at K to the left of this leg from P to Q. Using these four pairs, make a windmill and stick pin at Q, then remove pin K and draw up the threads neatly.

All the threads are now hung on and you can continue with the instructions from † onwards (see below).

Start of the repeating pattern at A. After the WS, twist, between the two RH pairs, followed by two extra twists of the RH pair, place pin A to the left of both pairs.

*Next, with the inner pair as workers, work two WS to the left (i.e. between the second and third pairs from the right, then between the third

Fig 57 *Working diagram*

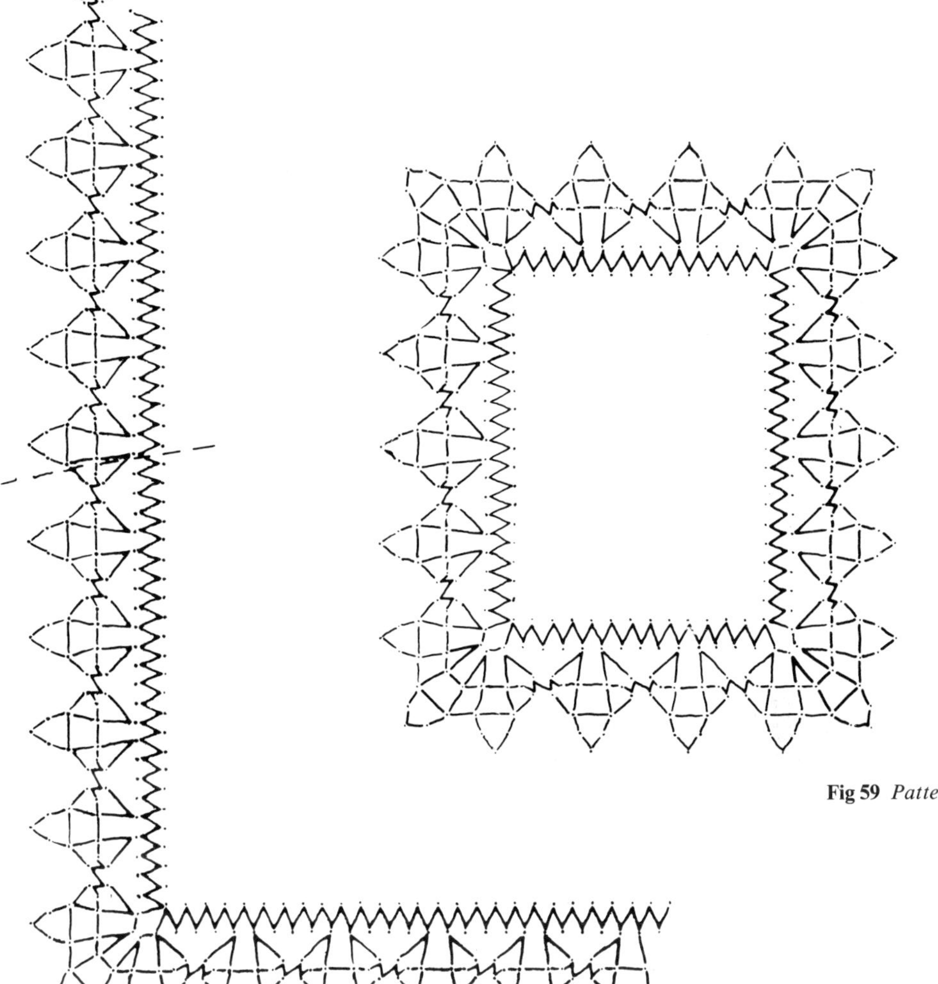

and fourth pairs from the right). Twist the workers twice and stick a pin B to the right of the workers. Make two WS to the right between the same pairs as before, then twist the workers once. Work WS, twist, with the edge pair followed by two extra twists of the RH pair then place pin C^1 to the left of both pairs*.

Now work from * to * at pins D^1 and E^1 and again at pins F^1 and G^1. Leave the footside.

Stick pin H^1 between the two pairs of the leg from V. After sticking pin H, make a WS between the two pairs, then the LH pair after this stitch becomes the worker pair and works through the two pairs of the leg from U in WS, then the worker pair is twisted twice, pin I^1 inserted to the right of the workers and the worker pair goes back in WS through these two

pairs, through the other original pair, then through the two pairs of the leg from W. Twist the worker pair twice and insert pin J^1 to the left of them. Work WS back through five pairs to the left. Twist workers twice and stick pin K^1 to the right of them. Work WS back through five pairs to the right. Twist workers twice and stick pin L^1 to the left of them. Work WS back through three pairs and twist once both the workers and the last pair worked through. Stick pin M^1 between them and work two or three $\frac{1}{2}$sts with them to leave these two pairs ready as a leg from M^1 to P^1.

Return to the two LH pairs hanging from K^1. Make about four $\frac{1}{2}$sts to form a leg from K to Q^1 and leave them. Return to the two RH pairs hanging from L. Make about six $\frac{1}{2}$sts to form a leg from L^1 to N^1.

Now leave these pairs to the left while you return to the footside workers, which will be the second pair from the right at G^1. (This pair will have one twist in it.) Make two WS to the left with these workers through the two passive pairs.

‡Catch in the leg from L^1 by working through both pairs in WS. Place a pin between the two passives (i.e. with two pairs to the left of it). Make a WS with these passive pairs to enclose the pin. After this stitch the RH pair becomes the new footside worker pair and will be used in a moment, but first make a leg to P^1 (about six $\frac{1}{2}$sts) with the two LH pairs, i.e. the former footside worker pair and the LH pair after the enclosing of the pin. Lay aside this leg while you return to the footside worker pair (fourth pair from the right). With it work two WS to the right through the passive pairs, twist once, then WS, twist, with the edge pair followed by two extra twists of RH pair‡.

Stick pin O^1 to the left of both these pairs then leave the footside while you work the head.

Return to the two pairs which made the leg from N^1 to P^1. With these two pairs and the two pairs of the leg from M, make a windmill and stick the pin at P^1. After this, make a leg with the two RH pairs to reach to V^1 (about four or five $\frac{1}{2}$sts) and leave them.

Return to the two LH pairs and make a leg to Q^1 (about three or four $\frac{1}{2}$sts). Using these two pairs and the two pairs of the leg from K^1, make a windmill and stick pin at Q^1.

†After this, make a leg with the two RH pairs to reach U (about four $\frac{1}{2}$sts) and leave them.

Make a leg to R^1 (about three or four $\frac{1}{2}$sts) and make a picot at R^1. Make a leg to S^1 (about three or four $\frac{1}{2}$sts) and make a picot at S^1. Make a leg to T^1 (about three or four $\frac{1}{2}$sts: the same as R^1 to S^1) and make a picot at T^1. Make a leg to U^1 (about three or four $\frac{1}{2}$sts: the same as Q^1 to R^1). Using these two pairs and the two pairs of the leg from Q^1, make a windmill and stick pin at U^1.

With the two LH pairs make a leg (about four $\frac{1}{2}$sts: the same as K^1 to Q^1) to reach to I^1 and leave them.

With the two RH pairs make a leg (about three or four $\frac{1}{2}$sts: the same as P^1 to Q^1) to V^1. Using these two pairs and the two pairs of the leg from P^1, make a windmill and stick pin at V^1.

With the two LH pairs make a leg (about two $\frac{1}{2}$sts) to H^1 and leave them.

With the two RH pairs make a leg to W^1 of equal length to the leg from N^1 to P^1 (about six $\frac{1}{2}$sts), then lay them to the left.

Return to the footside workers, which will be the second pair from the right at O^1. (This pair will have one twist in it.) Make two WS to the left with these workers through the two passive pairs. Now catch in the leg from V^1 at pin W^1 as in the instructions for pin N^1 from ‡ to ‡, making a leg from W^1 to J^1 in place of the one from N to P in these first instructions.

You have now exactly completed one repeat of the pattern and you go back to the beginning of the instructions and stick the pin at A^1.

The corner

At the corner the worker pair passes through the legs from the headside at the two central inner holes (near the inside point of the corner). The working of the corner is quite straightforward and clear from the marking on the pattern.

PATTERN 3   PLAITED TRAY-CLOTH BORDER

Materials

17 pairs of bobbins
Swedish linen thread no. 35

Note Pattern 3 was worked with linen thread, no. 25. This is no longer available but there is a simple remedy. Take the pattern to your local photocopiers and have it reduced a little. I would have three slightly different sizes photocopied, then at home you can try them with your threads to see which is best.

Hang on two pairs at A, one splayed outside the other, and work WS, twist. Twist the RH pair two extra times and lay it aside.

Hang on five pairs at B, side by side, and work through them in WS, using the LH pair from A as workers. Replace pin at B with workers, twisted twice, to the left of it.

Using this LH pair at B, work WS to the right through two pairs, then make a leg with these two pairs to reach to C and lay them aside.

Return to your workers (fifth pair from right) and work WS through three pairs to the right, then twist workers once, work WS with edge

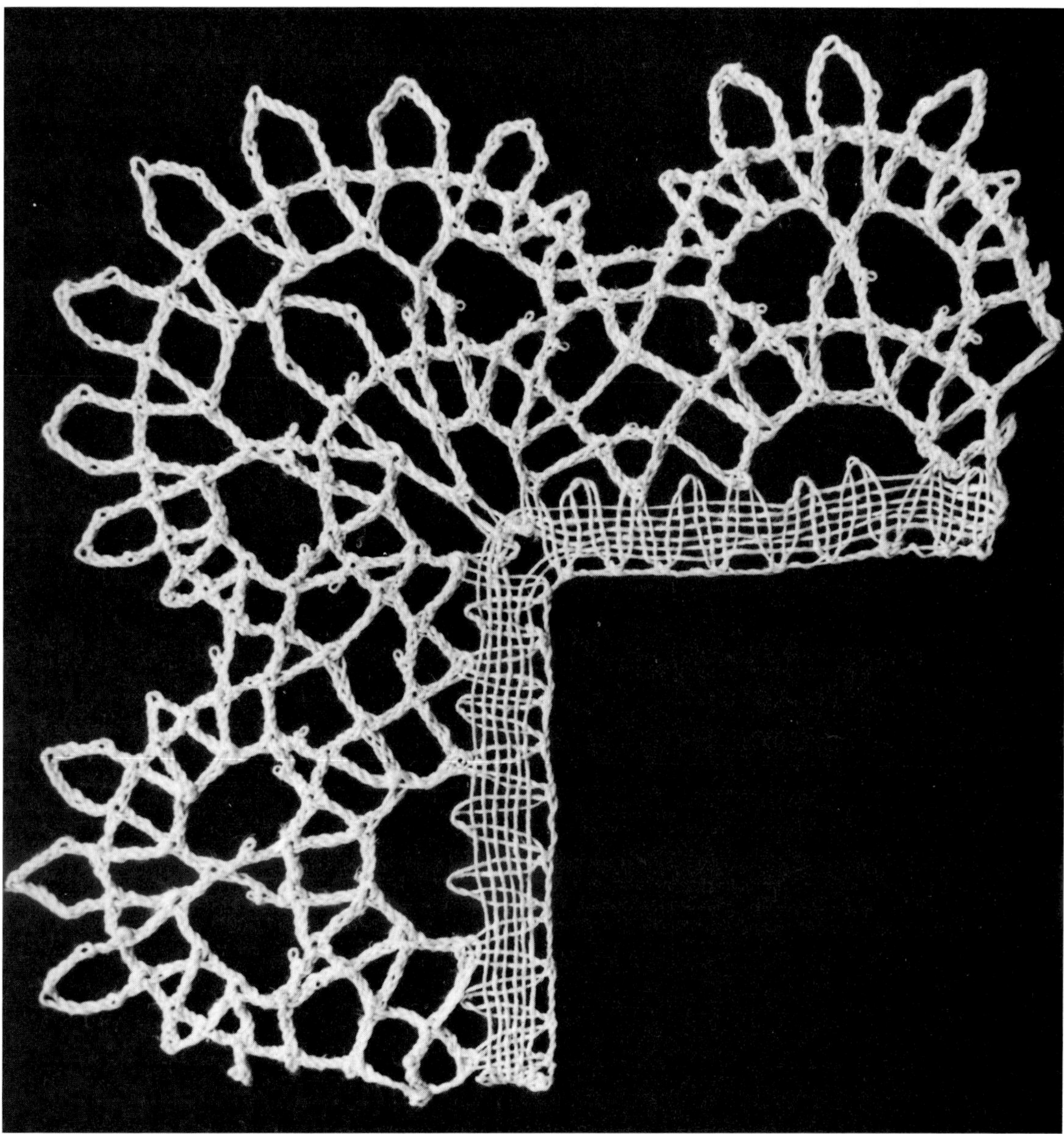

pair, twist RH pair two extra times and lay it aside. Stick pin at D with these two pairs to the right of it.

The footside now continues in the normal manner, except that there are three passive pairs as well as the edge pair, whereas in the two previous patterns there were two. The diagram (Fig 63) indicates where to take in and release pairs.

Return to the leg hanging from B and reaching to C. Hang on two more pairs at C, one splayed outside the other and make a windmill between these four pairs, replacing the pin at C in the normal manner for a windmill.

Make a leg with the RH two pairs to reach to E and a leg with the LH two pairs to reach to F.

Hang on four pairs at G, splayed outside one another and work a windmill stitch round the

pin. With the RH two pairs make a leg to reach to F. With the LH two pairs make a leg to reach to H. Hang on two more pairs at H, splayed one outside the other and make a windmill stitch with the leg from G, replacing the pin at H in the normal manner for a windmill stitch.

With the RH two pairs make a leg to reach to I. With the LH two pairs make a leg to reach to J.

Hang on two pairs at J, one splayed outside the other, and work a windmill stitch with the leg from H, replacing the pin at J in the normal manner for a windmill stitch.

All 17 pairs are now hung on and there should be no further difficulty if you have worked through the two previous patterns and if you refer to the diagram (Fig 63), which shows you the direction of the legs, in case you are in doubt.

At the corner, in the plaited section, you will

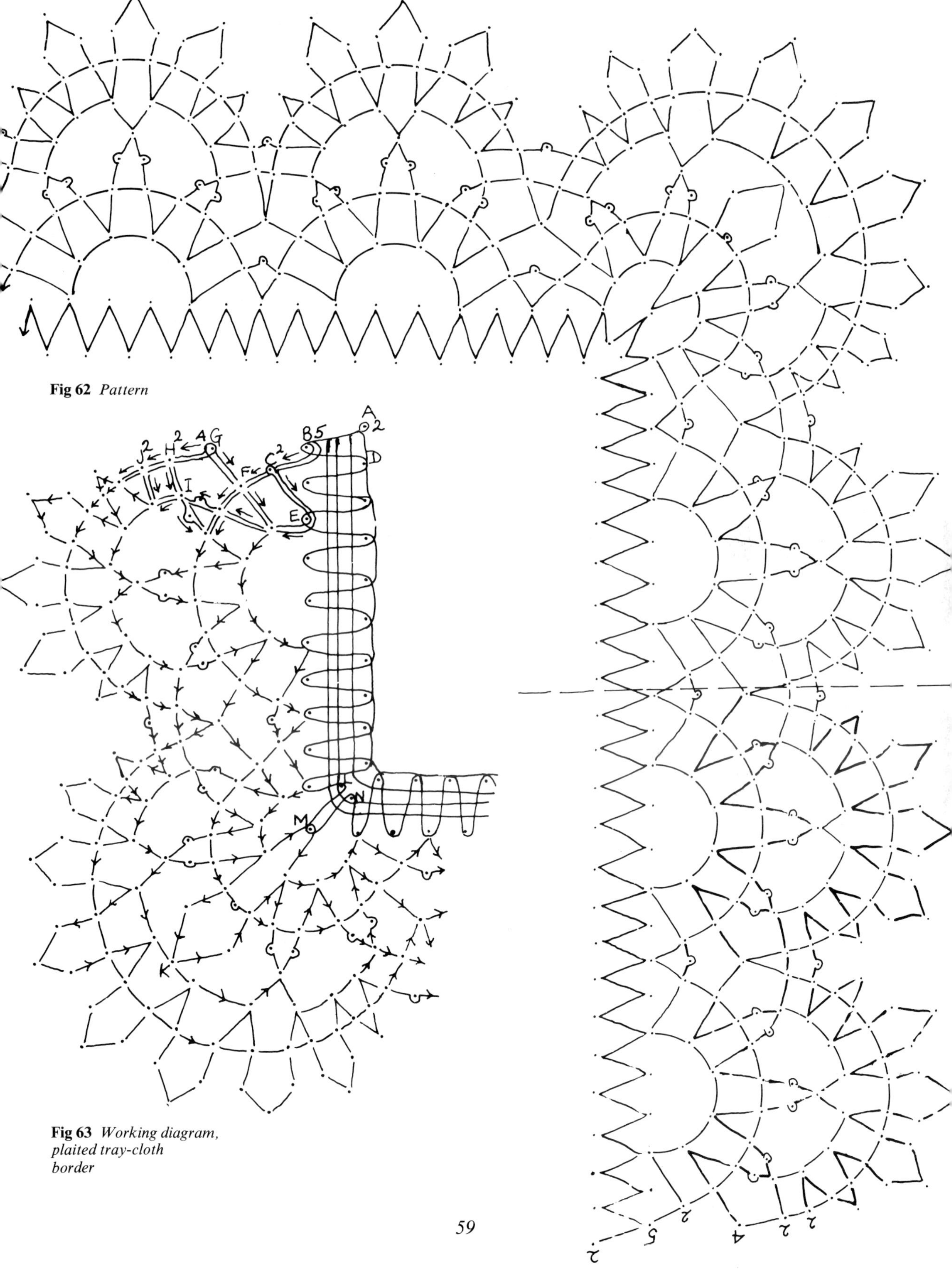

Fig 62 *Pattern*

Fig 63 *Working diagram,
plaited tray-cloth
border*

find that a leg is taken into part of the semi-circle and immediately released at K.

At the inside point of the corner, the footside workers only pass through two pairs of passives at L and N, between which they catch in the point of a leg at M. The workers should be twisted twice both before and after the stitches with the leg at pin M. (You will notice that this was omitted in the sample.)

Since the thread is coarse, it was thought preferable to use a typical Cluny edging, in which the pins are stuck between the two pairs of the leg and then the leg carries straight on after the pin, rather than making picots. These might have looked puny and out of place and would have rendered the finished piece less hard-wearing. A few single picots are included, as indicated, in the centre of the work.

PATTERN 4   THE SPIDER

Materials

24 pairs of bobbins and 1 extra pair at corner
DMC Cordonnet cotton thread no. 80
or Swedish linen thread no. 70

Hang on two pairs at A, one splayed outside the other. Work WS, twist, give the outer pair two extra twists and lay them aside to the right.

Hang four pairs on at B, side by side. With the LH pair from A, work through these four pairs in WS, twist workers twice, then replace a pin at B with the worker pair to the left of it and the other four pairs sliding into the gap between A and B.

Work back to the right through the four pairs in WS then twist workers once and do WS, twist, with the edge pair, then twist RH pair twice more. Stick pin at C to the left of both of these pairs. RH pair is laid aside to the right. LH pair works to the left in WS through two pairs only. (The other two pairs which were originally hung on at pin B are laid aside to the left in order to work the leg from B to E in due course.) Twist the workers twice and stick a pin to the right of them at pin D.

The footside will now continue as in the ninepin footside, taking in and releasing legs as indicated by the lines on the diagram (Fig 65). It is suggested that you use the method suggested in the basic instructions, Chapter 1.

When you have completed the footside as far as you can (i.e. until a leg is taken in) return to the two pairs left hanging from B. Work a leg with these to E.

Hang two more pairs, one splayed outside the other, at E. Make a windmill stitch between them and the two pairs of the leg from B and replace pin at E, in the usual way for a windmill (i.e. before the last movement of 2 over 3).

With the two RH pairs make a leg to G and leave them. With the two LH pairs make a leg to F, where you repeat from * to *.

With the two LH pairs make a leg to P and leave them.

With the two RH pairs make a leg to H and leave them.

Return to the footside and take in the two pairs at G, then release them. Work more footside until you reach the next place where a leg is taken in (at I) and leave it there.

Make a windmill at H then work a leg with the LH pair to Q and leave them and a leg with RH pair to I. Work this into the footside and release it and work on another bit of footside as far as you can.

Hang on four pairs at J, splayed outside one another, and four pairs similarly at K. Of these pairs work the three inner LH pairs through the three inner RH pairs in WS (i.e. do three WS to the right with the fifth pair from the right of this group as workers, then three WS to the right with the sixth pair from the right as workers, then three WS to the right with seventh pair from right as workers).

†Using the RH pair from J as the true workers work three WS to the left and, using the LH pair from K as true workers, work three WS to the right. These two pairs of workers are now in the centre. Twist each pair once, stick pin L between them and enclose with WS. Work the RH pair through three pairs to the right in WS, twist twice and stick pin M with workers to the right. Work centre LH pair through three pairs to the left in WS, twist twice and stick pin N with workers to the left. Now make a WS with the two centre passive pairs. These two pairs then make a leaf from L to O†.

The two trails should now be straightforward, the diagram (Fig 65) showing clearly where pairs are taken in and pairs left out.

The ninepin edge will be familiar to you with minor variations. I suggest the picots round the

Fig 64 *Finished lace, The Spider*

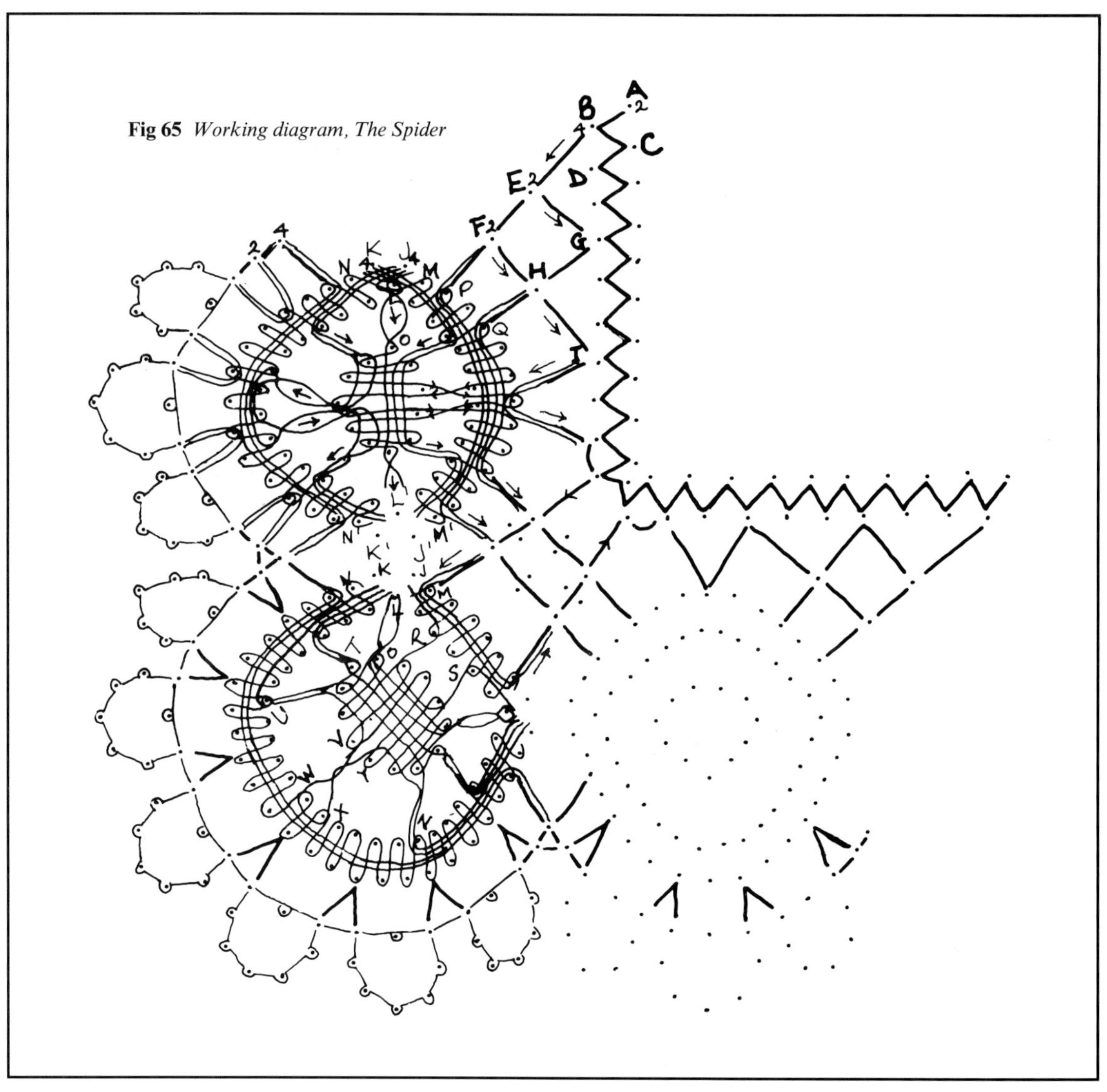

Fig 65 *Working diagram, The Spider*

edge are double picots and those on the inner row are worked as single ones.

Cross-over. Since the very first trail cross-over is slightly different from subsequent ones I will here describe the sequence of stitches at a normal trail cross-over (other than those which are at the beginning and end of the corner). I have named the last three holes of the preceding trail K^1, J^1 and L^1, as indicated at the end of the first trail in the diagram (Fig 65). Similarly, the two previous holes are named M^1 and N^1. Reference should be made to the enlarged diagram of the cross-over (Fig 67).

Bring the RH workers from M^1 to the left in WS through the two pairs of passives then through the RH pair hanging from the centre leaf at L^1.

Bring the LH workers from N^1 to the right in WS through the two pairs of passives then through the LH pair hanging from the centre leaf at L^1.

Twist each worker pair once then stick centre

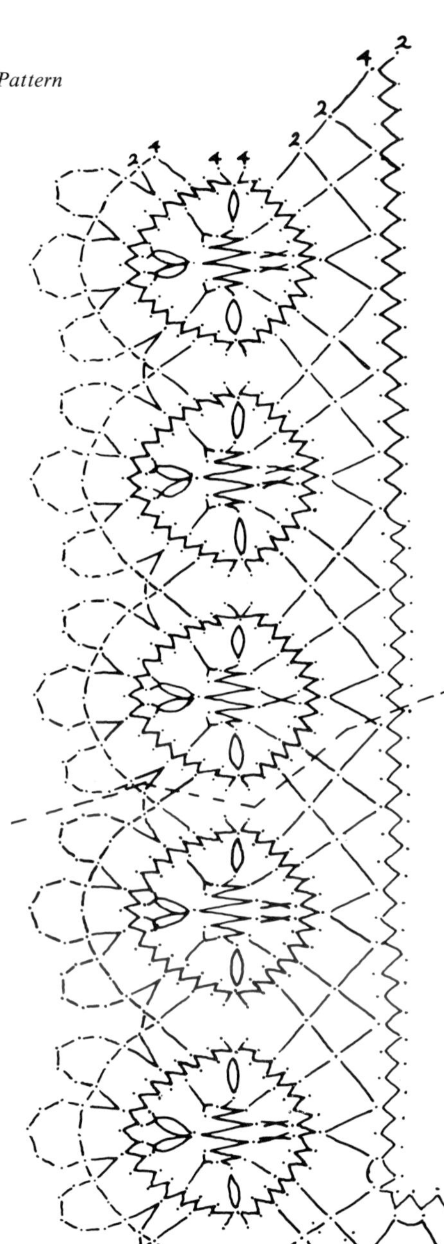

pin L[1] between them, enclose with WS. Pass the RH pair through three passive pairs to the right in WS, twist twice and stick pin J[1] with the worker pair to the right of it.

Pass the LH pair through three passive pairs to the left in WS, twist twice and stick pin K[1] with the worker pair to the left of it. With the remaining six pairs in the centre work the three LH pairs through the three RH pairs in WS (i.e. do three WS to the right with the fourth pair from the right of this group as workers, then three WS to the right with the fifth pair from the right as workers, then three WS to the right with the sixth pair from the right as workers).

Now bring the RH workers leftwards from J[1] to the centre through three pairs in WS, and the LH workers rightwards to the centre through three pairs in WS. These pairs now become passive pairs.

Of the eight pairs now hanging in the centre, twist the RH pair twice and stick pin J to the left of it. Twist the LH pair twice and stick pin K to the right of it. These are the new workers. Now finish the cross-over as described from † to † above.

The working of the centre of the spider should be clear from the diagram (Fig 65). The three sets of pairs coming in are no problem. On the centre right of the spider, the workers exchange with the workers from the RH side of the trail at two consecutive pinholes, using the 'kiss' as described on page 48.

On the centre left of the spider, two pairs go *outwards* to the trail, making a leaf, and then each pair is taken into the trail at consecutive pinholes. They are then left out again at the next

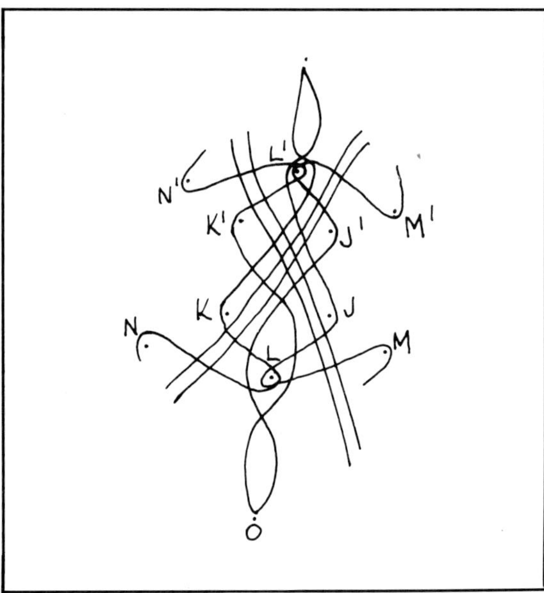

Fig 67 *Enlarged diagram of cross-over*

two pinholes, another leaf is worked and the two pairs are taken back in at the same place in the centre. The centre workers have to wait while the above manoeuvre takes place and then, when the two pairs are back at the centre, the centre can be completed.

Corner. The diagram should make the corner working straightforward if you note the following points: at the cross-over at the beginning of the corner you need two extra pairs on the outside trail; one of these can be borrowed from the inside (RH) trail, the other has to be added. So at the cross-over work one extra pair to the LH side, with one pair less on the RH side (i.e. four passive pairs to the left, two passive pairs to the right) at the junction just above K and J, after which, when the workers have continued, one to M and one to N, the inner passives (i.e. one on each side of pin L) are worked together for the leaf from L to the centre of the spider. That leaves one pair in the RH trail and three pairs in the LH trail. However, the RH trail is immediately augmented by two pairs coming in at M.

Notice that only *one* pair is left out of the RH trail at R (and then twisted three times before being taken into the centre of the spider). It returns in a similar way at S.

You should turn your pillow through a 45 degree angle to get yourself orientated for working the corner correctly. You will then see that the centre of the spider working starts at T and not at O, as you might have expected.

At U add the one extra pair necessary for the corner and make a leg with it and the inside passive to go to the centre of the spider, where the pairs are taken in, one at each pinhole.

At V in the centre of the spider, the LH passive pair is taken out to the left after enclosing the pin, twisted three times, and worked into the LH trail at W, then left out again after enclosing the pin at X. You now work the single pair 'kiss', as described in the basic instructions, page 48. The pair is returned to the centre of the spider at Y.

When the leg is returned to the LH trail at Z, one of the trail pairs is left out by laying it back out of the way and cutting it off later.

At the cross-over at the end of the corner, there will be four passive pairs coming from the left and two from the right. You must make sure that, as they go out into the next circle, there are the normal three pairs of passives on each side, of which the middle pairs become the leaf.

PATTERN 5   BOOKMARK

Materials

22 pairs of bobbins
Swedish linen thread no. 100 or 120

To start this pattern you must lay your bobbins across the pillow so that one of each pair lies to the left and one to the right. Turn your pillow sideways and start at the LH picot (A) of the top loop of the ninepin edge (Fig 68a). Hang two pairs across the pillow to the left of this pinhole and twist twice. Work a leg with the LH two pairs then leave it and turn the pillow round and work a leg in the other direction with the two RH pairs. Now manipulate the bobbins to make sure they are pulled up evenly. Work the picot (B) at the top of the ninepin, then a leg, then the next side-picot (C), then another leg. Lay four more pairs of bobbins across the pillow from left to right below these other bobbins. Work a windmill between the two pairs from pin C and the two LH pairs just hung on, sticking the pin at D. Work a leg with the two RH pairs to reach to E then leave them. Return to the two LH pairs and work a leg

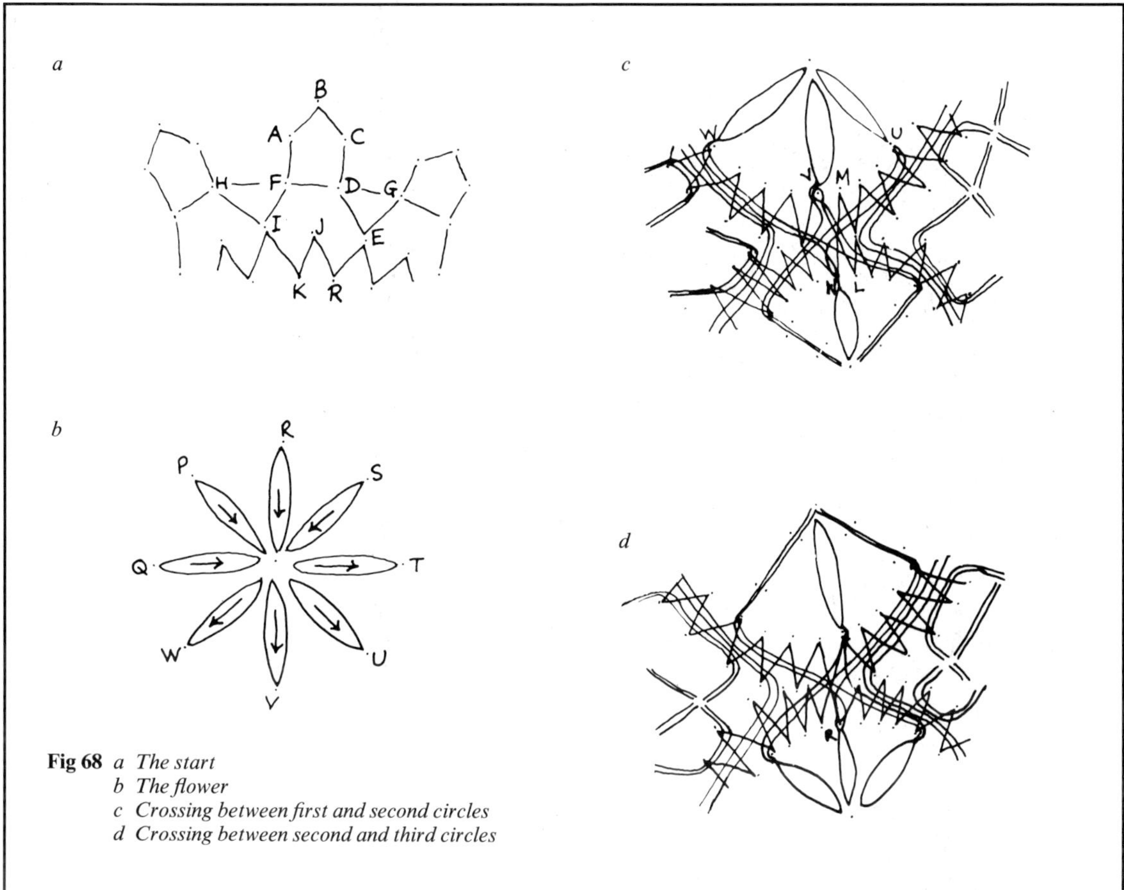

Fig 68 *a The start*
b The flower
c Crossing between first and second circles
d Crossing between second and third circles

to F. Turn the pillow round and work a leg from D to G with the remaining two pairs which have just been hung on and manipulate the bobbins to make sure the legs are firm.

Turn the pillow round again and return to the leg from D to F. Make a windmill at F between these two pairs and the first pairs hung on which are hanging from A. Now make a leg with the LH pairs to reach to H and leave them. Work a leg with the RH pairs to reach to I and leave them.

Lay two pairs from right to left behind pin at J and twist twice. These will be your two worker pairs for the trail. Lay four pairs across the pillow from left to right in front of the pin at J. These will be the passives for the trail in each direction. Turn the pillow and work the two LH threads from behind J in WS through the two LH pairs of passives. Twist twice and stick a pin at K to the

left of this worker pair, then work them back through the two passive pairs to I. At I work through both pairs of the leg hanging from F and from here continue round the circle to the left as far as Q (Fig 68b).

There should be no further problems until you reach the crossing at the bottom of the circle, but remember to hang on two new pairs for each of the leaves at P and Q. Once these pairs are hung on, do not work any more of the trail and ninepin on this side until you have completed the flower in the centre. But first you must return to the RH half of the trail and ninepin at J. Turn the pillow so that the passive pairs are hanging towards you and work through them in WS with the pair hanging from behind J. The next pinhole is R and here you must hang on two new pairs for the leaf. Then work back through the passives to E, where

Fig 69 *Finished bookmark*

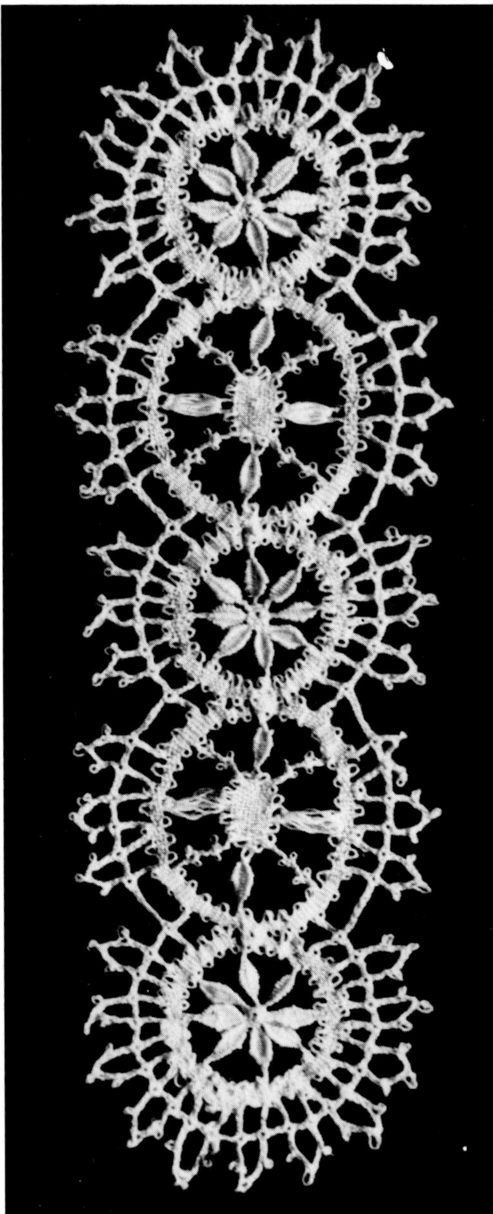

Fig 70 *Pattern*

you work through the two pairs of the leg hanging from D, then release them to go to G whilst your workers continue on round the trail to the right, hanging on two more pairs when you reach S.

Now that all the leaf pairs are hung on, work all the four leaves. Work an 8-pair crossing in the centre of the flower, then work four more leaves out to T, U, V and W, supporting each with a pin between the two pairs as you finish the leaf. The pairs from the leaf at T are surplus to requirements, so are worked into the trail for four rows. At T, throw back one pair of the passives from the trail (and cut them off later). After the four rows, throw back one of these two pairs from the leaf and cut it off later. (At each succeeding flower of this sort (i.e. in the third and fifth circles) two pairs are hung on at Q and two pairs taken out at T.)

Crossing

At the crossing the path of all the pairs should be clear from Figs 68c and d. Please note that the crossing between the first and second circles is slightly different from that between the second and third circles.

Differences

1. Between the first and second circles there are two pinholes which are used twice (by the upper and lower circles) and this does not happen between the second and third circles.
2. The leaf at V is slightly to the left of centre and the one below it slightly to the right, whereas in Fig 68b you can see that the leaf from the second circle is slightly to the right of centre with that below it being slightly to the left.

Points to note

Between the first and second circles the crossing occurs after the LH worker has taken in the two pairs from the leaf at V. After enclosing the pin at V, the worker and RH pair from the leaf both pass through the two LH passive pairs from the right. The RH of these two pairs becomes a passive pair for the next trail to the right, the LH pair (former worker pair) becomes the worker pair for the RH trail at L.

Return to V. The LH leaf pair works through two passive pairs from the left and becomes a passive pair in the LH trail. The RH worker pair from M works WS through the two RH passive pairs. Then those two passive pairs pass through the two former LH passive pairs in WS, after which the worker pair from M passes through these latter two passive pairs in WS to reach pin N, where, after enclosing the pin, it releases the inner pairs of the two passive pairs (which crossed over from each side), to be the new leaf at pin N.

At the centre of the second and fourth circles you will need to work a cucumber, as described on page 48.

The crossing between the second and third circles is basically the same but with minor variations, notably that it is the LH worker pair which works down to the pinhole at R and releases two pairs to work the leaf.

As you approach the end of the bookmark, where all the pairs meet together, throw back excess pairs in the trail when you can and, for the rest, meticulous darning in and judicious tying of knots is the answer. Finish to the side, not in the exact centre.

PATTERN 6   TOWN TROT

Materials

21 pairs of bobbins
Swedish linen thread no. 35

This is an old favourite Bedfordshire pattern and was the third pattern I myself was taught as a young girl by an old North Buckinghamshire lace-maker. I have always interpreted it as representing the wheels of the gig used to trot to town on Market Day.

This is a large pattern but, if it is too big for your pillow, I advise you still to prick it all and then, when you are approaching the end of the part on which it is comfortable to work, slip your pad underneath the next piece of the pricking (as you do when using a floating section in order to move on), work through this for a bit, then gather your bobbins into a 'bag' as usual, then carefully move the whole pattern up on your pillow, pushing your pins back into the pillow when you have reached the new position.

Hang two pairs at A splayed one outside the other. Make a WS. The LH pair is now the worker pair. Twist it once then hang on one pair at B and work through it in WS. Twist the

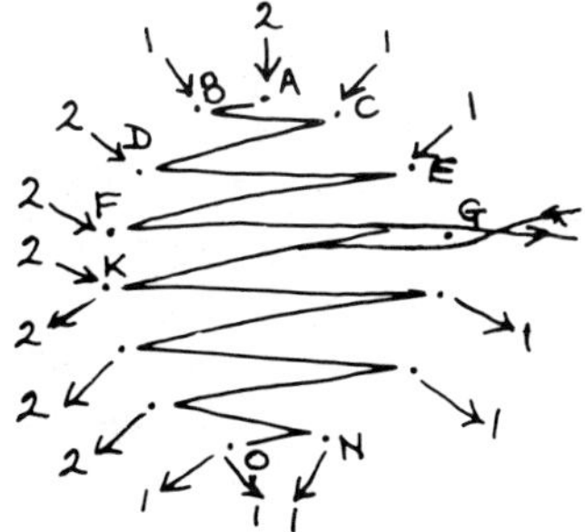

Fig 72 *Diagram for quick reference to see how many pairs come in and out at the holes in the oval junctions*

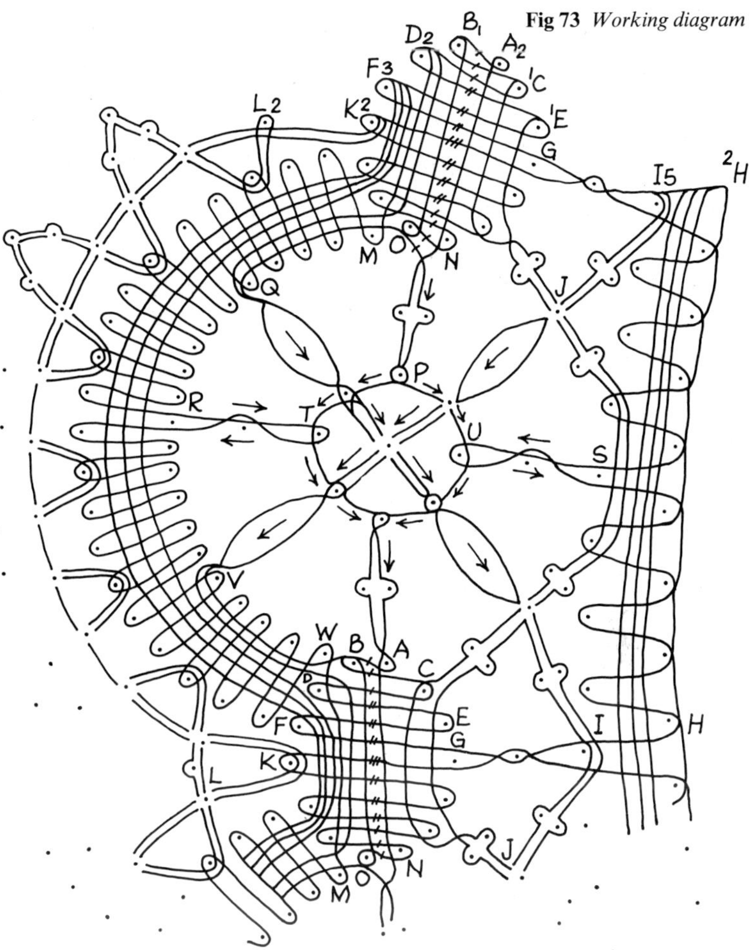

Fig 73 *Working diagram*

Fig 74a *Town Trot oval mat. Trace or photocopy this half of the pattern twice and make up as in Fig 74b*

Fig 74b *Reduced version of Town Trot oval mat for reader's reference*

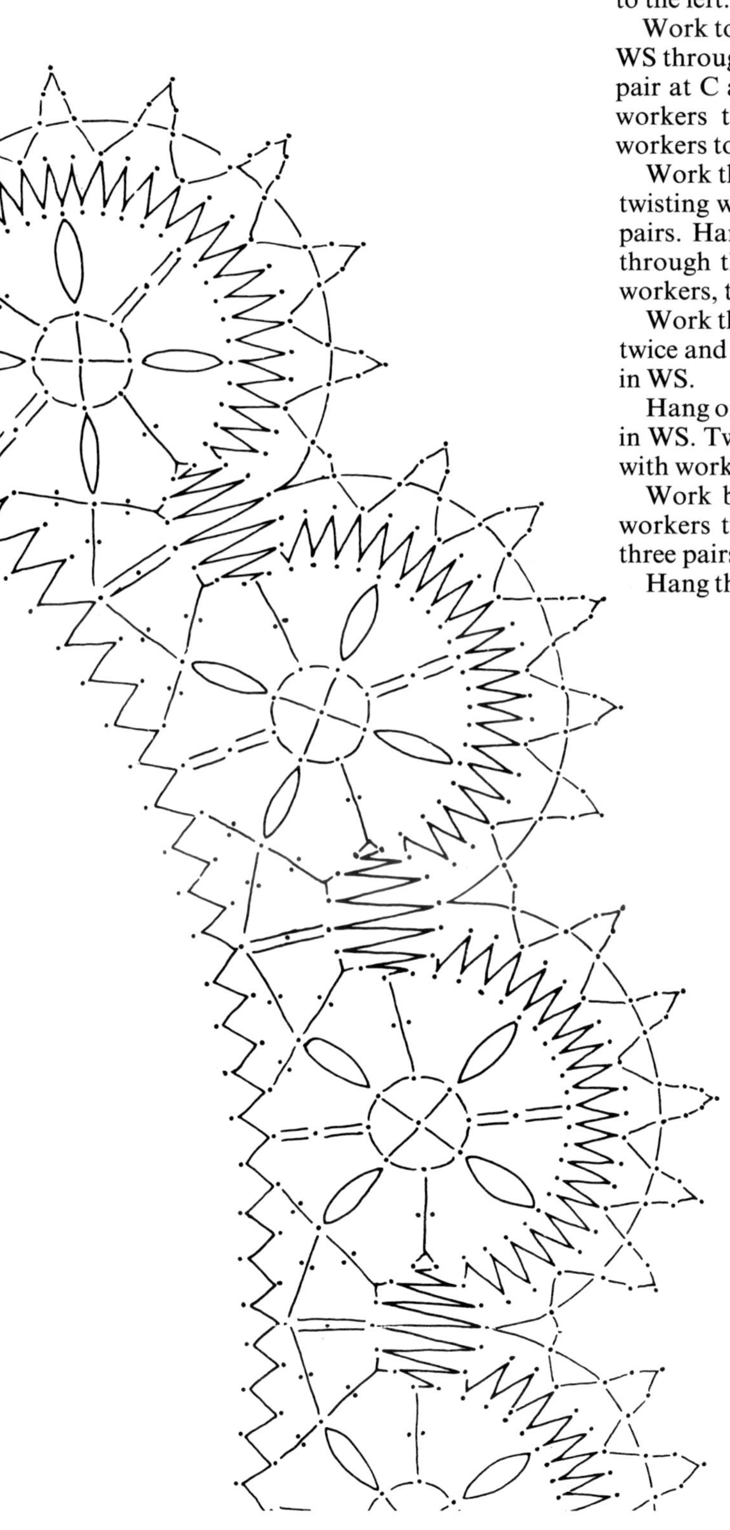

workers twice and replace pin at B with workers to the left.

Work to the right in WS, then twist once, work WS through the other pair then hang on another pair at C and work through it in WS. Twist the workers twice and replace the pin at C with workers to the right.

Work through the three pairs to the left in WS, twisting workers once between second and third pairs. Hang two pairs at D, side by side, work through them in WS and replace pin at D with workers, twisted twice, to the left of it.

Work through three pairs in WS, twist workers twice and work through the remaining two pairs in WS.

Hang on another pair at E and work through it in WS. Twist workers twice and replace pin at E with workers to the right.

Work back through three pairs in WS, twist workers twice, and work on through the other three pairs.

Hang three pairs on pin at F and work through

them. Replace pin at F with workers, twisted twice, to the left of it.

Work back through six pairs, twist workers twice, work through the three other pairs, stick pin at G with workers, twisted three times, to the right of the pin.

Return to the footside and work it up to this point by hanging two pairs, one splayed outside the other, on the pin at H. Work WS, twist, then twist the edge pair two more times and lay it aside to the right.

Hang five pairs on the pin at I side by side and work through them in WS with LH pair from H. Replace the pin at I with workers, twisted three times, to the left of it.

Work a kiss between these workers and the workers from G, as in the basic instructions, page 47, then lay the LH workers aside for a moment while you work a little more of the footside.

With the RH pair from the 'kiss' work through the next two pairs on the right. These are now released to the left to make a leg to J.

Return to the footside workers, and work WS to the right through the other three passive pairs, then twist workers once and work WS, twist, with the edge pair and two more twists of edge pair.

Return to the LH pair from the 'kiss' and work through three pairs to the left in WS, twist the workers three times, work through six more pairs then hang two more pairs side by side on pin at K. Work through them, twist the workers twice and replace the pin at K with workers to the left. Work back through two pairs then lay them aside to work the leg to L.

Continue working the workers to the right in WS. The finishing of this section will be simple enough, with the help of Fig 73. Note that the workers will have had three twists in the centre only once. The row you are now on and the following two rows have two centre twists, and the first three rows and the last three rows have only one centre twist.

Hang on the last two pairs at L, one splayed outside the other, and work a windmill stitch between them and the leg from K, replacing the pin at L in the normal place for a windmill stitch.

The ninepin edge will now continue in the normal way. All 21 pairs have now been hung on.

To start the semi-circular trail, return to the centre section. Not counting the leg released from pin K, the next six pairs will enter the trail; the workers will be the third pair from the left and they will work two WS to the right, twist the workers twice and stick pin at M, with the workers to the right of it. The trail then continues as in Fig 73, as far as R, leaving out two pairs for a leaf at Q.

The next two pairs, hanging from the centre at O and N, make a leg to P, which will be the start of the centre circle where, after enclosing pin P, the pairs will divide and one go to each side, twisting three times between pinholes and working round the circle. At each of the four points where the leaves go in and out, the single pair which meets the two pairs first works WS, twist, through one pair, stick pin between these two pairs, then work WS, twist, with the second pair, the workers then twist twice more and proceed to the next pin. The other two pairs work WS followed by twist and further $\frac{1}{2}$sts if a leg is the next stage, or followed by a leaf if that is the next stage. The legs work to the centre, make a windmill st, then another leg to meet the circular worker pairs.

Work the footside as required and, when the semi-circular trail has reached R, the footside has reached S, and the centre circle has reached T and U, they link by twisting the workers from R five times, working a WS, twist, with the twisted centre pair hanging at T, stick a pin at T, enclose with WS, then twist the RH pair (centre workers) three times and twist the LH pair (trail workers) twice, make a 'kiss' link (page 48) with themselves (when they were going into the centre), two more twists, and then these workers continue the semi-circular trail at R.

Bring the footside workers from S in and out in a similar manner.

The centre of the circle and leaves and leg can now be completed.

Next complete the semi-circular trail, bringing in two pairs from the leaf at V. After pin W, the workers work through two pairs then they themselves become a passive pair, entering the oval junction at D. It will be the same pair which reverts to being the worker pair after the oval junction is finished, starting the next semi-circular trail at M.

The footside is then worked as far as possible and thus one repeat is completed.

Fig 75 *Finished round mat*

PATTERN 7   ROUND MAT

Materials

54 pairs of bobbins
DMC Cordonnet cotton thread no. 100
or Swedish linen thread no. 70

Start at the top edge, as in the bookmark, laying pairs across the top so that one of each pair goes to each side.

Take two pairs into the centre each side of the middle point as well as the leg at the middle hole; these four pairs are for the leaves going round the circumference of the first circle. These meet again at the bottom centre and go into the top point of the middle circle with the leg. After a 6-pair crossing they go, two pairs to each side, as legs round the circumference of the sunflower in the centre.

For the two side motifs, four pairs are hung on

each side, as indicated by the arrows each side of the centre motif (two pairs per arrow), thereafter entering and leaving as indicated by the arrows, so that they can be used in successive motifs.

The centres of the six outside motifs are in $\frac{1}{2}$st. The centre of the sunflower in the middle is worked in WS.

At the centre sunflower, the top seven leaves go inwards and the bottom seven go outwards. The two centre pairs on each side go out then in, as indicated by the arrows.

The mat is quite straightforward and further instructions should not be necessary. You will need to finish off the pairs very neatly towards the end when they are no longer needed.

PATTERN 8   MOTIF

Materials

42 pairs of bobbins
Swedish linen thread no. 100 to 120
or Brok 36/2

Hang on pairs for the outer ninepin edge and outer trail, as in the bookmark and the round mat patterns, starting at A.

As you work the trail, hang in pairs as indicated in Fig 78. There are also many places, as you will see, where a leg is taken in and either released immediately, or at the next pin. Keep a close watch on the arrows in the diagram (Fig 78), where it has all been worked out for you.

Fig 78 *Working diagram, motif*

When you have worked as far as B and C, you will have hung on 30 pairs. You now need to hang on another six pairs for the inner trail at D and, at E, another two pairs for the leaf.

Continue mainly on the centre trail, but keeping pace with the other parts as well, adding on two pairs each side at F and G to make two more leaves. Once these are all added on work the three leaves to the centre, where you do a 6-pair crossing, then work the three leaves outwards to H, I and J, where you should support them on pins until the trail has eventually been worked round to those points to take in the pairs. Two pairs in place of the pairs from H and J are immediately left out again at K and L.

At M, work a 6-pair crossing, after which the two LH pairs make a leg to N. Of the remaining four pairs use the LH pair as workers and work through the other three pairs to the right in WS to start the small trail. By the time you reach O you will have cut off a number of pairs, so two pairs can be re-used to hang on at O to work through to P then back again from Q to R where they are finished with.

Fig 79 *Pattern*

4 Bucks Point Lace

INTRODUCTION AND BASIC INSTRUCTIONS

Bucks Point lace has been made in that county (soon to be followed by the neighbouring counties of Bedfordshire and Northamptonshire) since the first Flemish Protestant refugees, fleeing from Catholic persecution, arrived at Olney, Newport Pagnell and Cranfield in 1568. In style and technique it is virtually identical to lace from Lille, where many of these refugees came from.

It is a very fine, closely-worked lace, for this reason being slow to work, and also it is generally considered to be the most complicated of the English laces. The lace consists of a footside (for attaching the lace to the fabric it is ornamenting); an ornamental headside, usually scalloped, consisting of a flowing, usually rounded pattern; and, in between the head and the foot, the ground, which is traditionally rounded net, although it is sometimes worked in honeycomb stitch or kat stitch.

Bucks Point is a trolly lace. That is, you keep the same number of bobbins in the lace throughout (admittedly, with exceptions, as the lace becomes more complicated) and these pairs travel on the diagonals from one section of lace to another, thus uniting the sections as you go along. The word 'point' which was misused in Victorian times to describe a different kind of lace, means that there is a fine net ground (or background) filling the sections between the main part of the pattern and the foot, whereas in a guipure lace, such as Bedfordshire, this section would consist of holes traversed by linking bars or leaves.

For the beginner to Bucks Point, difficulties occur for several reasons. It should, however, be stressed here that lace-makers should master the making of torchon lace, e.g. by working through Chapter 1, before they get involved with Chapter 3.

These patterns are so designed and graduated that, if the student progresses through them in order, she will work through the different skills in easy stages and no undue difficulty should be encountered. By the end of the chapter, he or she will be capable of tackling almost any Bucks Point pattern.

The main reason for the difficulty beginners suffer from Bucks Point is, in my opinion, due to the pinholes being so close together that the pins already stuck more or less touch one another. Thus, if students make a mistake, it is very difficult, particularly for the inexperienced, to see where they have gone wrong because they simply cannot see through the pins. This difficulty is bypassed in this book by the simple expedient of working the first three patterns in a larger size and coarser thread than normal. It must be emphasized that these patterns are a means to an end and, although this large lace is not as beautiful in itself as a finer lace, this does not matter as long as the aim is achieved of acquainting students with the basic techniques so that they can progress confidently to the subsequent fine patterns, having mastered the footside, ground, picots, honeycomb, gimp and scalloped headside.

As these first three patterns are a means to an

end, I suggest that students only work a length of each, sufficient to make them feel quite familiar with each pattern before they proceed to the next and that they do not spend valuable time edging a complete article except perhaps a small mat, when they could be progressing to finer and more beautiful patterns.

The second reason for problems with Bucks Point stems from the fact that the patterns are based on angles which are not 45 degrees, as in torchon. The 45 degree angle, being half of a right angle lends itself to totally straightforward corners where the pattern is cut diagonally at a suitable place and then repeated in mirror-image: this is easy to understand and straightforward to work, normally requiring no extra bobbins. Bucks Point patterns, on the other hand, are designed on a variety of different angles between about 50 and 70 degrees. The latter, steeper angles are used for patterns requiring very fine thread and result in a very close cloth stitch, as the sections are squashed. If you do not understand this fact, a simple experiment will demonstrate it to you: cut four pieces of card approximately 10cm × 2cm each, or $3\frac{1}{2}$in × $\frac{3}{4}$in. Lay them together in two pairs. For each pair sew through the two pieces about 1cm in from the end. To sew, just pass the needle through the two pieces of card and tie a knot each side of the card so that it is firm yet you can move the pieces of card sideways. Now open each pair out to make a right angle and lay the two pairs down together to form a window shape, then sew together the two sets of overlapping ends in the same way as before so that the window is fixed at each corner.

Keep the window as a square with 90 degree angled corners and lay it down with one corner pointing towards a ruler to represent the footside. If you do this symmetrically the sides will be equivalent to the diagonals in torchon lace (where the diagonals are at 45 degrees to the footside but 90 degrees to each other).

Draw outwards the top and bottom corner and the side corners will come closer together, leaving the space inside an elongated diamond (called a lozenge by lace-makers and heralds alike). You can see that, with the same number of threads and of rows as the fatter diamond, the cloth stitch will be much closer.

This question of the angle of working leads on to the problem caused by it, namely the corner.

To design a corner, as in torchon lace, you metaphorically cut the pattern diagonally and then repeat this last section in mirror image, but the snag arises when you realise that these two sections do not fit together: in between is an empty space shaped like a slice of cake or old-fashioned cheese. Into this wedge-shaped space the designer has to make an extra piece of pattern. In some patterns that you may come across this has not been drafted accurately and there is no way of working it correctly as it stands. Having seen the intense frustration suffered by really good lace-makers who have wasted countless hours working at these patterns, only to find subsequently that, however skilful they are, with an incorrect pattern they cannot achieve the near-perfect lace which is their normal standard, I cannot stress too strongly the need to study a fresh pattern very carefully before starting, to make sure it reaches your exacting standards. If not, throw it out or completely re-draft it from scratch. The patterns in this chapter will not, I hope, disappoint you in this way.

Another problem to beginners is the gimp, but I hope soon to reassure you that gimp is a sort of non-event and, once the simple procedure is understood, you will think nothing of it. I can promise you that it serves a very useful purpose. Without it a Bucks Point pattern would be immeasurably less beautiful and the pattern sections would be blurred. With a gimp (and top designers like Thomas Lester often used a really thick one for definition) the shape of the pattern is clearly delineated and stands out against the net background. Where, by the nature of the work, a flowing pattern is in reality a series of steps, the gimp will overlook all this and flow smoothly in the intended design. It would be wise to experiment with different sizes of gimp, to see the different effects, in both these and other patterns.

In your very first pattern, probably the catch-pin will muddle you but, hopefully, you will master that small detail early on before you progress to the finer patterns, where it would be harder to identify your mistake.

Instructions for working the ground, footside, picots, etc. will be given the first time each of these is encountered. I will here attempt to solve the gimp problem at some length before it rears

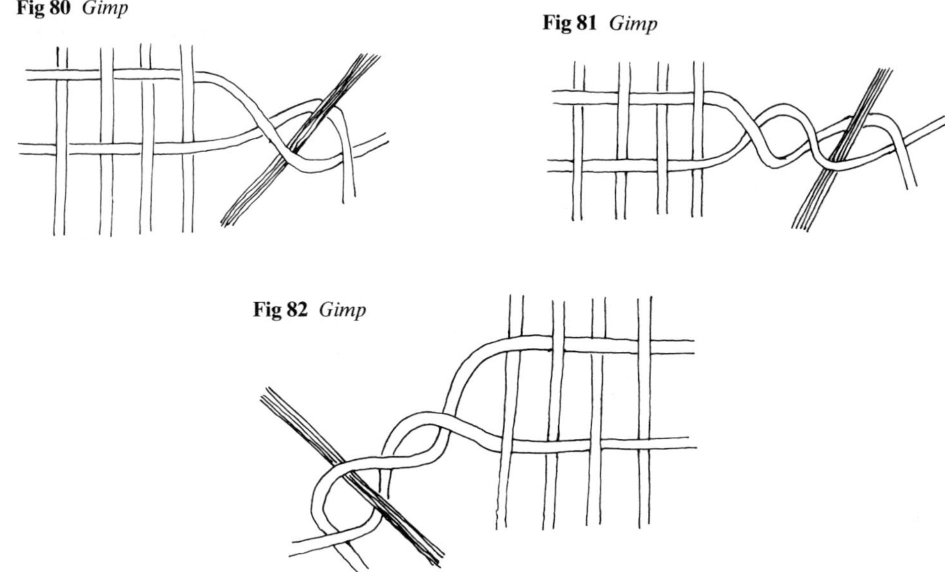

Fig 80 *Gimp*

Fig 81 *Gimp*

Fig 82 *Gimp*

its ugly head. First I will show you how to manage your gimp then we will discuss how many twists you should give the pairs before and after the gimp has passed through them.

Instructions to show you how to obtain one twist each side of the gimp: gimp travelling from right to left; if you only twist the worker once after the last stitch before the gimp, the result will be as in Fig 80 where, if you try it yourself, you will find that you lose the twist to the left of your gimp. You must, therefore, twist the workers twice, then lay the gimp (from right to left) *over* the first worker thread and *under* the next, then twist the worker threads once, right over left. Your result will be as in Fig 81. Strange though it may seem from the diagram, in 'real life' you will find that you only have one twist each side of the gimp. The same result can be obtained by twisting the worker threads once, then laying the gimp (from right to left) *under* then *over* the worker threads, then twisting the workers twice.

Gimp travelling from left to right; the procedure is reversed. Namely, first twist the workers twice then lay the gimp (from left to right) *under* the first thread and *over* the second thread then twist the workers once more, as in Fig 82. The same result may be obtained by first

twisting your workers once only then laying the gimp (from left to right) *over* the first worker thread and *under* the next, then twisting the worker pair twice more.

Although in each case I have given an alternative method of working, it is strongly advised that the student adopts one system and sticks to it consistently.

Now the question: How many twists? The student may well wonder, as some books say one, some say two and some differentiate, quite rightly, between different sections of lace. The answer is this: always have at least one twist each side of the gimp, as in Figs 81 and 82. That is all you will require on the headside, where you have first the picots on the outside, then the block of passive pairs, then the twisted workers, which will thus slightly separate the gimp from the passives. Where the gimp follows ground stitches on one side, you will realise that these ground pairs already have three twists, so you do not add any extra twists when the gimp *follows* the ground stitches, but you must twist three times after the gimp where it immediately *precedes* the ground work, except as specified below. After passing the gimp through these pairs, however, if a cloth stitch section (known by old workers as a bud) is to be worked, only twist the worker pair once more. If a honeycomb section were to follow, instead of the cloth stitch, you must realise that, as the pair go *out* of the honeycomb they will be twisted twice, so you must similarly twist twice when going *into* the honeycomb section.

There are exceptions but, once you have understood the reasoning behind this rule, you will be in a position to decide for yourself what is best. The reason for exceptions is this: between two holes, in a space where you would normally have a maximum of three twists, you are now having, perhaps three twists, a gimp and two more twists. If the pricking is very fine or your thread a little coarse for the pattern, this may well be too bulky and then you must decide what is best for you in that situation. You must, however, remember that, if you twist less going *in* to the ground, you must *untwist* the pairs coming *out* of the ground so that they have the same number of twists as each other.

Another difficulty in Bucks Point is when you progress to what are known as floral patterns (as opposed to geometric). Geometric patterns are, like torchon patterns, completely logical and work out mathematically with two pairs of threads meeting at every hole, no more and no less. The more simple Bucks Point patterns are geometric, but the most beautiful of the old Bucks Point patterns are floral and can be recognised by their *rounded*, flowing, often unsymmetrical shapes. The patterned part, the headside, appears to have been just dumped down on to a background of net and, indeed, this is precisely how they were designed. The holes for the net are so close that there was nearly always one where it was needed to bring a pair into the 'bud'. The lace-maker had to work out for herself which ground threads went best into which holes of the patterned section – no diagrams for her – and undoubtedly the pairs had to be 'fiddled' to some extent. The number of bobbins used had to be constant and accurate for the ground: there could be no fiddling there, but pairs could easily be added and removed at will from the patterned section.

Although it will not occur in this book, I will explain here how to add and subtract pairs because the student will be fully equipped to progress to floral patterns once Chapter 3 has been completed. In this book, only the bookmark *approaches* a floral pattern and you will see that, in the cloth stitch sections, there are frequently more than one pair coming in or going out at the holes, which could not happen in a truly geometric design.

A pair can be added: 1. by a false picot (described in Pattern 3); 2. by hanging it over the gimp then twisting it and working through it with the workers; 3. or by hanging it temporarily on to the next pin to which the workers are moving, then work through it as the workers arrive there, twist the workers twice as usual then remove the pin from the extra pair and replace it in the normal position with the worker threads behind.

A pair can be removed: 1. by laying it back if it occurs in a cloth stitch section and then cutting it off after you have worked an inch or so further; 2. or by running it round with the gimp for a few stitches then cutting it off. This is most easily effected if you actually tie the pair to the gimp bobbin either by a rubber band or tape, then you cannot inadvertently forget to incorporate the extra pair.

Your attention is drawn to various points, details of which are described in the Introduction, Chapter 1, particularly the following:

1. The sample of Pattern 5 is worked in a larger size than the normal pattern so that the student can easily see the way it was worked. This pattern is a preparation for Pattern 8, where the sections of the motif are the same as the pattern sections (other than the corner) of Pattern 5. In case some students decide that they would prefer to work it in a large size like the sample, a pattern of that size has been included as well as the fine one.

2. A mark has been made across the edge of continuous patterns, where the student can cut off a 'floating section' of pattern to fit at both the beginning and end to facilitate moving back to the beginning when you reach the end of the pricking.

3. It can be surprisingly difficult to mark correctly the necessary lines on a Bucks Point pattern. Whilst there is no way of escaping the *pricking* of a pattern, it *is* possible to avoid the marking of it, by the simple expedient of tracing off the selected pattern from this book, sticking it on to your pricking card, then covering it all with coloured sticky-backed plastic film. You then only have to prick the holes, and the lines are

marked for you. Do not be tempted to leave the pricking of holes until you reach them when working, because this is both more inaccurate and more time consuming.

PATTERN 1   LITTLE RUNNING RIVER

Materials

15 pairs of bobbins wound with
Filato di Cantu thread no. 30
or DMC Cordonnet cotton thread no. 50
and 1 gimp bobbin wound with
Coton Perle no. 8

This is an old Buckinghamshire pattern which, in a much reduced size, was often made by children (including me) as one of their first patterns and was also frequently used to trim babies' garments.

Hang two pairs of bobbins at hole A and work WS then twist both pairs three times.

At B there is not a hole. You can prick one if you wish, to be used only this one time when hanging on the two pairs indicated and not at any subsequent repeats of the pattern; or you can instead hang them on to C and drop them off as soon as you have worked through them. I prefer the first alternative, in which case you should prick the hole halfway between A and C on the line joining these two holes.

Lay aside the RH pair from A and work through these two passive pairs from B in WS with the LH pair from A. Twist workers three times and stick pin C with the worker threads behind it.

Now hang one pair on this pin C to the left of the workers and work $\frac{1}{2}$st, then twist both pairs twice.

*Hang one pair on pin D and, using the LH pair from C, work $\frac{1}{2}$st then twist both pairs twice. Take out pin D and replace it in the same hole but *between* these two pairs*.

Repeat from * to * for holes E, F, G, H and I. Lay the LH pair from I well over to the left. I suggest you stick a glass-headed pin in front of these bobbins. This will remind you that you will not use this pair again until you start to work the head.

Lay the other pairs from the ground over towards the left ready to work the next diagonal row from the footside.

‡Starting with the fourth pair from the right, work two WS to the right. Twist the workers three times and work WS with the edge pair then twist both pairs three times. Stick pin J with both pairs to the right of it.

Lay the RH pair aside to the right and using the LH pair, work to the left through the two passive pairs in WS. Twist the workers three times and stick pin K to the right of the workers. Now work $\frac{1}{2}$st, followed by two twists of both pairs, with the next pair on the left, but *do not stick in a pin*. This pin (K) is the catchpin and is always worked in that way. Note that pin K is a 'pin without a stitch' and is immediately followed by a 'stitch without a pin'.

†Laying aside the RH pair from K, use the LH pair with the next pair on the left to make a $\frac{1}{2}$st, followed by two twists of each pair. Stick pin L between both pairs but *do not enclose it*†.

Repeat this last section from † to † along the remainder of the diagonal line, finishing at pin M‡.

For evermore, your Bucks Point ground will be worked as in the above instructions, working from ‡ to ‡.

Note In the early stages of Bucks Point one can almost guarantee that students will make a mistake over the catchpin. I am sure this is because they do not understand why they are doing certain actions. All that is, in fact, happening, is that your footside workers are going *round* the catchpin, as in Fig 83, instead of sticking the pin between the two pairs *after* making a stitch, as in Fig 84. You can see that, if you were to do as in Fig 84, which at first your instinct tells you to do, you would have a messy line on the footside, as the stitch pulls to the right away from the pin. Although it is traditional (and easier) to stick the catchpin *before* making the stitch, the result is that you have stuck the pin to the right of the two pairs instead of in between them. The result will be that, whereas in the rest of the ground, one pair hangs between every pair of pins, between pin K and pin L and at every subsequent catchpin, two pairs will hang.

If you seem to have gone wrong at any time, check along the diagonal to see that there is one edge pair, two passive pairs, two pairs between the catchpin and the next pin and one pair to the left of all the other ground pins.

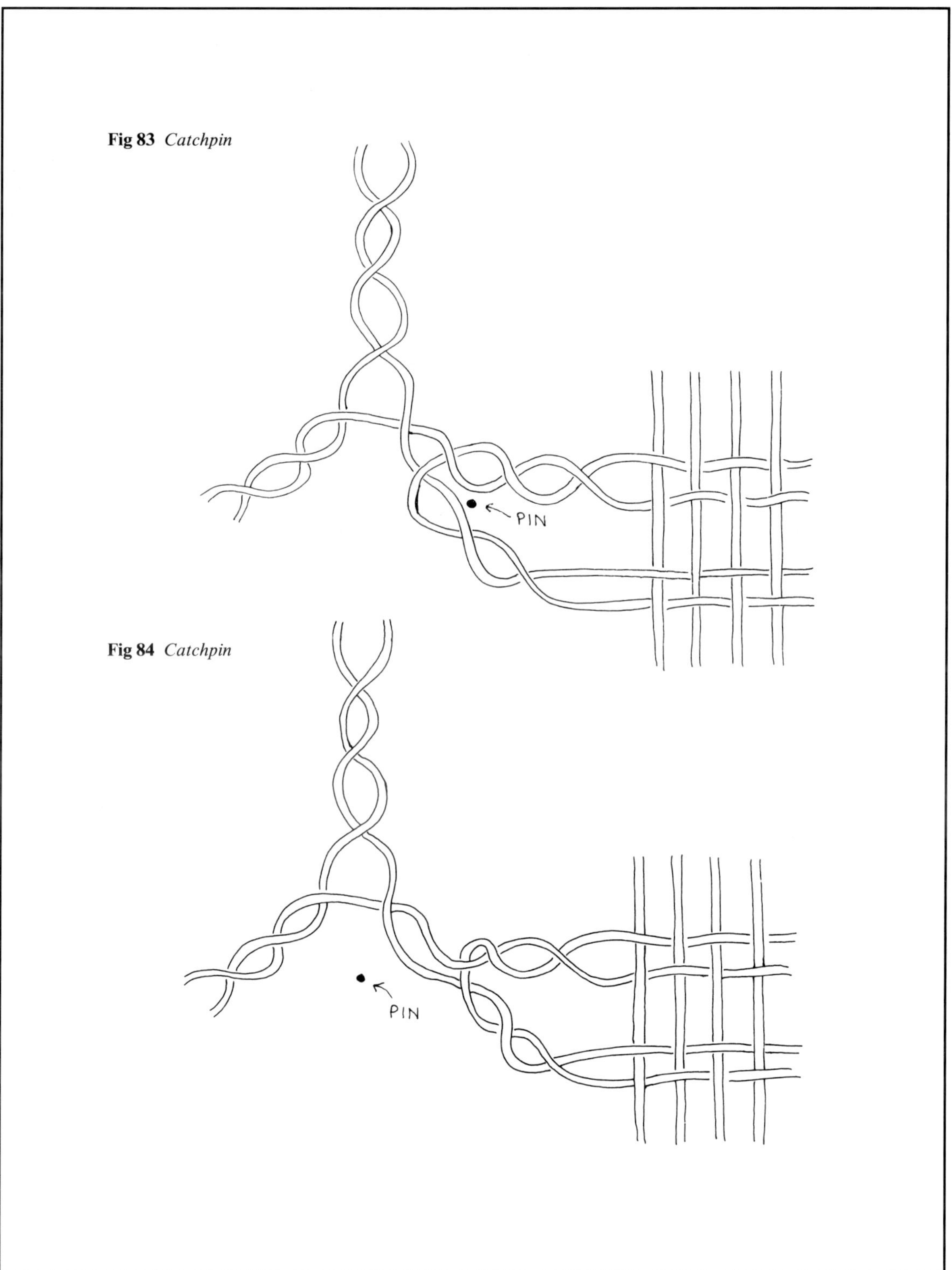

Fig 83 *Catchpin*

Fig 84 *Catchpin*

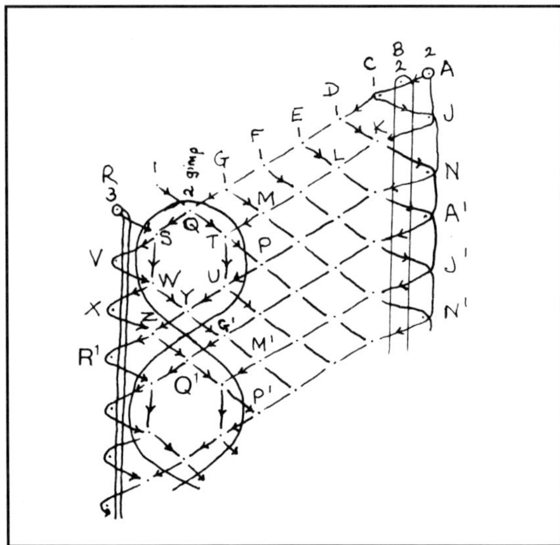

Fig 85 *Working diagram, Little Running River*

Repeat from ‡ to ‡ for the diagonal lines starting at N, O and P. When the four-hole diagonal line from P has been finished, you are ready to insert the gimp and start working the head.

Study the Introduction, page 78, for details of how to manage the gimp. As there is only one gimp thread and not a pair, you will have to wind the thread round and round a pin and anchor it firmly behind the work near where the gimp starts.

Lay the gimp from left to right through the five pairs hanging to the left of pins I, M and the next three pins on the diagonal, as described in the Introduction. Leave the five pairs with one twist, waiting to enter the headside at pinholes R, T, V, X and Z.

The headside is now worked like the headside in the basic torchon fan pattern: hang four pairs on a pin at Q. (The two RH pairs should be side by side and the two LH pairs should be splayed one outside the other.) Starting with these two LH pairs, work WS then, with the RH pair after this stitch, work two more WS to the right then work one more WS through the LH of the waiting pairs through the gimp. Twist the workers twice, stick a pin at R to the left of the workers, then work WS through all four pairs to the left. Twist the workers twice and stick pin S to the right of the workers. Work in WS through

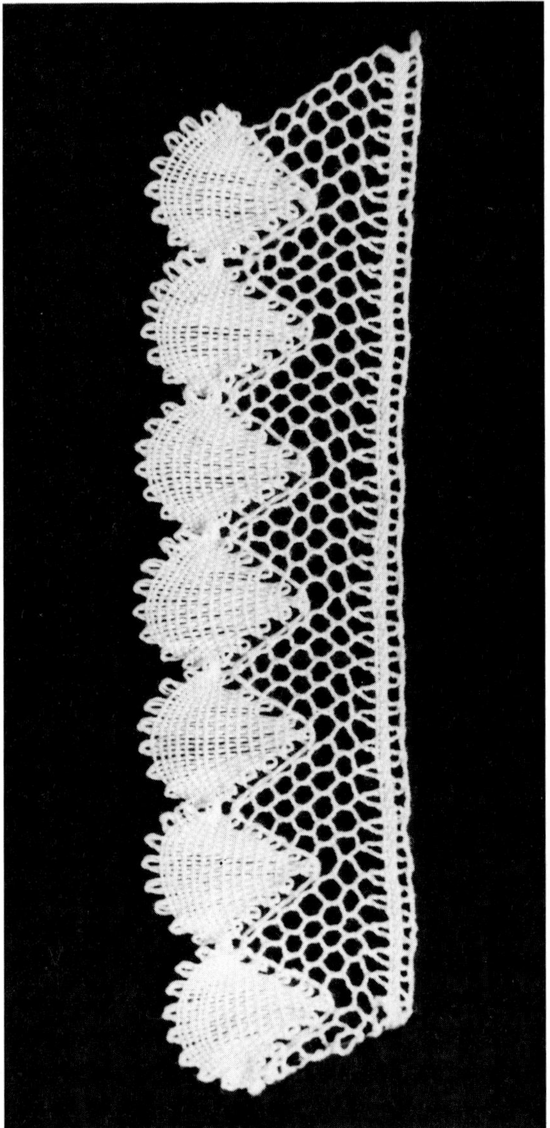

Fig 86 *Finished lace, Little Running River*

four pairs to the right, then through the LH of the waiting pairs through the gimp. Twist the workers twice and stick pin T to left of them.

Continue thus from side to side, the pins following alphabetically. After sticking the pin at Z, work a WS with the next pair on the left and then lay it well aside to the right (preferably behind a glass-headed pin) as it will not be used again for a time. Continue with the workers,

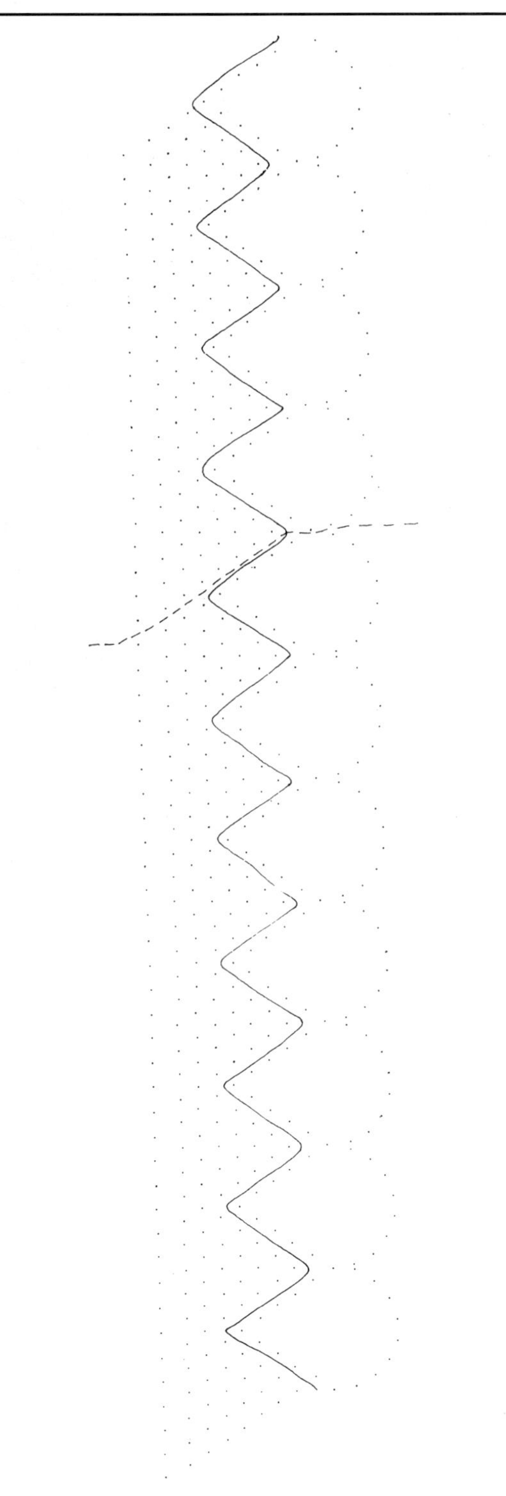

doing WS through the remaining seven pairs to the left, twist twice, stick a pin, then work WS through seven pairs to the right. Twist the workers twice, stick a pin to the left of them then work a WS with the next pair on the left. Lay it well aside to the right (preferably behind the glass-headed pin) as it will not be used again for some time. Continue with the workers, doing WS to the left through all the remaining pairs, etc., dropping off one pair at each of the inner pinholes. Go on until you have stuck pin Q^1. Leave the workers there to the left of the pin and leave three passives to the right of the pin. Lay these four pairs well over to the left behind a glass-headed pin while you return to pin A^1 and repeat the whole pattern again as before. Don't forget to start with the fourth pair from the right.

Remember also that, in the first row, you will not have to move and replace the pins as you did on the hanging-on row originally, as the pairs are already hanging there correctly.

But first, you must pass the gimp through the five passive pairs which are hanging from the 'bud' ready to work holes E^1, F^1, G^1, H^1 and I^1. To pass the gimp through these pairs (from right to left) read the instructions in the Introduction, twisting the pairs twice before laying through the gimp to ensure that you will end up with one twist.

PATTERN 2   THE PEA

Materials

13 pairs of bobbins wound with
Filato di Cantu thread no. 30
or DMC Cordonnet cotton thread no. 50
and 2 gimp bobbins wound with
Coton Perle no. 8

This, in reduced size, is another traditional old Buckinghamshire pattern. The footside and ground are worked in an identical manner to those in Pattern 1, so the instructions will refer to Pattern 1, and the holes will be given the same letters. The difference here will be three-fold:
1. There is less depth of ground so that, for example, the first diagonal row is lettered A to G instead of A to I, as in Pattern 1. The letters H

Fig 87 *Pattern*

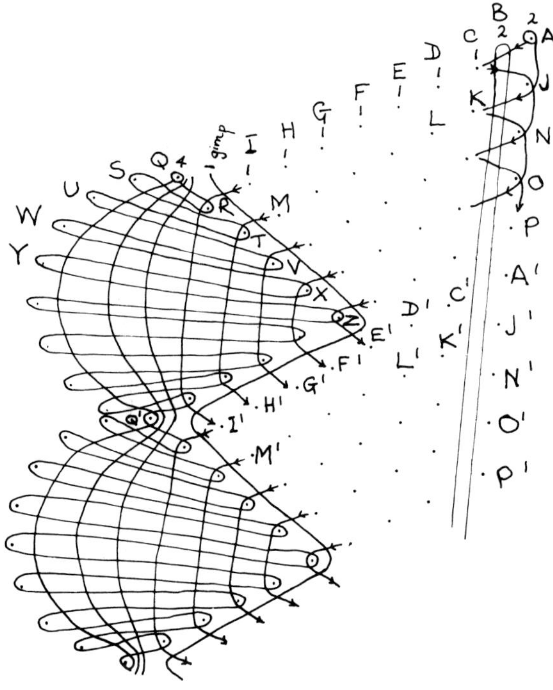

Fig 88 *Working diagram, The Pea*

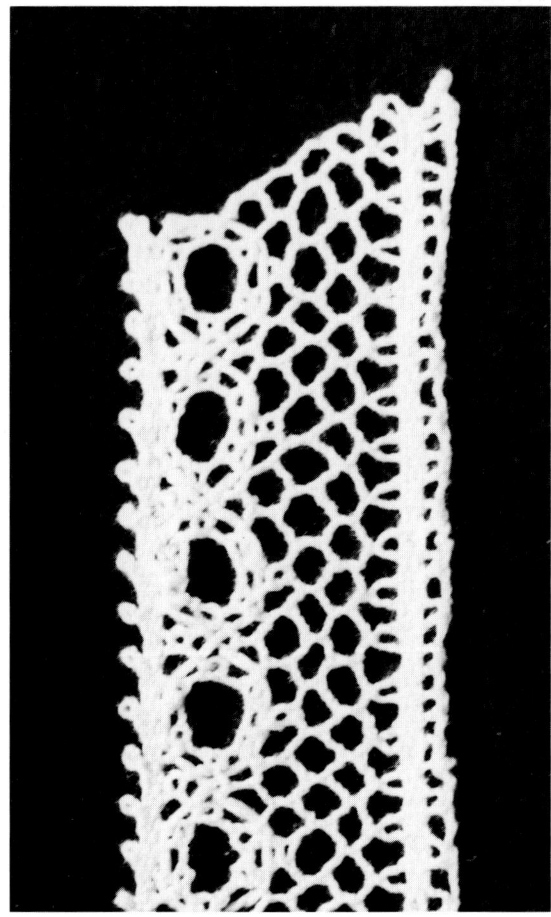

Fig 89 *Finished lace, The Pea*

and I are omitted so that the foot starts again at J. You should, in any case, be so familiar with the ground and footside after Pattern 1 that you will probably not need to refer to the instructions.

2. There are less diagonal rows to work in each ground section before you work the headside. In Pattern 1 there were five such rows and in this pattern there are three in each repeat but only two in the very first section that you work.

3. The other difference here is that you cannot work all three rows consecutively after working the headside, as you did the five rows in Pattern 1. First you must work the two diagonal rows starting with A and J, or A^1 and J^1, etc. Then you must work the head from hole Q, at least as far as T and definitely no further than W, but you cannot work pin U yet. Next you leave the headside and work the third ground row, starting with N or N^1, etc. Only after that can you complete the headside to pin Z.

The headside is the simplest of the Bucks type because it is straight and not scalloped. It is an easy stage towards learning the scalloped edge

because you will practise picots and taking your workers through the two passive pairs and the gimp without having to master the principles of 'uphill' and 'downhill', as in the next pattern. In this pattern you will learn to manage a pair of gimps, not just one. Finally, this is your first introduction to hc st. These six-hole rings are a very basic ingredient of Bucks Point lace.

Let us consider the headside in detail. When you have worked the two ground rows starting at A and J and finishing at G and M you are ready to begin the head at Q. Hang your pair of gimp threads temporarily on to pin Q. (It is normal to list the number of gimp bobbins separately, not in pairs as with the other bobbins, but nevertheless they are wound in pairs if they are to be hung on at a crossover point, as here. There must *never*

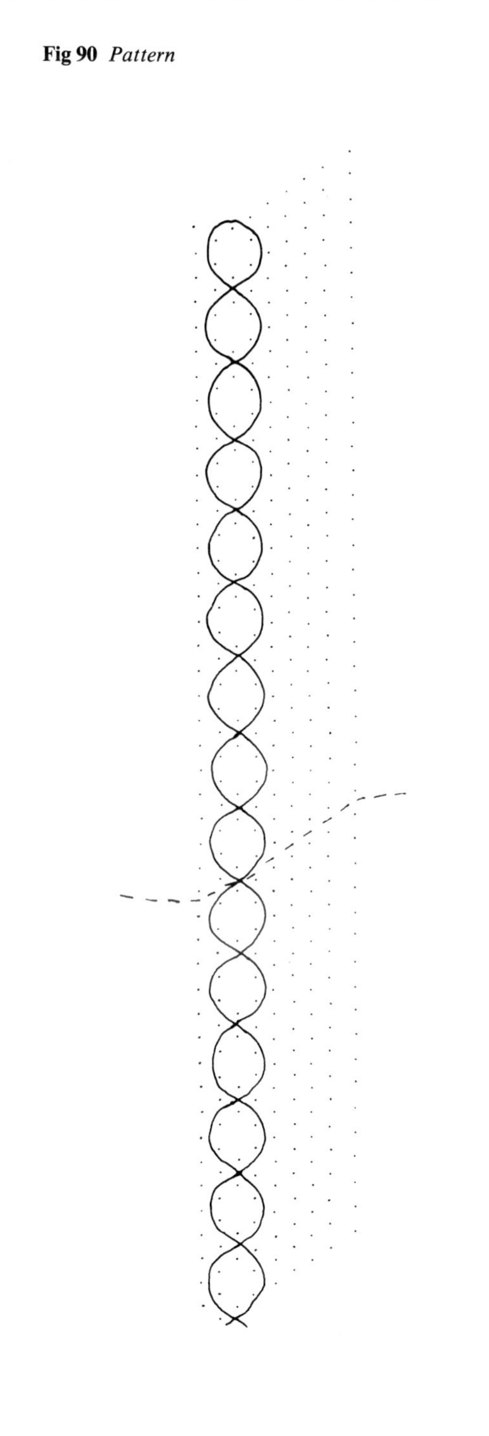

Fig 90 *Pattern*

be a knot in a gimp thread in your lace. You should so plan that you do not run out of gimp thread unless you are on a very long or complicated piece of lace, when it cannot be avoided, but, if you do run out, join it by working the old and new threads alongside each other for a time.)

The RH gimp passes from left to right through the two pairs hanging from G and M, then these two pairs are twisted twice.

To the left of pin Q a new pair of bobbins is hung over the LH gimp then twisted twice to work a ½st, twist, with the pair from G, which is hanging through the RH gimp. Then replace pin Q between these two pairs and enclose it with ½st, twist, between the same two pairs. To hang a pair of bobbins over the gimp you do literally that, as if you were hanging a rope over a clothes-line to dry.

Return to pin R and hang on three pairs of bobbins, the RH pair hung first separately then the two LH pairs hung splayed one outside the other. Start by twisting these two pairs three times, then work a WS between them then, using the RH pair, make a WS through the third pair hanging from pin R. Now follow the instructions in the introduction to pass the gimp from Q from right to left through this pair.

Next make a hc st at S between this pair and the LH pair hanging from Q. (A hc st is ½st, twist, pin, ½st, twist.) Leave both of these two pairs and go to pin T to work a hc st between the RH pair from Q and the pair hanging through the gimp from M. After this stitch you can, if you wish, work holes V, W and X but I suggest that instead you do as follows: take the RH gimp from right to left through the RH pair from T then twist this pair three times and leave it ready to work pin P. Now work the footside and ground row from pin N to pin P. Now pass the RH gimp from left to right through the LH pair hanging from pin P. Work pin U in hc st between the pair hanging from pin T and the LH pair from P which you have just brought through the gimp. Lay both pairs well over to the right and return to the pairs hanging from pin S.

*Take the LH gimp from left to right through the LH pair from S. Now, using this pair as workers, work in WS through the two passive pairs to the left.

Make a *picot* with your worker pair (now the pair on the left of your work) thus: twist the pair three times then lay the pin on top of the outside thread, point to the left, twist the thread once round the pin and stick the pin into the appropriate hole (V). Take the other bobbin of the pair and wind its thread once round the pin clockwise, twist the pair three times, then draw up both threads. The loops should now be twisted round each other round the pin. Do not draw up the threads tightly until this last stage or they will not twist together round the pin*.

Now take your worker pair back in WS through the two passive pairs then twist twice and pass the gimp through them from right to left, as in the Introduction, twisting the pair twice after the gimp has passed through.

Work pin W with the pair hanging from S and this worker pair, after which the RH pair stays waiting to work pin Y later. Meanwhile, work from * to *, reading pin W for S and pin X for V. Now take your worker pair back in WS through the two passive pairs then twist once and lay it aside to wait.

Return to the hc ring and, using the RH pair from W and the LH pair from U, make a hc st at pin Y.

Bring the LH gimp through the LH pair from pin Y from left to right.

Bring the RH gimp through the RH pair from pin Y from right to left.

Cross the gimps, left over right. Actually, it does not matter whether you cross gimps left over right or twist them right over left, as long as you are consistent. I cross them because that is how I was taught by the old Buckinghamshire lace-makers.

There is one more thing to do before you start to repeat the pattern at A^1. This is the pin Z. It only occurs once in every repeat and is a hc st *outside* the hc ring but inside the headside passives. You frequently get a similar pinhole in Bucks Point, at the narrowest point of the headside section, where the gimps cross. It is worked with the worker pair from X, which works in WS to the right through the two passives then is twisted twice, and the LH pair from Y, which must have two twists after the gimp, not the usual one on the headside. Work hc st at Z, then the LH pair is ready to work in WS through the two passive pairs to the left to do a picot at R^1 and repeat the pattern. The RH pair from Z is equivalent to the pair which you hung

on to the gimp when you started. Now the LH gimp passes through it from right to left and it is then hanging ready to start the next head at Q^1. But first you must work the footside and ground by starting again at A^1.

PATTERN 3   HONEYCOMB FAN

Materials

20 pairs of bobbins wound with
Filato di Cantu no. 30
or DMC Cordonnet cotton thread no. 50
and 4 extra pairs of bobbins at the corner
and 2 gimp bobbins wound with
Coton Perle no. 8

This is an old favourite Bucks Point pattern, but I have enlarged it and added the corner. It was not normal for old patterns to have corners because the lace-makers worked to sell their lace and the lace-buyer came round once a fortnight on 'cut-off day'. The lace-makers would sell him all that they had on the pillow at so much a yard, and so it was known as yard lace. This was much more adaptable and could be put to any number of different uses, unlike a piece with ready-made corners. The lace was gathered round the corners and old (usually very large) handkerchiefs can still be found like this. Nevertheless, it is prettier now that we make lace for our own pleasure, to have a special corner and to make the sides of lace any length we like.

If you wish to make a complete piece of lace which does not take too long, it can look very attractive to make an edging for a very small mat with perhaps only two heads between each corner, so that the actual linen is not much more than an inch square. In this case it is best to prick all the mat as one, so that there is no moving up of the lace while working. To do this, trace the corner section and a small part of each adjoining head (noting that the corners of these adjoining heads have been flattened to fit into the corner). You can then superimpose this corner section over your pattern at each of the corners, remembering to adjust the shape of the adjoining heads at the same time. You can cut out two heads for each of the remaining sides from the spare heads down the long side. The use of the traced corner will ensure that you maintain the correct space between corner and adjoining head, because you can see through it to the extra parts you had already traced at the sides of the corner.

Such a pattern is included here.

Start this pattern in exactly the same way as the preceding two patterns. Work the two diagonal rows A to E and F to H. When you work the third row, starting with hole I, you will find something different. Instead of the sixth hole there is a space with a tally marked. You work this tally with the two pairs which would have worked the normal ground stitch. To make a tally, the threads being twisted a total of three times from the previous stitch, you use the second thread from the left as the weaver and take it first to the right over the next thread and under and round the RH thread. *Bring it back in front of the RH thread, behind the centre thread, in front of then round and behind the LH thread, in front of the centre thread, then behind and round the RH thread. Draw up the threads carefully so that they are taut, drawing the outside passive threads outwards to manipulate the weaving thread, which is held under tension, particularly against the LH thread*. Repeat from * to * about five times, depending on the size of your thread in relation to the pattern. You want a good firm little square (see Fig 91). Remember the number of rows you have woven and always weave the same number of rows for the tallies in the same piece of work. When you are working a tally in ground like this, you will normally be working along the diagonal from right to left, therefore the next stitch after the tally will be at pin J. After a tally it is necessary to work the following stitch with two of the passive threads, not the pair containing the weaver.

You must therefore leave the weaver on the right, as in Fig 91. You must lay the weaver thread across the pillow with the thread slack until you are ready to use it in the next row. Any pressure on this thread will spoil the shape of the tally. After working pin K, work the next four diagonal rows, finishing at pin-hole L. You are now ready to work the headside.

Hang a pair of gimps temporarily on the pin at M. Pass the RH gimp down from left to right through the line of seven waiting pairs, hanging from the pinholes E, H, K and down to L, as in the Introduction.

Hang two pairs on pin N, splayed one outside the other, twist both pairs twice and work WS,

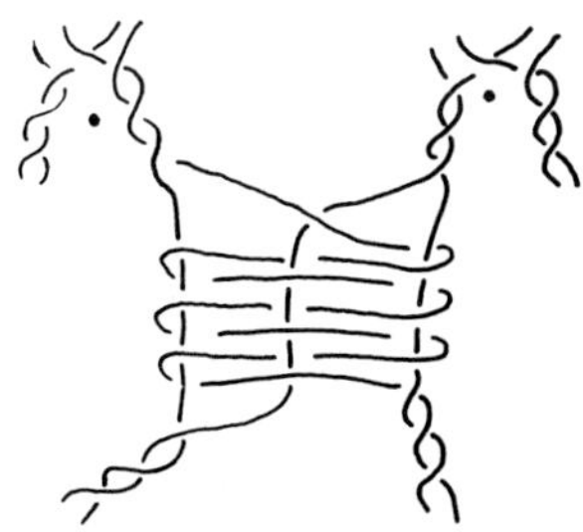

Fig 91 *Working diagram, Honeycomb Fan*

twist twice. (Future repeats of this pinhole will be in hc st.)

Pass the LH gimp through the RH pair from N from right to left.

You can now start working the hc fan. Work $\frac{1}{2}$st, twist, at M between the RH pair from N and the pair from E, replace pin M between these pairs and cover the pin with another $\frac{1}{2}$st, twist, between the same two pairs. Now work down the diagonal to the right, making hc sts at the next six holes until pin O has been worked. Lay the RH pair from O well over to the right behind a glass-headed pin, as it will not be needed again in the head.

Lay the other bobbins to the right and go over to pin P, where you should hang two pairs. Twist both pairs three times and work WS. Lay aside the LH pair which will become the outer of the two passive pairs which remain constantly round the headside. Only at the corner will the inner pair of the two change with another pair when you work a false picot.

Now take the RH pair from P and work it in WS through three more pairs which you can either hang on to P, side by side, or you can make an extra hole from which to hang them halfway between pin P and pin N. Work it also through the LH pair from N.

Now pass the LH gimp from right to left through this worker pair.

You now work the 'short row' of the hc, which consists of alternate long and short rows. (The first row you worked was a long row, which means the holes are closer together, so there are more of them.) Work pin Q in hc st with this worker pair from P and the pair hanging from M. Now here is the difference; *lay both pairs aside to*

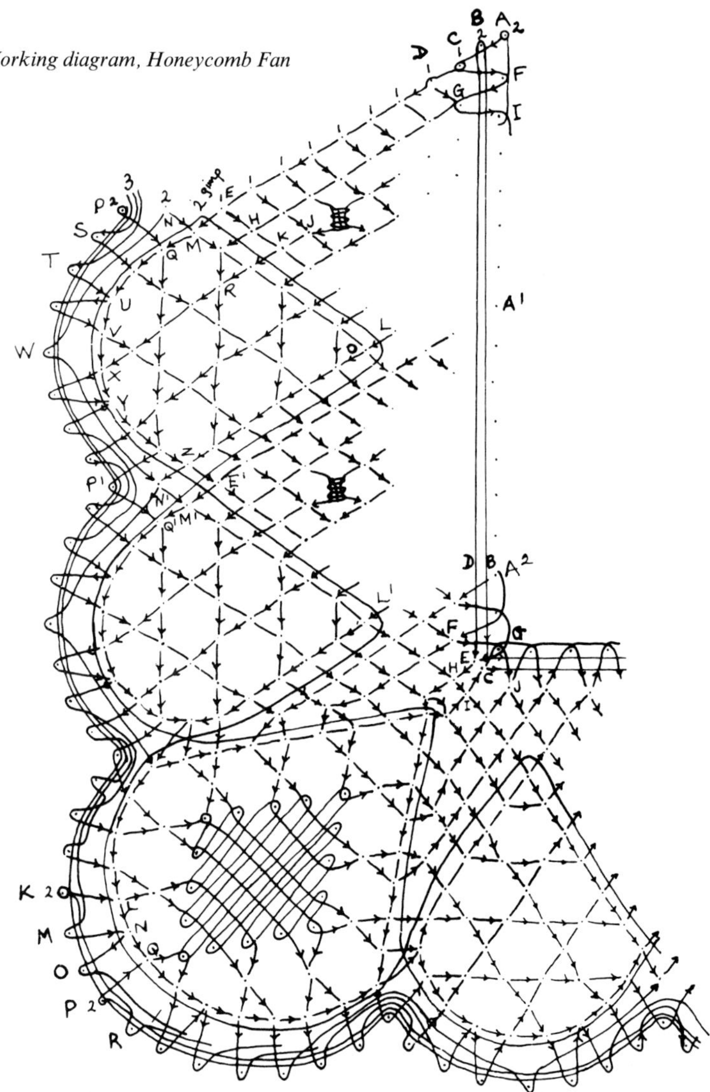

the left and work pin R with two fresh pairs, after which you lay them both aside again. Work two more holes to the right, using two fresh pairs each time, after which lay the RH pair well over to the right behind the glass-headed pin, as it will not be used again in the fan.

Have you grasped the principle of hc? Remember the following facts:

1. Hc st consists of $\frac{1}{2}$st, twist, pin, $\frac{1}{2}$st, twist. (Some workers call just the $\frac{1}{2}$st, twist, a hc st, but, as the pin is always enclosed with $\frac{1}{2}$st, twist, it

seems more logical to call the whole movement a hc st.)

2. You work alternately long and short rows.

3. In a long row (holes close together) you carry one pair of threads from the previous stitch on to work the next stitch.

4. In a short row (holes with spaces between) you leave both pairs aside after working the stitch and use two fresh pairs to work the next stitch.

Now you must learn the principles of the 'uphill' and 'downhill' on the headside. You are

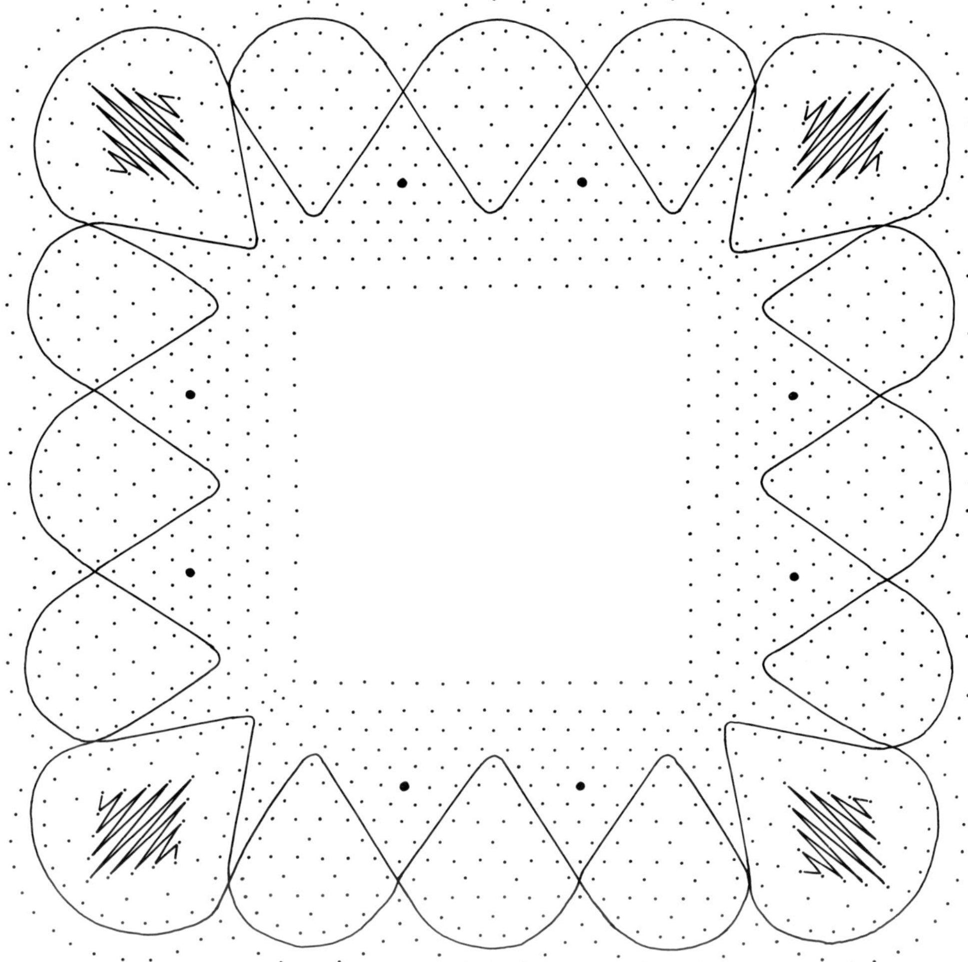

Fig 93 *Pattern*

going uphill at the moment and this means that you use one of the group of passives to work the picot then work it through the remaining passives, then through the gimp to work in the hc fan. As you need to keep the two outer passive pairs intact to make a crisp, neat edge, you use the third pair of passives from the edge to work the picot. Take it out to the left in WS through the two passive pairs, then make a picot at S (described in Pattern 2), work the pair in WS to the right through four more pairs of passives, pass the gimp from right to left through this worker pair and it is ready to work the stitch inside the gimp with the LH pair hanging from pin Q. Work the remaining six stitches of this long row and, after the last stitch, lay aside the RH pair to the right behind the glass-headed pin.

Return to the left and, again using the third pair from the left, work two WS to the left through the two outside passive pairs, make a picot at T, then work the pair in WS through three pairs to the right, then pass the gimp through from right to left, then work the stitch at U inside the gimp with the LH pair hanging from the row above. This is the beginning of a short row, so you lay aside both pairs after the stitch and take up the next two pairs on the right for the next stitch. This is followed by two more stitches, each time with two fresh pairs of bobbins and, after the last stitch, lay aside the RH pair to the

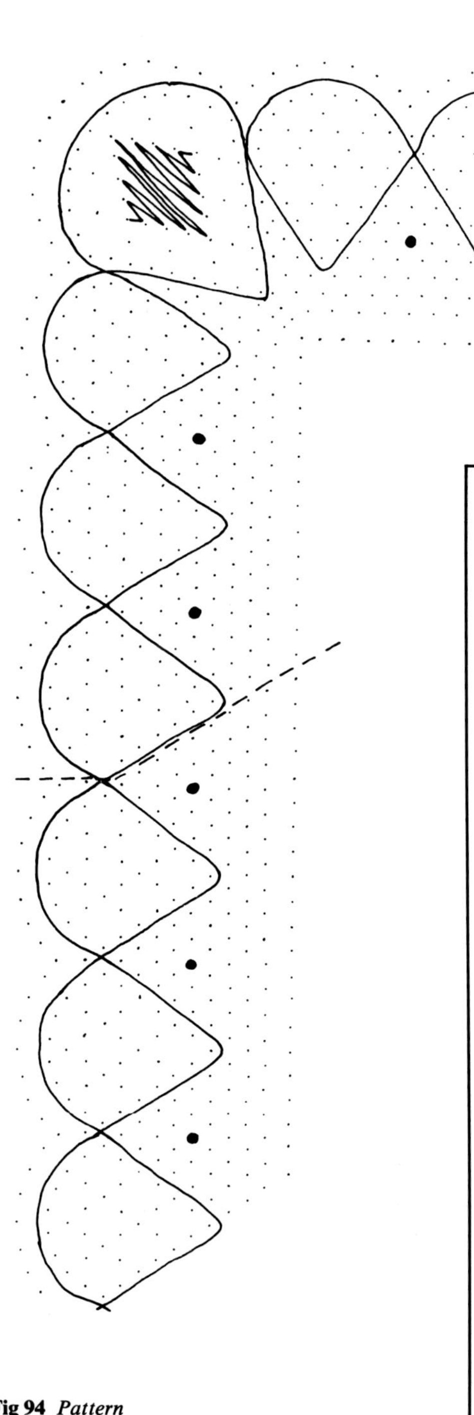

Fig 94 *Pattern*

right behind the glass-headed pin.

Return to the left. This time you use the LH pair from U to work the picot, so first you must pass the gimp from left to right through this pair then the pair works three WS to the left, makes a picot, then works 3 WS to the right, the gimp passes through from right to left and the pair is ready to work at V.

After working V there will be five more hc sts to the right and, after the last stitch, the RH pair should be laid aside behind the glass-headed pin, as it will not be used again in the fan.

At pin W take the third pair from the edge and work to the left through the two outside pairs in WS, then make a picot at W, but this time only work the pair back to the right through the two outer passive pairs then leave it.

Having finished the uphill section of headside, where the picots were worked *before* you could work the corresponding section of fan, you are now at the downhill section, where you must work the fan first *before* you release the pair to work the picot. Thus you must work pin X and the remaining two stitches of the short row, after which the RH pair is laid aside behind the glass-headed pin.

Return to the headside and the LH pair from X. Pass the gimp from left to right through this pair then work the pair to the left through three

Fig 95 Working diagram, Honeycomb Fan

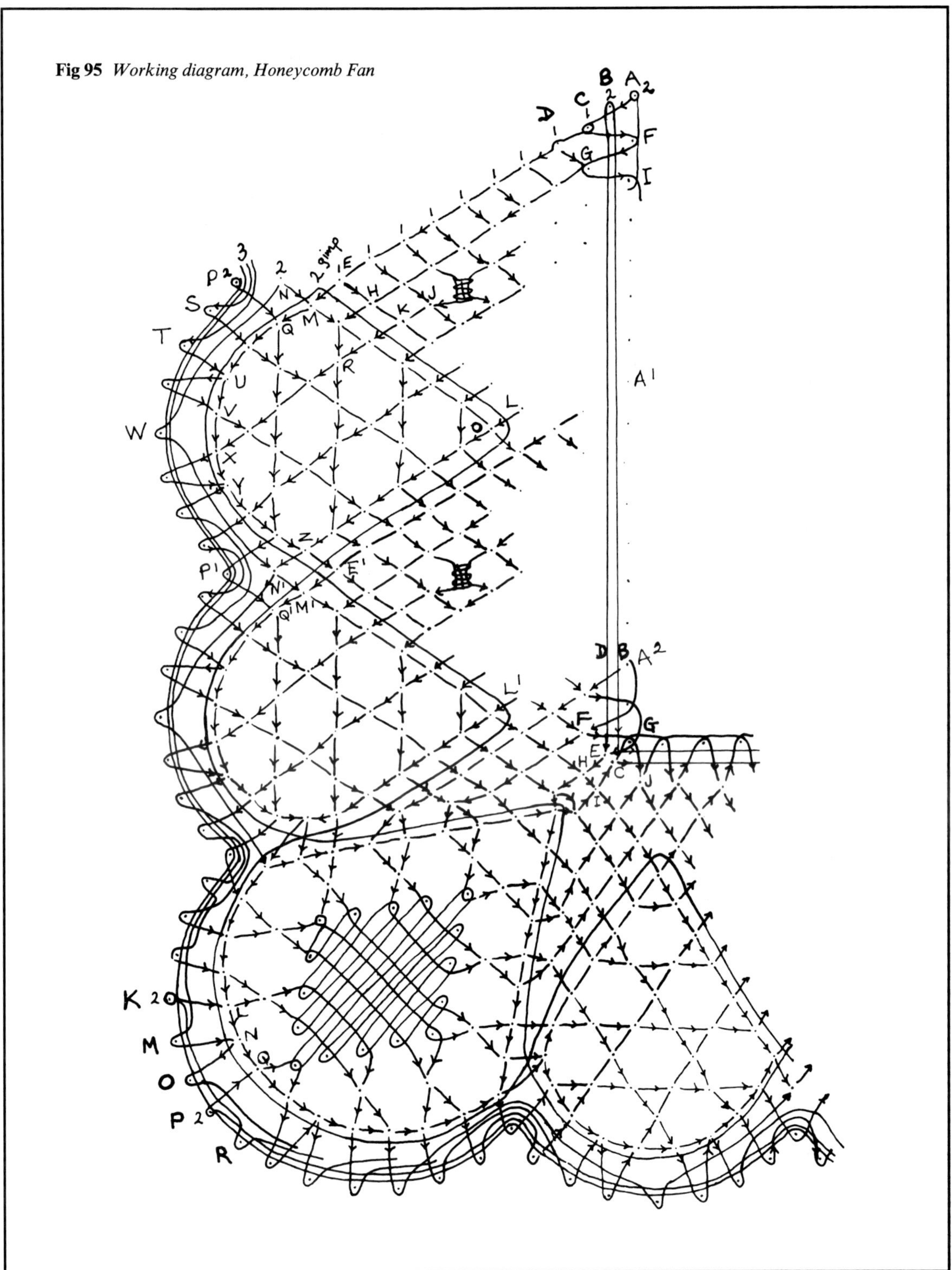

pairs in WS, make a picot, then bring the pair back in WS through the three pairs. Pass the gimp through it from right to left and work the next hc st at Y inside the gimp with the pair hanging from X. Work the remaining three pinholes of the long row, finishing at Z, when the hc fan will be complete.

The gimps now need to cross between the two pairs hanging from Z. First go to the RH gimp and bring it from right to left through seven pairs, ending with the RH pair from Z.

Go to the LH gimp and bring it from left to right through four pairs, one hanging from Y, one each from the next two holes and one from Z.

Now cross the gimps, left over right, and leave them over to the right while you complete the headside.

Take the LH of these four pairs, i.e. the pair hanging through the gimp from Y and work it in WS through three pairs, work a picot, then work WS back through two pairs and leave the pair lying inside the two constant passive pairs.

Take the next pair hanging through the gimp and work it in WS through four pairs, work a picot, then work WS back through two pairs and leave the pair lying inside the two constant passive pairs.

With the next pair through the gimp work out to the left in WS for five stitches, then make a picot at P^1 and leave the pair there.

Now with the LH pair hanging through the gimp from Z, twist it twice instead of the usual once. Take the inside passive pair, twist it twice, and work a hc st between these two pairs at pin N^1.

After this pin, the RH pair is ready for the gimp to pass through it, then it can work pin M^1 in due course.

The pair left at the outside at pin P^1 will be the worker pair and it now works to the right in WS through five pairs then the LH gimp passes through it from right to left.

You now have pairs waiting on the left for the first two rows of hc.

You now lay aside completely all the LH side of the lace and return to the footside at A^1, where you work the first diagonal from A^1 to E^1, followed by six more diagonal rows, finishing at L^1. Instructions for all this have already been given. All will now be plain-sailing, apart from the corner.

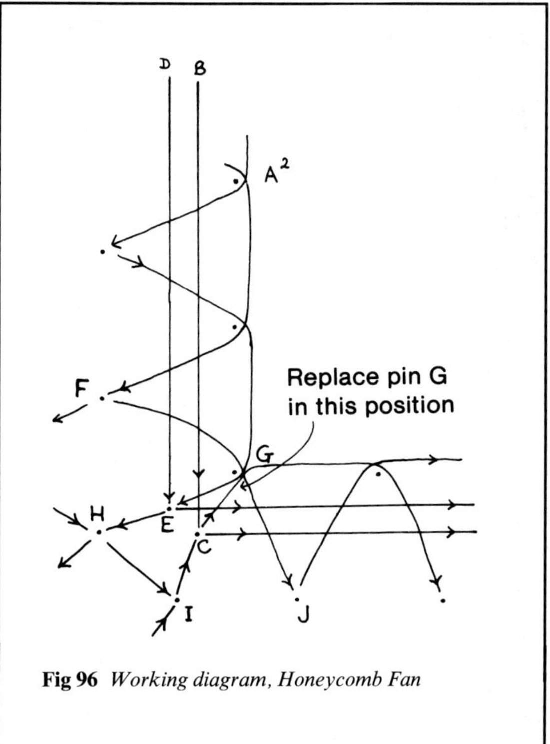

Fig 96 *Working diagram, Honeycomb Fan*

The corner

When you reach A^2 things will start to be different. On the whole, you should be able to manage satisfactorily as long as you work from Fig 95 and *follow the direction of the arrows* carefully. The diagram shows you exactly where each pair goes and in which direction. You yourself know where you will be working ground stitch and where you will be working hc st, so I will only list here a few points where something slightly different happens.

As I have used up all the letters, these new uses of the letters bear no relation to the previous sections.

The inside corner

The enlarged diagram (Fig 96) will help you to see the exact path of each pair. In principle, the edge pair of passives (BC) becomes the inner pair after the corner and the inner pair (DE) becomes the edge pair after the corner.

Thus, after sticking pin F and working the next four pinholes on that diagonal, return to the pair hanging from F.

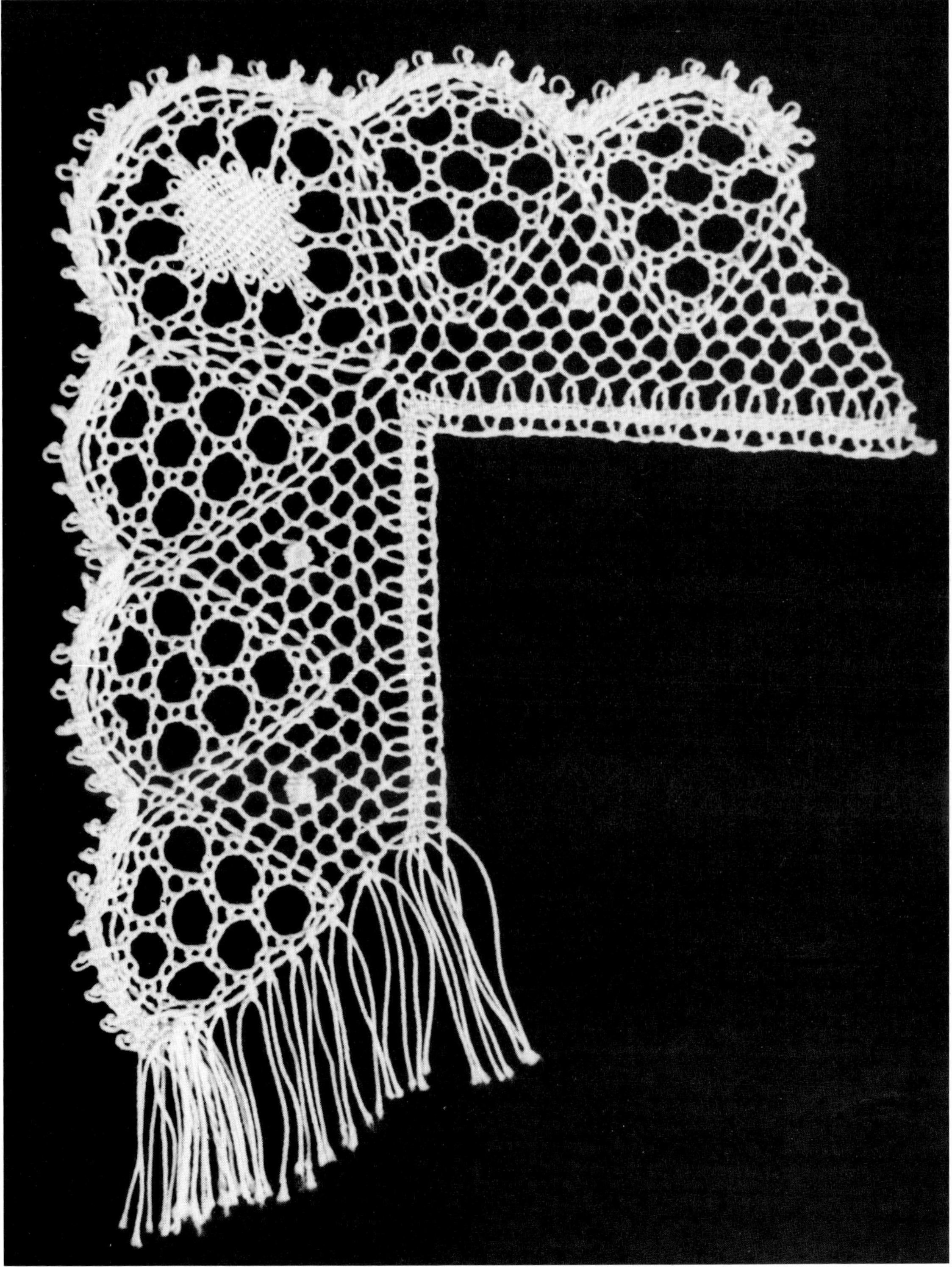

Fig 98 *Small mat*

Work WS through the two passive pairs to the right, twist three times and work WS with the edge pair. Twist only the LH pair three times and leave the RH pair untwisted and stick the edge pin at G as usual with both pairs to the right of it. Work the LH pair through one passive pair in WS then, at E, work a $\frac{1}{2}$st with the inner passive pair, stick the pin, then cross no. 2 thread over no. 3 to complete a WS. Twist the LH pair twice and leave it (it will continue to H in due course).

Work the RH pair through the edge passive pair in WS so that they change places.

Hole C cannot be worked until the corner section is finished but I will describe it here to save going back to it later. Hole C is worked between the pair coming from left to right from I and the former edge passive pair from B. Work a $\frac{1}{2}$st between these two pairs at C, stick the pin then complete a WS by crossing the centre pairs as before, 2 over 3, after which the LH pair is left to become the inner passive pair and the RH pair works in WS through the new edge passive pair from E, twists three times, then works WS with the edge pair which is waiting at G. Twist both pairs three times then replace pin G to the left of both pairs. The RH pair stays at the edge until the next pin and the LH pair works back in WS through the two pairs of passives to J.

There is only one other point I need mention as the rest of the diagram (Fig 95) is straight-forward.

At the edge there are two picots where there is a '2' written (K and P). At each of these pinholes you need to hang on two pairs and work a *false picot*. This is worked as follows:

†Hang two fresh pairs of bobbins on the pin at K, one splayed outside the other and twist both pairs three times. Work a WS then twist both pairs twice. Work the RH pair through the two passive pairs. It is then ready for the gimp to pass through and then the pair can work the stitch inside the head at L.

The second pair hung on at K is at present on the outside. Work it to the right in WS through two pairs and leave it lying inside the two pairs.

Take the second passive pair from the edge and work it to the left in WS through the outer passive pair. It is now ready to work the picot at M in the normal way, then pass in WS through the two passive pairs, then the gimp will pass through this pair from right to left so that the pair can work inside the head at N†.

After the stitch at N the LH pair passes through the gimp, through the two passive pairs in WS, then works the picot at O, after which it works through the two passive pairs in WS and is left inside the inner passive pair, to be laid back (and in due course cut off) after three more rows.

Repeat from † to †, reading hole P for K, Q for L and R for M, only the pair that worked the picot at R will not, in fact, work at a pin inside the head but will stay inside the two edge passive pairs for three rows then be laid back and eventually cut off.

The centre section of the corner fan is worked in cloth stitch (WS) (*see* Fig 95).

The diagram shows where the other two extra pairs are laid back and eventually cut off, amongst the passive pairs on the headside.

PATTERN 4   HONEYCOMB DIAMONDS

Materials

23 pairs of bobbins
and 1 extra pair at the corner   } wound with
Swedish linen thread no. 90 or 100
and 2 gimp bobbins wound with
Coton Perle no. 12

Note: The gimp is not fully indicated at the end of the pattern, the reason being that the final three holes in the last diamond are already indicated at the beginning, being the hanging-on holes.

This pattern is quite straightforward and consolidates your present knowledge. There is nothing really new. The diamonds are much like the pea, only that the points of the diamond are included within the gimp instead of being outside it. The exceptions to this are the two flattened diamonds at the highest point of the head, where the top point of the diamond is, in fact, the edge picot.

The footside is started in the usual way at A and three diagonal rows are worked from A to B, C to D and E to F.

Now hang your gimp pair temporarily on the pin at G. Three pinholes are marked on the pattern, where you can hang the three pairs which enter this first diamond from the left but, after working the hc st inside the diamond, each pin should be removed to avoid a large loop in the threads. The result will be that the pair will be hung round the gimp, a manoeuvre that you did in Pattern 2.

After you have completed this first diamond, the gimps must be crossed and run alongside each other in the same channel with the pairs containing them only twisted before and after *both* gimps, not in between the gimps. The pairs which they pass through are the pairs hanging from H and I and the LH pair from J.

The cross-over after each of the diamonds will be in this manner, as indicated in the diagram, except between the two at the top of the headside, where the gimps cross in the same way as those in the pea pattern and do not run alongside each other.

After the first diamond you work a section of headside. Hang two pairs on the pin at K and work a false picot. Hang six pairs side by side on

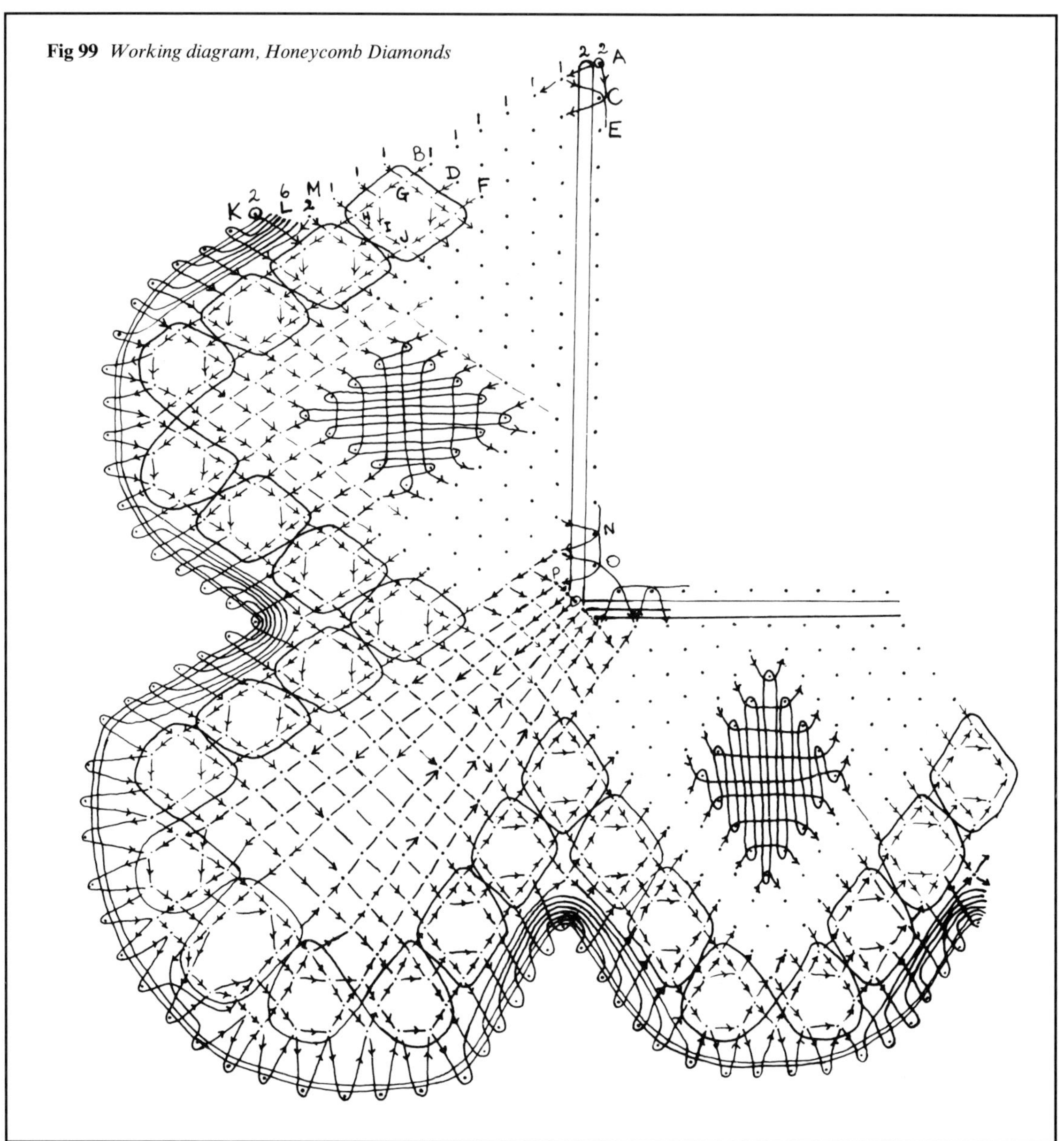

an extra pin stuck at L between pin K and pin M. This method of hanging on can later be compared with that given in Pattern 5 and then you can choose for future use the method you prefer, remembering that the method which gives the best final effect when the work is complete and joined up is the one for you.

Work the RH pair from K to the right through the six pairs at L in WS.

Hang two pairs at M, one splayed outside the other, twist both pairs twice and work WS, twist twice. (This pinhole will be worked in hc st in future repeats.) The RH pair from M will work the top pinhole of the second diamond after the gimp has passed through it. The workers from K now work through the LH pair from M, then they will work the second stitch of the diamond when the gimp has passed through them.

98

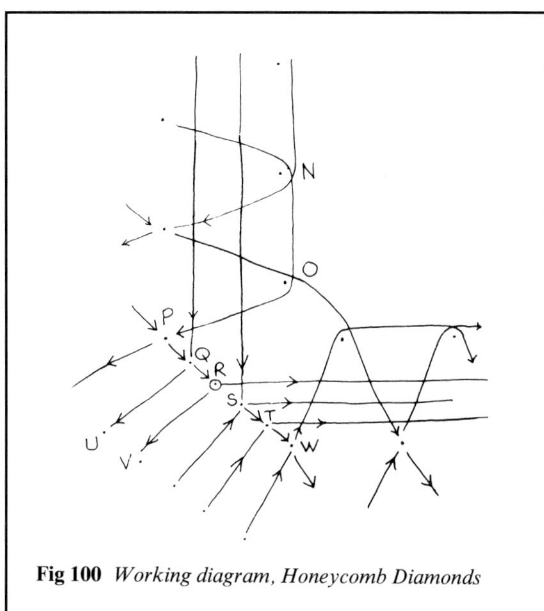

Fig 100 *Working diagram, Honeycomb Diamonds*

The remainder of the edging should present no problems if you follow the diagram (Fig 99). It has the usual uphill section where all the pairs go *into* the work from the picots, the downhill section where all the pairs come *out of* the work towards the picots and the flat top where the workers go both out of and into the work before and after the picots.

The corner

This is an unusual and simplified corner, in which the ground is not at the normal angle. It is very easy to work as long as you follow the direction of the arrows, noting that the first three long rows of ground work from the inside towards the edge and the second three rows work from the edge towards the inside.

Only one extra pair is required to work the corner and your only possible problems might occur at the inner corner, so an enlarged diagram of this section is given (Fig 100). The diagonals starting at N and O are as usual. After working them, bring the LH passive pair to work WS, twist, pin at Q, WS with the pair from P. Twist the LH pair three times. This will then work up the long row from U onwards. The RH pair is not twisted but works at pin R with a new pair hung on the pin to the right of this passive pair (the passive pair being taken to the left of the pin before the stitch). The pairs work WS, then twist the LH pair three times and don't twist the RH pair. The LH pair will now work up the long row from V onwards.

The RH pair now changes places with the outer passive pair by working a WS between them. Thus the former inside passive pair becomes the edge passive pair. The pair that was the edge pair will work at hole S after you have worked the main part of the corner, since the pair it works with at S comes from left to right down the long line from the corner.

When you are ready, this is what happens: the two pairs work WS, twist, pin at S, WS. The RH pair is laid over to the right with the other passive pair and the LH pair works at pin T with the pair coming down the next long row from left to right. It works WS, twist, pin at T, WS. The RH pair is laid to the right with the other two passive pairs and the LH pair will work a catchpin stitch at hole W with the pair coming from left to right down the next row from the corner, at which point the corner is finished and you are back into your normal edging.

All that remains is to lay back and cut off the central passive pair on the footside after three or four more rows.

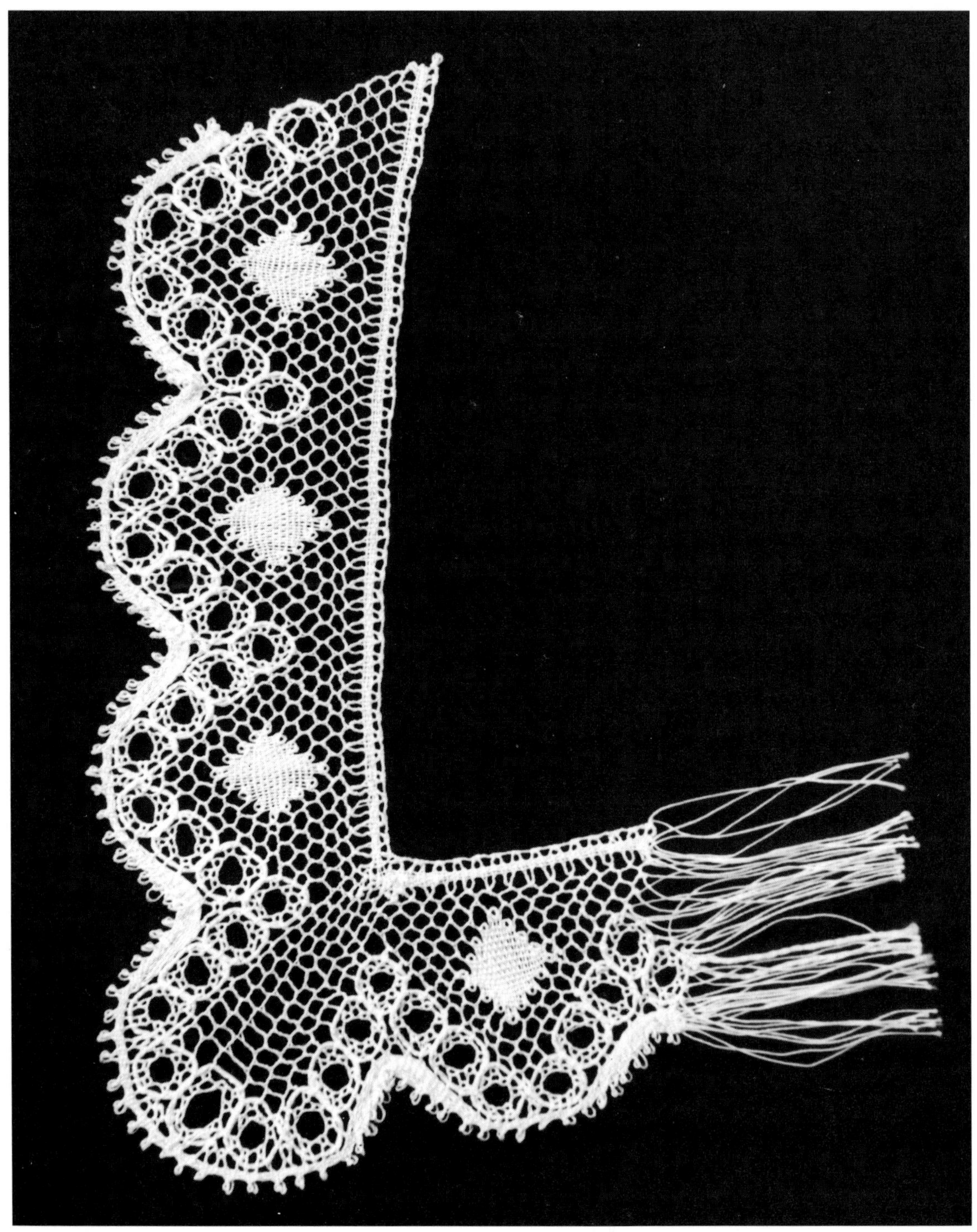

Fig 101 *Close-up of lace, Honeycomb Diamonds*

Fig 102 *Small mat*

Fig 103 Pattern

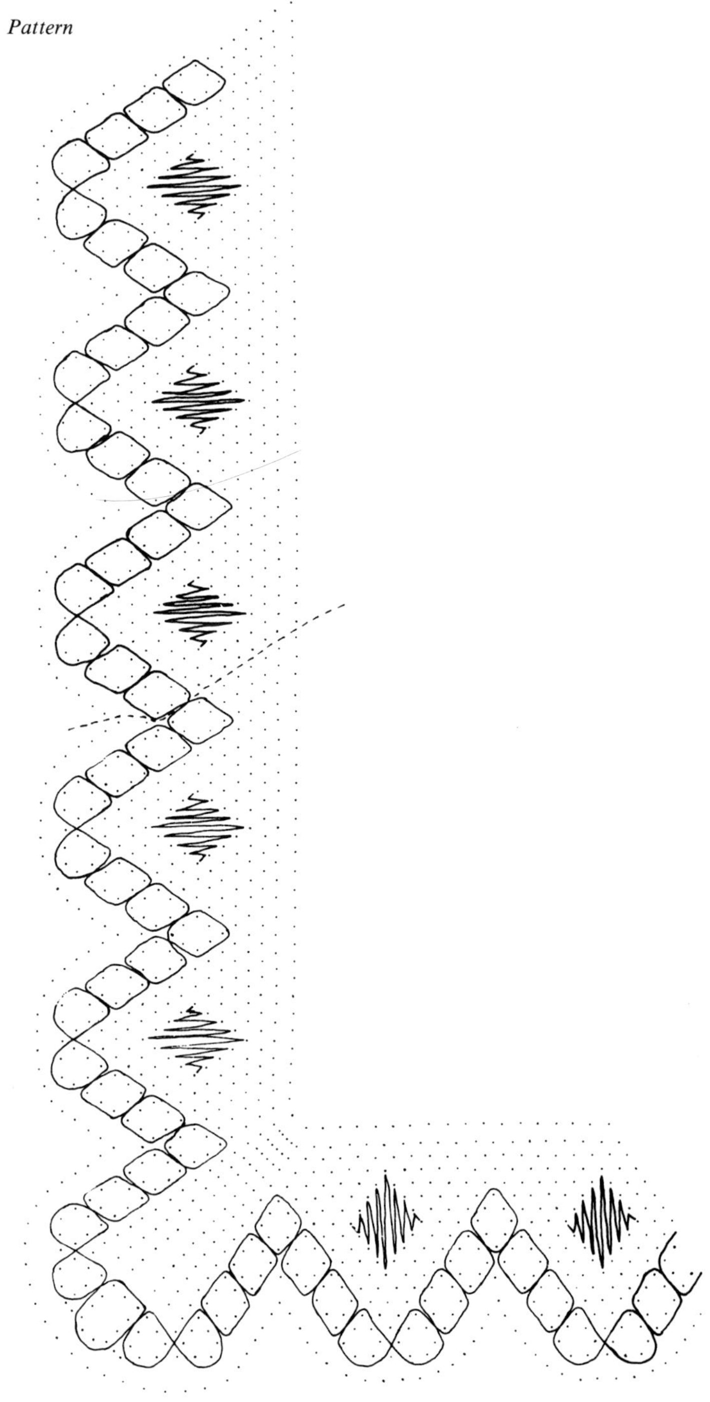

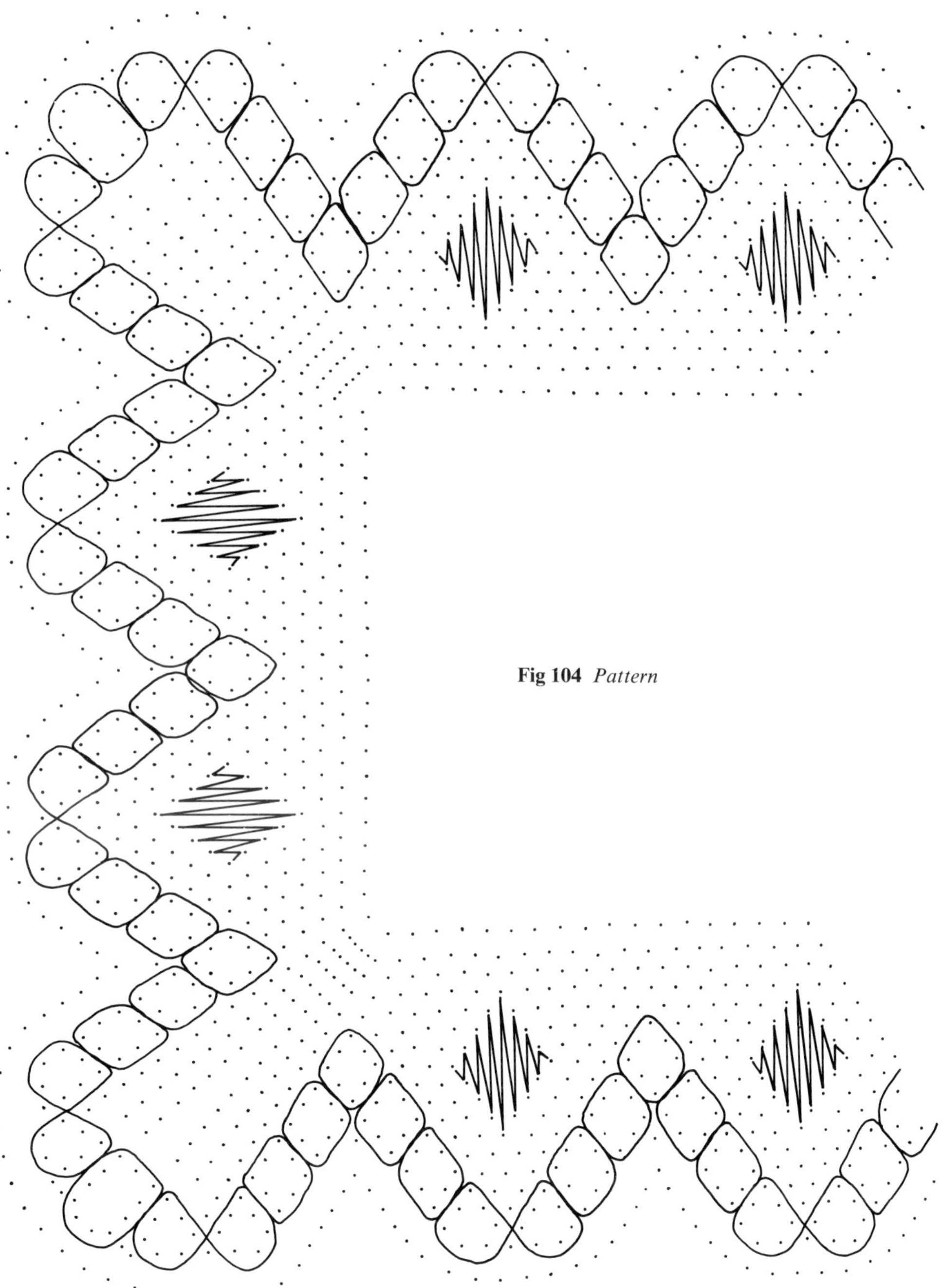

Fig 104 *Pattern*

PATTERN 5   WINGS

Materials

33 pairs of bobbins
and 8 extra pairs at the corner } wound with
DMC Cordonnet no. 50
or Filato di Cantu no. 30
or Swedish linen thread
no. 50 or 60
} for the large size
or Swedish linen thread
no. 100 or 120
or Unity Glace cotton
no. 150
} for the small size
and 4 gimp bobbins wound with
Coton Perle no. 8 for the large size
or Coton Perle no. 12 for the small size

This pattern is by way of introduction to the
motif, Pattern 8, since the motif consists of this
pattern section repeated six times. This will make
the motif easier to tackle since the main part will
be familiar, leaving you free to master the other
problems peculiar to a motif. This pattern was
designed to be worked in the smaller size with the
finer thread but, after working the sample in a
larger size in order to show the working more
clearly, it was felt that some people might wish to
make it up the same size as the sample and might
be disappointed if that pattern were not included.

The headside has the classic uphill and downhill parts, with a flat piece on the crown, all of
which works in just the same way as the previous
pattern.

In the rather squashed 'valley' between the two
heads, you will notice a different treatment of it.
In Pattern 4 a hc st was worked between the two
inside passives. These inside passives need to
change places by the simple expedient of working
through each other in WS, with no pin.

You start the pattern and work the ground
section in the same way as usual. At the headside
the small figures indicate how many pairs will be
hung on at each pinhole.

The first part of a false picot is worked at each
picot where a 2 is marked, in order to get the
needed pairs quickly into the work (so that the
head matches subsequent heads where there will
be a lot of passive threads in the valley). Thus,
*firstly you hang the two pairs, one splayed
outside the other, twist three times then work WS
and twist twice. The RH pair then works through
all the passives to pass through the gimp and the
LH pair works through the two constant passives
and is left lying there as a passive*. Repeat from *
to * at the next three pinholes. All the bobbins for
the edge will by then have been hung on.

Fix two separate gimp threads to pins behind
your work, so that about 4in of thread extend
beyond the work. (This is to darn a short way
into the other side when the work is complete.)
These are the two gimps which run all along the
headside just inside the picots. They are a
characteristic feature of some Bucks Point laces
and have a hc st sandwiched between them all the
way round. (Some patterns have three or more
such threads round the headside.) Mainly you
will work this by retaining one of the threads
after the stitch inside the sandwich to work the
stitch in the next row with the next pair that will
either come through *from* the picots on the uphill
side or go through *to* the picots on the downhill
side. Where the gimps make a wiggle or change
shape, as at A, B and C, you will see from Figs
106 and 107 that the pair which usually remains
in the sandwich goes out and a different pair
takes its place. Look carefully at the flat section
of head and you will see that *no pair* remains in
the sandwich between stitches. This is because
you will in any case have two pairs to work the
stitch because the workers are going in and out at
every stitch (instead of in only or out only, as is
the case with the uphill and downhill sections). It
is therefore not possible to keep a constant pair in
here or you would have three pairs meeting at the
pinholes, which would not work.

For the large motif surrounded by gimp you
will need to hang on a fresh pair of gimps each
time, as these sections do not join up with each
other. As already explained, the best system is to
knot the threads together after the first time you
have used them, then wind one knot sufficiently
far back on to one bobbin so that you do not
reach it in the next section. This is easy to
calculate as the sections are small, and this way
you can keep using the same pair of gimps, yet
never have a knot in your work.

To work this section, hang on the pair of gimps
temporarily at D. Work the stitch at D, replacing
the pin between the pairs in the usual way. The
gimp then follows the path outlined for it. When
you finally complete pin Z the two gimps cross
each other between the pairs coming from pin Z,
then overlap each other, the one going leftwards

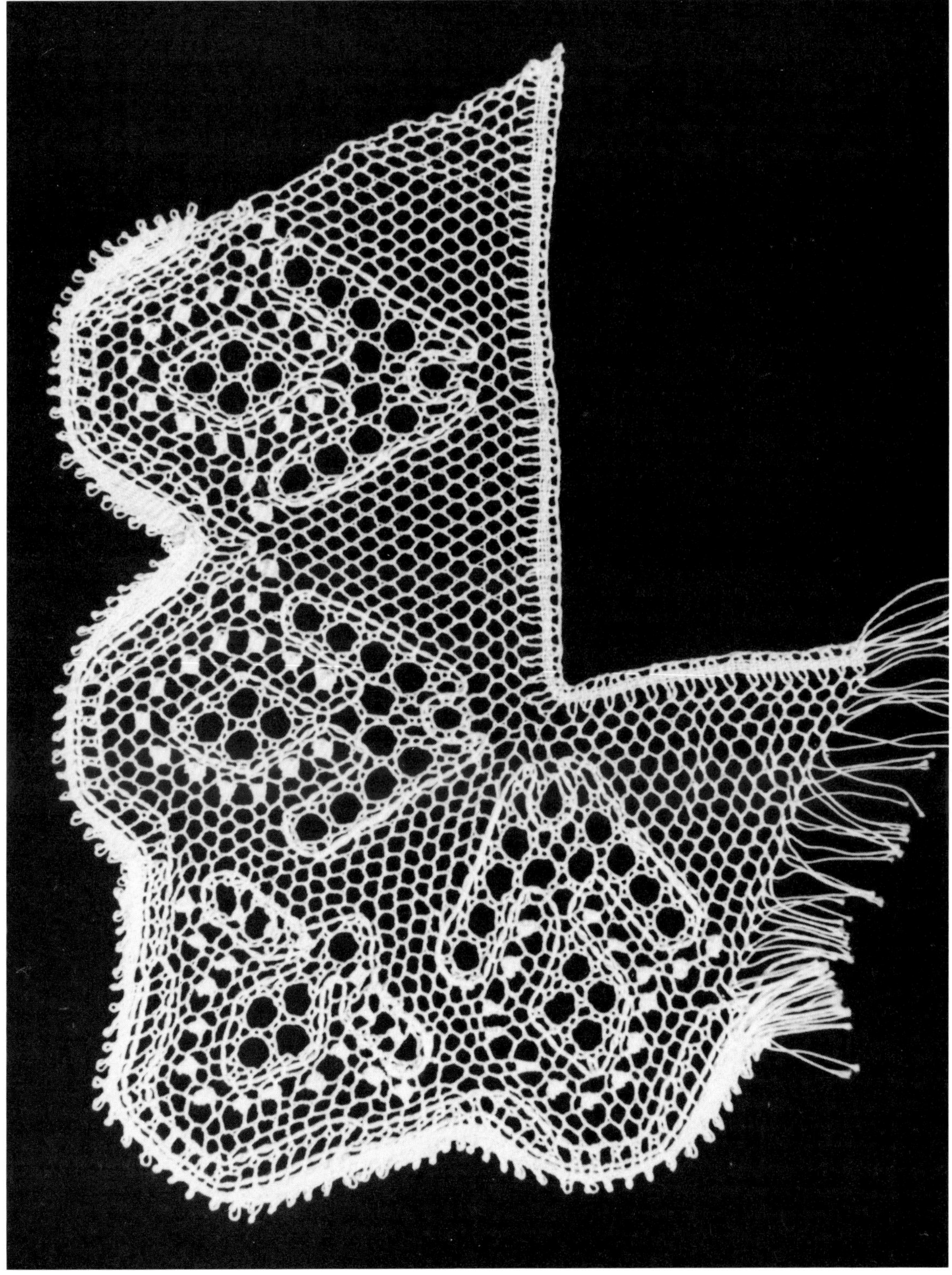

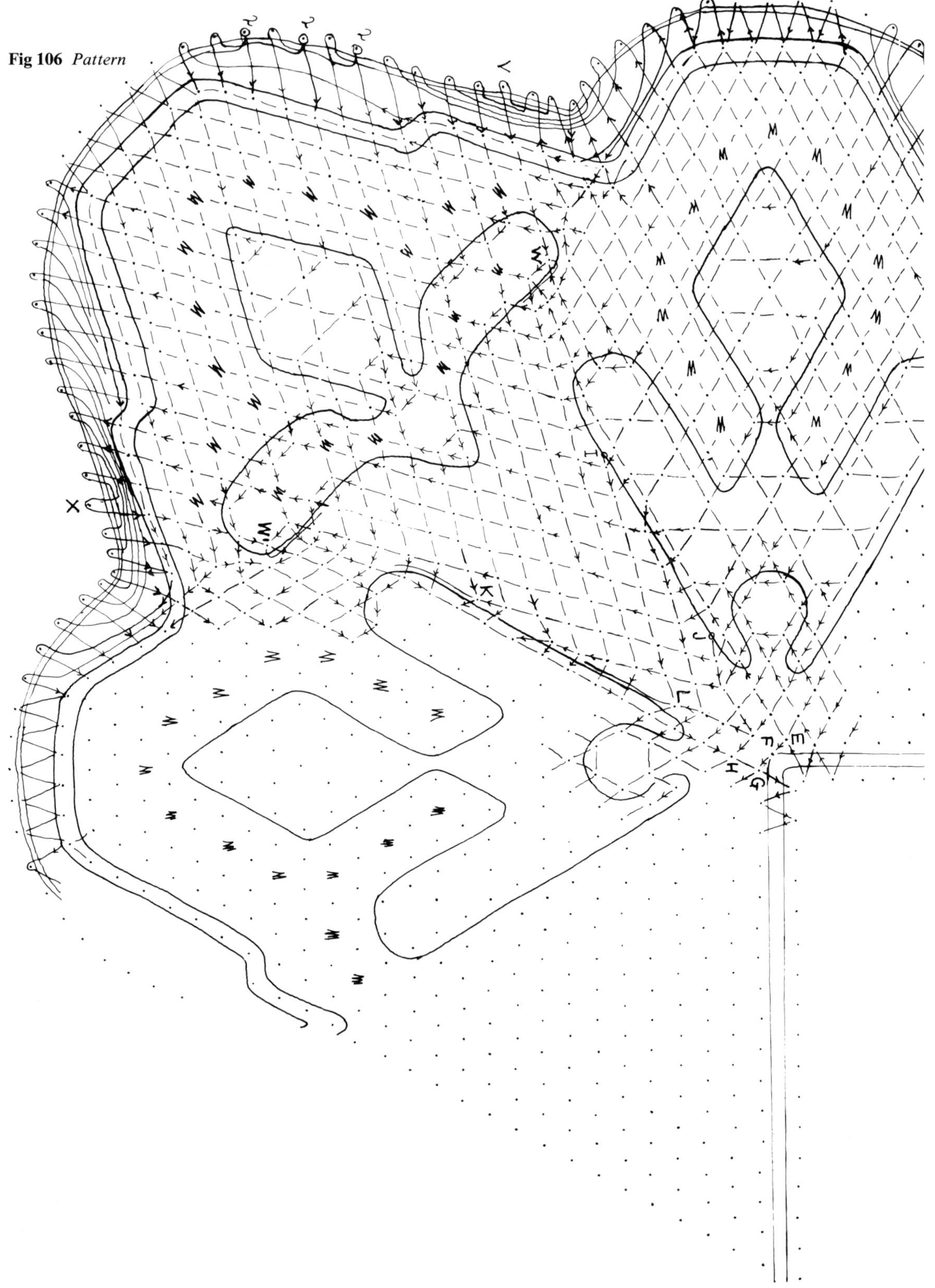

Fig 106 *Pattern*

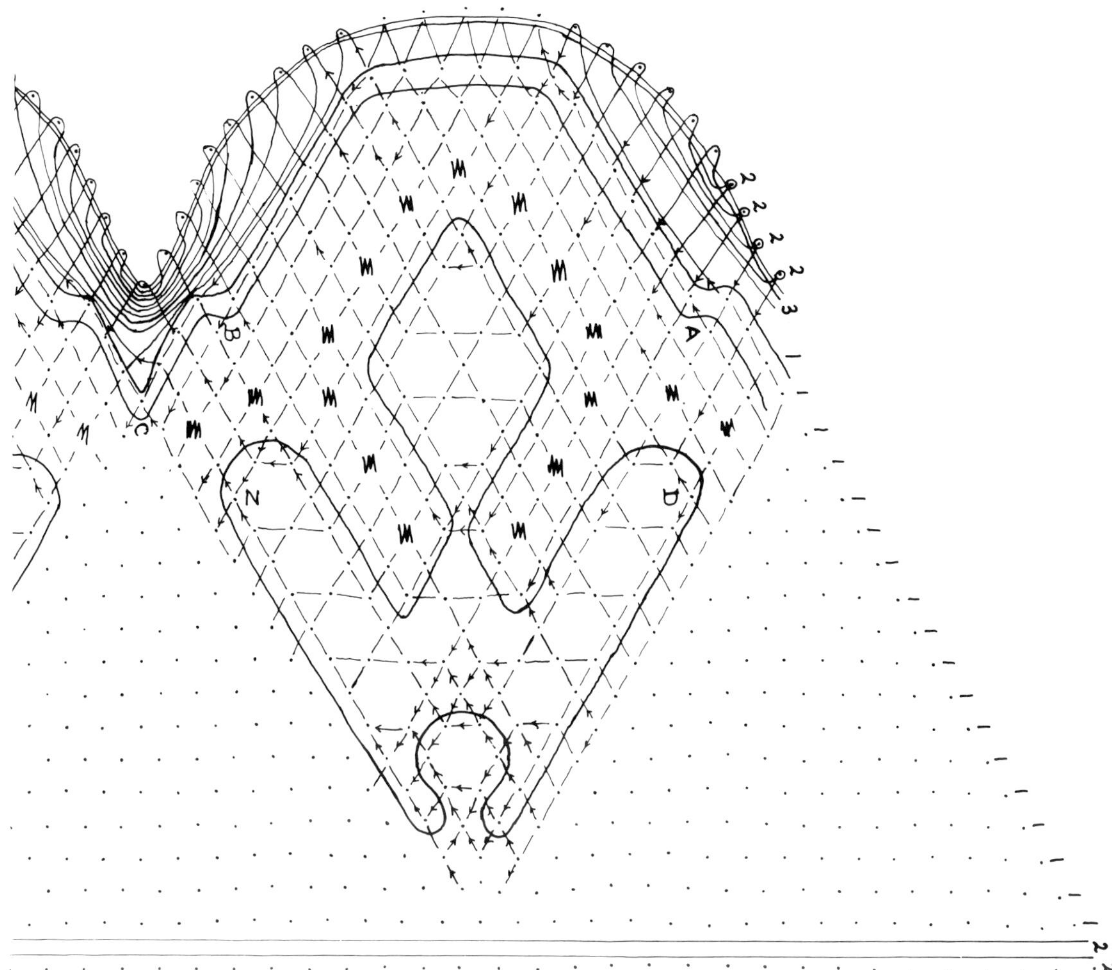

going between one more pair (the next stitch outside having already been worked so that it can go no further) and the one going to the right can go through another three pairs. When gimps overlap in this way as, indeed, at any other time when two gimps continue for a while alongside each other, they stay in the same channel as each other and the pair they pass through does not twist between each gimp. The gimp on the left should be cut off with a 4in tail; this is to enable you to darn it in a little way after the lace is finished, since it was not possible to overlap it sufficiently to make it secure. The other gimp can then be laid back and in due course cut off. I do not cut off really closely until the work is off the pillow and I am working in a good light with good scissors.

The corner

This corner is a good example of a Bucks Point corner, and from Fig 106 you can see the way the ground changes its angle. This means that the diagonals do not exactly fit together where the two angles meet. However, if you refer closely to the diagram, *ensuring that you follow the directions of the arrows*, it will all work out correctly.

After the 'valley' immediately preceding the corner, you will notice that two pairs go *out* to the picot on the uphill section instead of going *in* as normal, but from V onwards they go *in*. At X, on the other side of the corner, the threads from the picots start going *in* instead of *out*, as would be normal for a downhill section.

The inside corner is more simple than usual. At F the footside worker from E works a hc st with

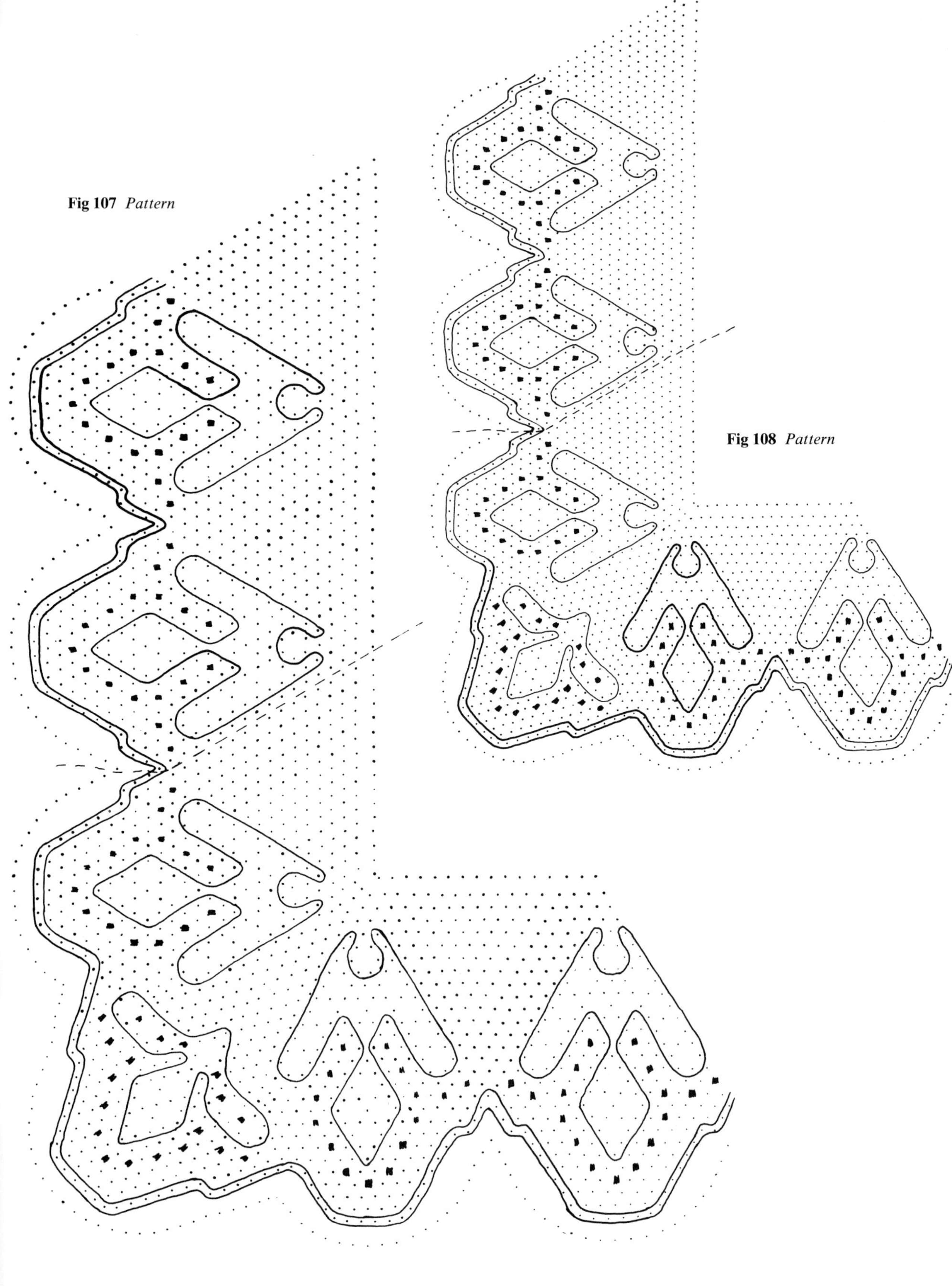

Fig 107 Pattern
Fig 108 Pattern

the inner passive pair, after which the RH pair goes to the right as the inner passive and the LH pair goes to G to work a catchpin stitch (i.e. ground stitch but with the pin to the right of both pairs instead of between them) in due course (after the corner has been finished) with the pair from H.

Add pairs
1. At the edge where twos are marked (doing false picots).
2. Down the gimp immediately before the corner in two places where a small o is marked, at I and at J.

Take out pairs
1. At W and W[1] near the beginning and end of the corner motif: run these threads alongside the gimp for three or four stitches, if possible but, where it is not possible because the stitches have already been worked, as at W, lay the bobbins back, cut them off in due course and darn in the threads along the gimp after the work is complete.
2. Four pairs at the downhill edge where indicated by the threads ending.
3. Two pairs down the gimp which follows the corner, equivalent to where they were hung on, at K and L, both pairs being run along the gimp in the same channel for three or four stitches.

Finally, I would again stress that you must follow the direction of the arrows closely or it will not work out.

PATTERN 6   LOZENGE MOTIF

Materials

26 pairs of bobbins wound with
Unity Glace cotton no. 150
or Retors d'Alsace no. 50
and 4 gimp bobbins wound with
Coton Perle no. 12

The motif is designed to be looked at sideways to the way of working. You will realise that it is a simple matter to make a motif like this into a bookmark. Trace the pattern as it is, without the bottom lines of pins outside the gimp, and move it up so that the bottom section is on top of the top section. Trace a new lower part and so on for

a total of five heads or thereabouts. Similarly, you can make the bookmark (Pattern 7) into a motif by only tracing the top and bottom heads, i.e. tracing the top section, then moving it down to rest on top of the bottom but one section then tracing the bottom section. You then prick your pattern through the tracing paper.

Bucks Point motifs are generally made in one of two ways. In this type, you start at the top and work down, making it all in one piece. In the other type, as in Pattern 8, there are six sections, each of which is completed before moving on to the next.

You hang on two pairs along the top lines at the pinholes where a 2 is marked. At each of these pinholes you will work a false picot: i.e. hang the pairs, one splayed outside the other, twist both pairs three times, make a WS, twist both pairs twice. After the first hole the pairs go, one to the left, one to the right to become the outside passives round the edge. From the second hole on each side, after the false picot, the inside pair crosses the inside pair from the opposite second hole in WS and becomes the inner passive pair down the opposite side to where it was hung on. The other pairs from these second pinholes will work the top stitch of the first bud. (A 'bud' is the Bucks Point name for any pattern section, usually surrounded by gimp.) Before this top stitch you will need to hang a pair of gimps temporarily on to the top pinhole of the bud, then take the gimps through the pairs and work a hc st at this top hole, replacing the pin in the usual way between the pairs.

Other points where you may need guidance are:
1. There is a line of eight hc sts on each side outside the gimp and inside the picots and headside passives. These stitches are worked between the pair coming down from the first bud and each pair as it travels in from its picot to the honeycomb diamonds.
2. The second pair of gimps is hung on at the lower side of the first spider, being the dotted line indicated in the spider diagram (Fig 109).
3. The 'spider' may be a little unexpected in Bucks Point lace, seeming to have escaped from torchon lace, but, indeed, these spiders are to be found in old Bucks Point lace and, as you can see, are worked differently from the torchon variety (see Fig 109). The spider is surrounded by hc sts

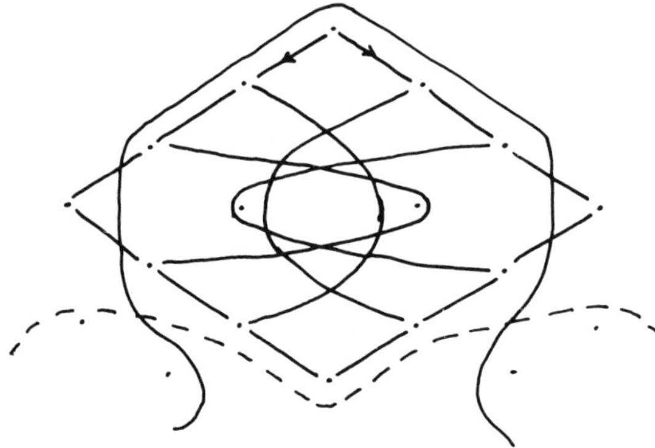

Fig 109 *Spider diagram*

Fig 110 *Finished lace, lozenge motif*

on all sides. These are the stitches which make up the spider.

Twist the four legs once more (a total of two twists).

Work WS between the following pairs in this order:

2 and 3;

1 and 2, 3 and 4;

2 and 3;

1 and 2, twist LH pair four times, twist RH pair twice, stick a pin between them at left centre;

3 and 4, twist LH pair twice, twist RH pair four times, stick a pin between them at right centre;

1 and 2, 3 and 4;

2 and 3;

1 and 2, 3 and 4;

2 and 3.

Twist the four legs twice each.

4. The large cloth stitch lozenge with the tally in the centre: the pathways of all the pairs are clearly shown on Fig 112. At A the sides separate, the worker pair continuing in the RH portion and the centre passive pair becoming the LH worker pair. At B, where the two sides rejoin, the

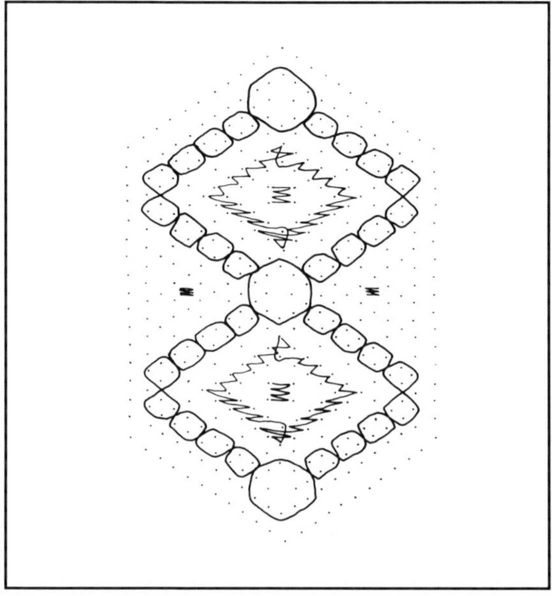

Fig 111 *Pattern*

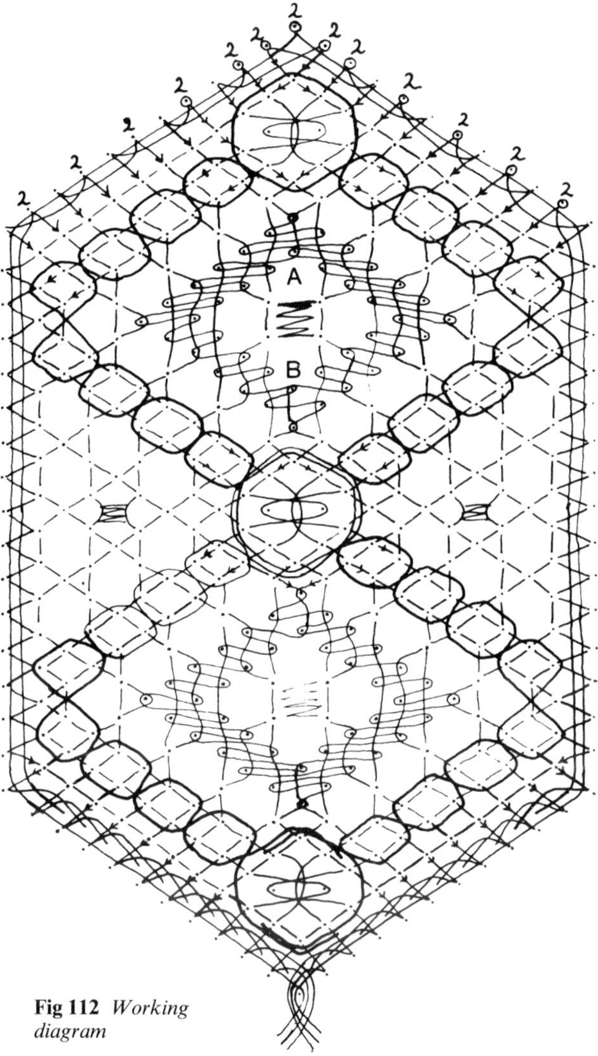

Fig 112 *Working diagram*

RH worker becomes the central passive pair and the LH worker continues to the end.

5. At the bottom, you start laying back pairs (and in due course cutting them off), as shown by the cut-off ends in the diagram (Fig 112), the principle being that, once a pair has stayed with the passives for four rows it is safe to lay it back. This way you only have a small number left at the end, which you can tie in a tassel, as in the sample, or can carefully darn in with a needle. As in the sample, you can then thread the tassel ends carefully through a small hole to the back of your mounting material, if you wish.

PATTERN 7   BOOKMARK

Materials

30 pairs of bobbins wound with
linen thread no. 120
or Unity Glace cotton no. 150
or Retors d'Alsace no. 50
and 4 gimp bobbins wound with
Coton Perle no. 12

This pattern can be worked in a slightly coarser thread if, for example, you wish to use it as a bookmark on its own. If you are going to mount it on ribbon then you are better with a finer thread, because you do not want it so thick that it leaves an impression in the pages of the book. The worked sample is in linen 120. This whole question of choice of threads does depend on the end use. For example, a pattern used to edge the collar of a dress would need a thicker thread than the same pattern used as a bookmark.

To start the pattern, hang on pairs and work a false picot wherever a 2 is marked, just as in Pattern 6. The second gimp is laid in underneath the first bud then each side crosses the first gimps to go above the second bud on each side, in exactly the same way as in Pattern 6 (shown in the spider diagram (Fig 113) for that pattern).

In Fig 113, only the top and bottom sections are shown since the other sections are repeats of these, other than the fillings, which are shown separately in Figs 114, 115, 116 and 117.

Points that might help you when working:
1. The top ring and all the other junction rings are in hc st.
2. A suggested gimp arrangement for the junction rings between each head is given in Fig 113.
3. You will notice that, as mentioned in the introduction, two pairs, instead of the usual one, enter and leave at some of the holes of the cloth stitch buds. This is because this pattern is a 'halfway house' to the floral patterns, which are the crowning glory of Bucks Point and where, in order to get the rounded appearance of the buds and because the cloth stitch must not be too thin, extra pairs are added in the working of cloth stitch sections.
4. A hc st is worked to right and left of the junction rings down the centre, the pairs working it being indicated in the working diagram.
5. The pathways of all the pairs are shown in Fig

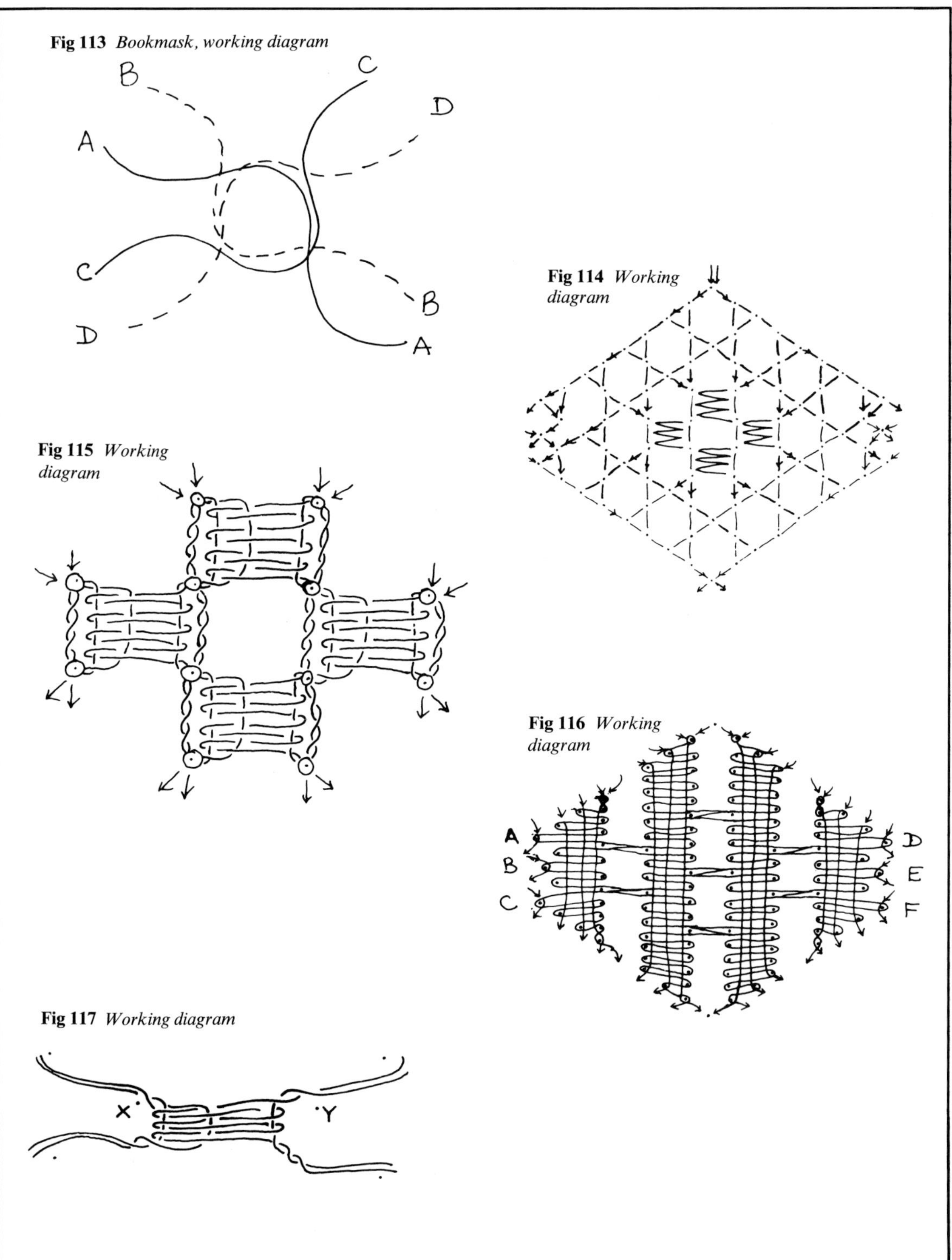

Fig 113 *Bookmask, working diagram*

Fig 114 *Working diagram*

Fig 115 *Working diagram*

Fig 116 *Working diagram*

Fig 117 *Working diagram*

113, if you study it closely.

6. At the end, pairs are laid back (and in due course cut off) after they are finished with. The cut ends are indicated here where the pairs are laid back after they have been lying with the passive pairs for four rows. The pairs that remain are worked through each other in WS, the last pin stuck in the centre between them and they again work through each other in WS. One thread can then be used to bind round the rest to form a tassel.

Fillings

The first and fifth fillings are in hc st. The second filling (Fig 114) is in hc with a central pattern of four tallies, worked as in Fig 115. You will see that a pair runs down each side of each tally, twisted three times, to meet the pair from that side of the tally in a hc st (four hc sts surround each tally). The weaver thread has been taken from the right to start each tally and has been taken into the RH stitch at the bottom of each tally. Actually, this is not crucial since each pair works a stitch at the end of the tally, so the weaver pair is fixed anyway, but one should, nevertheless, work the tallies in a regular manner.

The third filling (see Fig 116) is of cloth stitch bars linked with cucumbers. The bars are worked in cloth stitch throughout with one worker pair and three passive pairs. The workers of the two outside bars extend their range by incorporating the three holes further out (A, B and C and D, E and F) whilst working their bar. The holes linked by the cucumbers are indicated on the diagram by zig-zags. The enlarged diagram (Fig 117) and the following instructions explain the working. (To simplify the appearance, this enlarged diagram does not contain passives in the bar.) To those familiar with leaves a cucumber can best be described as a sideways leaf: the stitch is the same but, whereas a leaf is long and thin with a lot of short rows of weaving, a cucumber is short and wide with a small number of longer rows of weaving. It is, by its nature, looser and less solid than a leaf and it normally *links two worker pairs* from adjoining sections.

To work a cucumber

Stick pin X to the left of the workers and pin Y to the right of its workers and twist both pairs twice.

Thus far is the same as a normal pinhole. Now, using the LH thread from Y as the weaver and the two threads from X and the RH thread from Y as passives, *weave under the centre thread, over, round and under the LH thread, over the centre thread, under, round and over the RH thread* and continue from * to * two or three more times, depending on the size of your thread. Keep pulling the two LH threads well up and out to the left or the cucumber will slide down. At the end of the cucumber (making sure the weaver thread is on the right) twist both pairs twice (the weaver thread will now have three twists to help push the cucumber into place), then lay the weaver temporarily across the pillow with the thread slack and work through the passives with the LH pair until the next pin is stuck, then work the RH pair through its passives to fix all the pairs firmly in place.

The fourth filling, the flower filling (see Fig 120) is unusual in having no pin at the place where the stitches are made (i.e. the centre of each cross) but, instead, pins are placed between the pairs as they approach the cross-over. By this method a pretty, petal-like shape is given to the two pairs which travel together from the centre of one cross to the next. In the pattern, the cross-over point is marked by a cross.

The stitches are worked thus:

1. Using the pairs from A and B, work WS then twist both pairs twice. Stick pin C between both pairs.

2. Using pairs from D and E, work WS, twist both pairs twice, stick pin between at F.

3. Using these four pairs, work WS with pairs 1 and 2 then with pairs 3 and 4 (numbering from the left).

4. Work WS with pairs 2 and 3, then with 1 and 2, then with 3 and 4. Make a WS with pairs 2 and 3 then pull up the pairs firmly, particularly these last two pairs.

5. Using the two LH pairs, work WS then twist both pairs twice. Stick pin G between the two pairs.

6. Using the two RH pairs, work WS then twist both pairs twice. Stick pin H between the two pairs.

7. Work WS between the two LH pairs. Work WS between the two RH pairs.

Note Stages 1, 2 and 3 coincide with stages 5, 6 and 7 in the flowers within the mesh and will

Fig 118 Working diagram, bookmark
Fig 119 Pattern

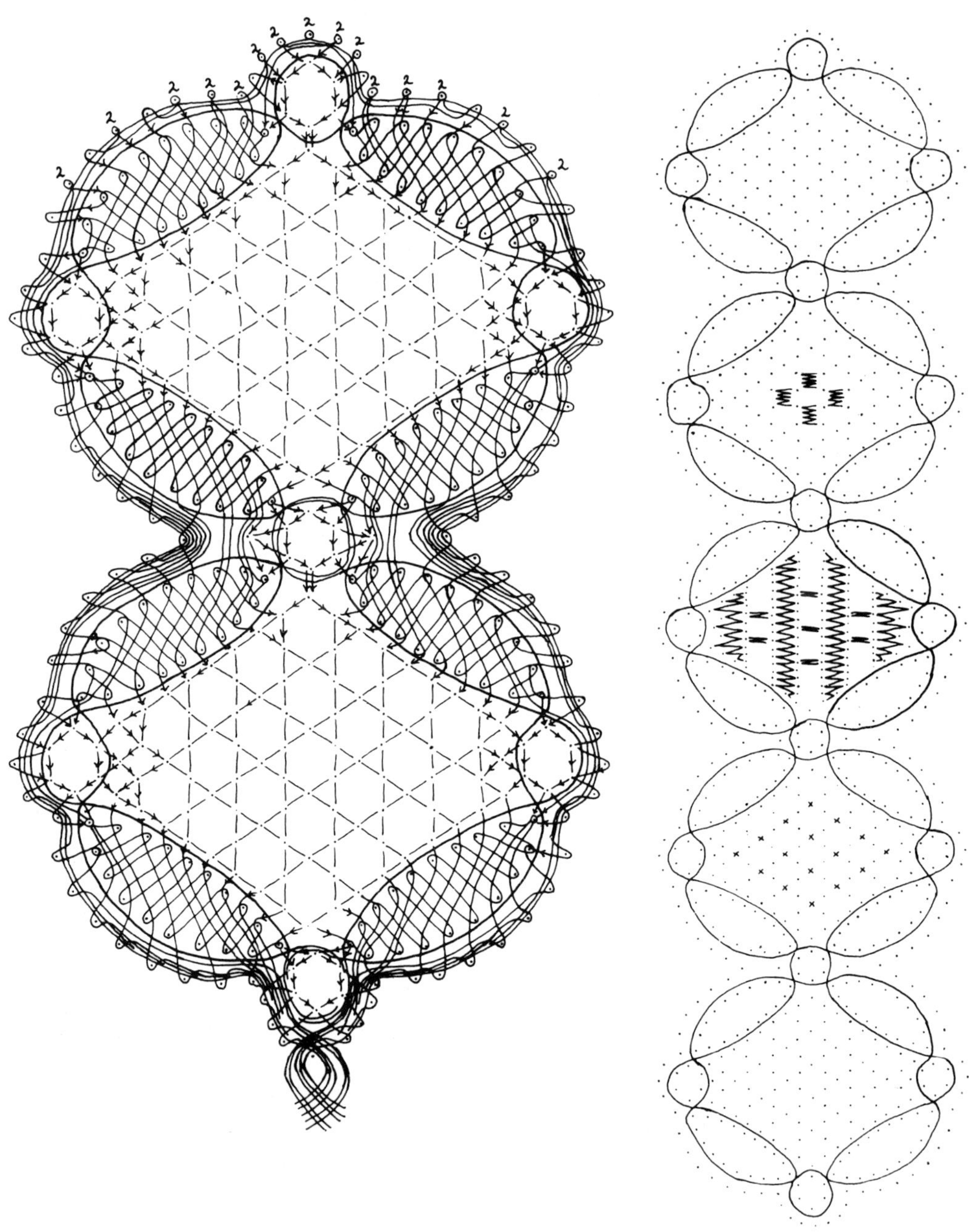

Fig 120 *Working diagram*

Fig 121 *Finished bookmark*

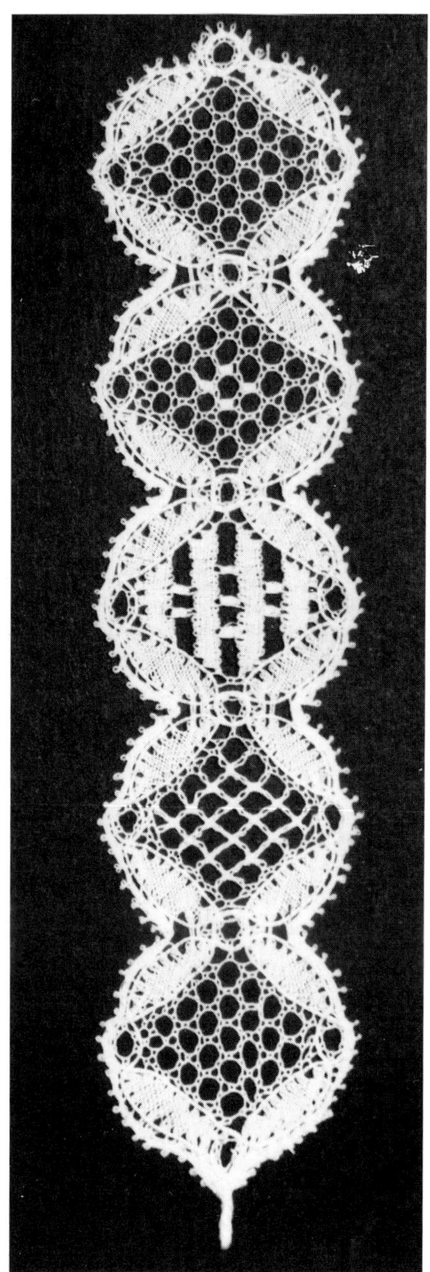

therefore be omitted in that situation whereas it will be obvious that all round the edge of the filling these stages must be completed.

The bookmark would probably look better with all the fillings the same or, perhaps, just the central one different. However, the four different fillings were given here mainly as a sampler, so that the student would become acquainted with as many different fillings as possible. You can then choose, for future occasions, which filling you like best for that application. You will realise that, not only in this pattern but many others, the lace-maker can imprint her individuality by her own choice of fillings.

PATTERN 8   STAR MOTIF

Materials

31 pairs of bobbins wound with
Unity Glace Cotton no. 150
or Retors d'Alsace no. 50
or linen no. 120
and 6 gimp bobbins wound with
Coton Perle no. 12 or equivalent

Note It is strongly recommended that you work Pattern 5 before embarking on this pattern.

Hang on two pairs at A, do a false picot, and take RH pair (in WS) through the three passive pairs hung temporarily from B.

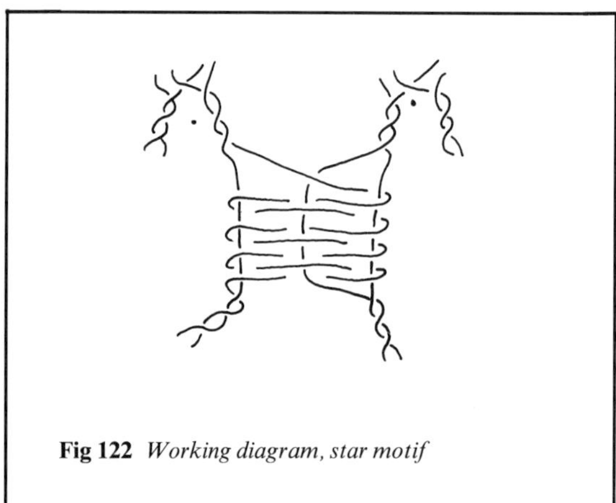

Fig 122 *Working diagram, star motif*

Fix two separate gimp threads to pins behind your work, so that about 4in of thread extend beyond the work (enough to darn in when the work is finished).

Pass the workers through one of the gimps. Hang a pair of bobbins on to C and work through them in hc st ($\frac{1}{2}$st, twist, replace pin, $\frac{1}{2}$st, twist). Then pass the RH pair through the second gimp to work at D.

At D, hang on another pair of bobbins and work hc st then, laying aside the LH pair, use the RH pair to work another hc st with another pair hung on at E. Continue down this diagonal doing exactly the same up to and including F.

Hang on another gimp (to a pin behind the work, with a 4in end) for the inner ring.

Pass the RH pair from F through this gimp to work G with another pair hung on at that pin, work hc st and replace pin at G.

Pass the LH pair from G to the left through the gimp and leave it waiting there while you return to the LH side of the work, laying the bobbins well over to the right.

Make a false picot at H (instructions in Pattern 3) then work the RH pair through four passive pairs then through the gimp to make hc st at I then through the other gimp and make a ground stitch at J ($\frac{1}{2}$st followed by two twists). Take out the pin at B and draw up the three passive pairs gently to avoid loops.

Next make a tally with the pair hanging from E. Use the second thread from the left as weaver of the four threads – two from J and two from E. Make sure that, at the end of the tally, that

thread is on the left so that after the tally, when both pairs have been twisted three times, the weaver bobbin is laid sideways to the left across the pillow. Keep the thread slack (not pulled by the weight of the bobbin) whilst you continue down the row, first making a ground stitch at K. Normally, with a tally in ground, you are working diagonals from right to left, so you leave the weaver on the right and use the other pair first. In this case, you are working the diagonals from left to right, so you must leave the weaver on the left, then the RH pair will work the next stitch. Now hang a pair of gimps temporarily on pin at L.

Bring the LH gimp thread through the pair from K (following instructions for gimps travelling from right to left). Bring the RH gimp thread through the pair from M. Work these two pairs in hc st and replace pin at L. The gimps will now be held back automatically.

Continue down the row, making hc sts up to and including pin N. Now pass the RH pair through the gimp in order to work pin O in ground stitch.

The gimp now does a U-turn and passes (from right to left) through the LH pair from N. The six pinholes inside this small circular shape are done in hc st.

The motif should now be straightforward with close reference to Fig 123 and, particularly, the direction of the arrows and the fact that you work hc sts within the gimp and ground stitches outside it, other than the link row between each section, which is worked in hc st.

The headside is worked in the normal manner once all the pairs are hung on: on the 'uphill' side the pair from the picot continues through the gimps and down the diagonal. On the 'downhill' side the pairs from the diagonals coming outwards go out, one at a time, to the picots. Whilst hanging on, where a 2 is marked near a ringed pinhole, hang on two pairs and work a false picot, but do not work the normal second half at the next pinhole. You will in this way add the necessary pairs as soon as possible.

At A[1] the pair from the picot goes in towards the centre. This might at first seem obvious, since that is what happened at A. In fact, you will have noticed that the pattern needs 31 pairs, whereas so far you have only hung on 30 pairs. This is because the pair going into the centre at A was

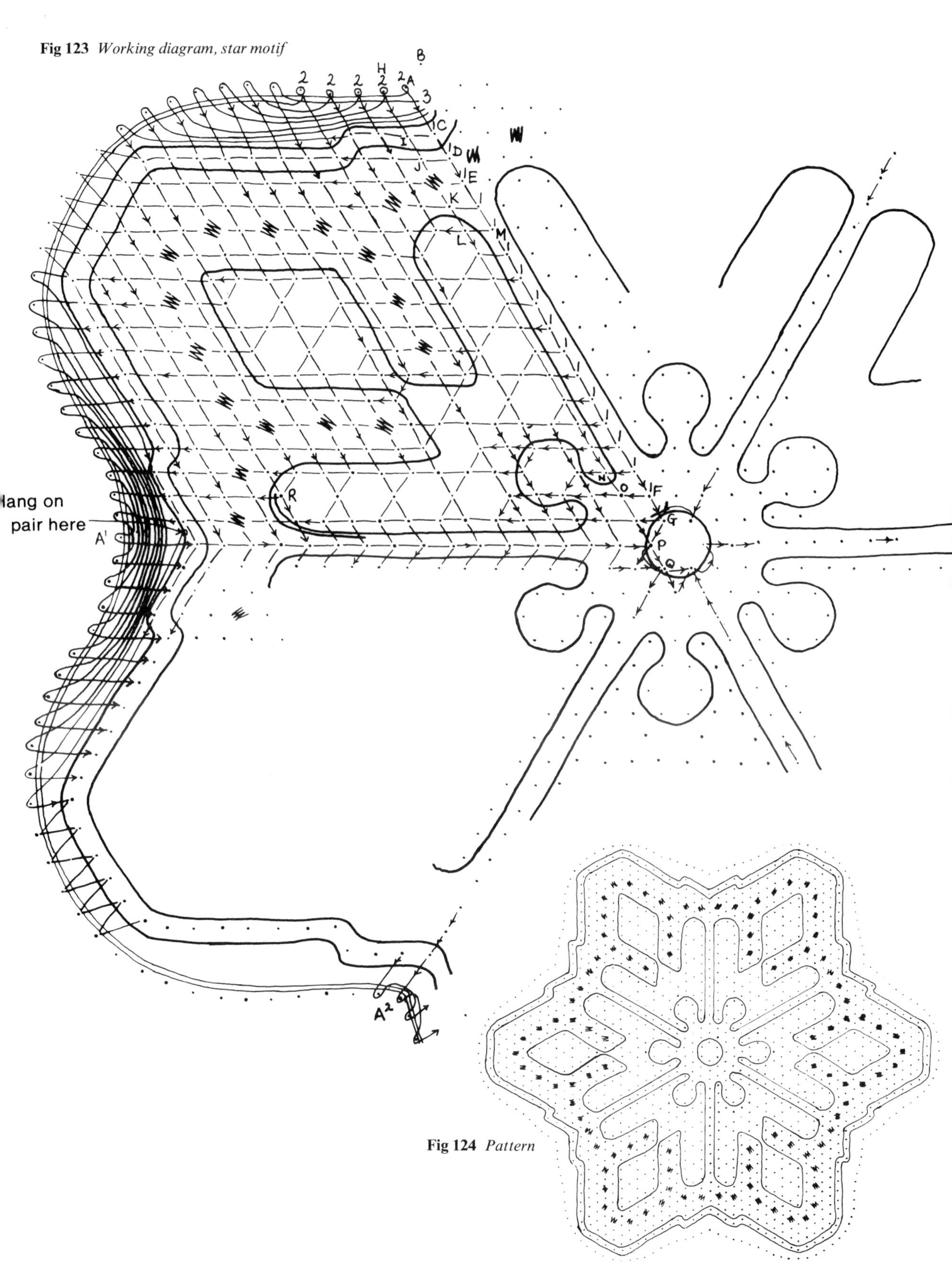

Fig 123 Working diagram, star motif
Hang on pair here
A'
A²
Fig 124 Pattern

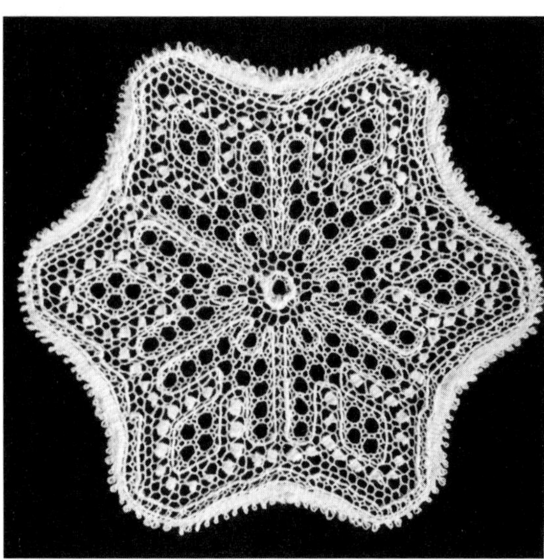

Fig 125 *Finished star motif*

only in the process of being hung on and it was convenient to work it all the way down the row.

An extra pair is hung round the gimp near A^1, as indicated, then left with the main group of edge passives, gradually working its way nearer to the edge as other pairs are used and eventually being used for a picot. You only do this once, not in subsequent repeats of the pattern.

The pair you have just hung on is to replace the pair you are taking into the centre from A^1. From now on a pair goes *into* the centre at the junction pin A^1, then *out from* the centre at Q, then in again at the next link row between sections, thus the hc link row is worked inwards then outwards alternately, from A^1 onwards, as indicated in Fig 123.

The pair which goes inwards from A^1 is an extra pair, used only in the link rows and not used in the rest of the section, thus, having gone *in* from A^1, it is the third pair to arrive at pin P. As you will know, you can only have two pairs working at any one pinhole, thus one of these pairs (the middle of the three being most convenient) is taken round in exactly the same channel as the gimp, from P to Q. As you see from Fig 123 there are two other pairs going *in* to Q but three pairs coming *out*, therefore this extra pair must be released to work outwards to A^2, from where it is carried along with the edge passive pairs until it comes *into* the centre again at the next link row.

Note: it will not be identically the same pair which is carried along then used at the next link row. It has already been indicated that a different pair was used on the *inside*. So it will be on the outside where, after working the picot A^2 the pair will pass through the two outer passives then be left among the passives, whereas at A^3 it will be the fourth passive pair from the edge which works WS to the edge, works a picot, then works through the passives and gimps in order to work the link row (as shown at A^1).

Finish off the gimp at R by overlapping the two ends for three or four stitches then laying them back out of the way and then cutting them off after the next row, at first with ends an inch or so long and then closely when the motif is finished.

A new gimp will need to be hung on at the same place as before when you get to this equivalent place in the next section. As you only need such a small amount of gimp each time, it is easiest to tie the two gimp threads together with a knot after you have cut them off from the previous section then wind the knot on to one of the bobbins a little way so that you have sufficient knot-free thread to complete the next section.

5 Pictorial Lace

INTRODUCTION (Please read before working any patterns)

The laces in this chapter could well be grouped under the heading of 'picture laces' since most are more or less recognisable for what they are, some being more stylised than others and Patterns 6 and 7 being very naturalistic.

As an introduction to the freedom of sectional lace, the student is first introduced to braid lace, often called Russian lace, as it is the type of lace still widely made today in Russia and Eastern Europe. The other patterns are sectional laces, namely Milanese, Valenciennes and Honiton, and they consist of $\frac{1}{2}$st sections and WS sections, with a straight or picoted edge, where an edge pair is usually separated from the main block of passives by three twists of the worker pair.

Sectional lace or 'pieced' lace is above all pictorial and the instructions will enable the reader to work eight different items, including a rose, a Christmas tree, a butterfly and a cockerel.

Unlike trolly lace, in which all the threads stay in the design throughout, in sectional lace, each section is worked independently and bobbins can be added and thrown out as required. Work can therefore proceed in any direction, including round in a circle.

For the remaining five patterns I have drawn inspiration from such different sources as a seventeenth-century flounce from Milan, in my possession, and a nineteenth-century piece from Brabant, Belgium, as well as the more obvious Honiton lace.

Apart from the two historic ones, which were adapted and redesigned, the patterns were all designed by me.

Students need no preliminary expertise beyond that acquired in Chapter 1.

Many different fillings are used to add variety to the appearance and patterns are designed with empty spaces where the worker can choose her own fillings. For this reason many old patterns did not have the pin-holes for these fillings marked, but that calls for a very good eye and excellent technique in order to get a good result. In these patterns I have chosen and designed the fillings in with the patterns and I advise any but the most experienced to prick their fillings before they start working any pattern. A whole range of fillings are described in the standard texts on Honiton lace and computer-drafted prickings can be obtained from lace suppliers. Students should trace off or work out on graph paper their chosen filling (transferring this to tracing paper) then, holding the tracing over the space to be filled, should move it about slowly until the very best position and angle is obtained, trying to get the holes of the grids in line with the pin-holes of the framing lace. If there are two corresponding sections, it is vital that the angle of the grid should be mirrored in the second section: this is very difficult to do accurately by eye if this pre-pricking is not carried out.

The mystique of 'raised and rolled work' is nothing more than, for raised work, working in one direction along an edge in 'ten-stick', then coming back over the top of it, making a normal edge one side and making 'top-sewings' into the cross-threads of the rib on the other side. This is described in detail in Patterns 5 and 6. The rolled work, as in Pattern 8, is a simple form of bringing the threads from one part of a pattern to another to save cutting them off. The only difficulty in the past has been the fact that it does not seem to have been described clearly in books on the subject. Certainly at least one old book condemns the practice as being shoddy workmanship.

Pattern 4 is a good introduction to the sectional laces, such as Brussels, Bruges and Honiton, because all use similar techniques and it is easier to work your first piece on a bigger pattern with thicker thread. One might guess that the reason so much of this early Milanese lace survives today may be because of the sturdy linen threads, compared with Brussels and Honiton.

Basically trolly laces, such as Bucks Point and torchon, keep the same number of threads in the lace throughout its length, threads criss-crossing on the diagonals from one section to another, tending to lead to angular, geometric designs, masked to some extent by curving gimps. Whereas sectional laces are worked one little piece at a time, then all the threads cut off and started again in another section. This way you can get more rounded and naturalistic designs.

There is a much more pronounced 'wrong' side in sectional laces, as there are many knots and ends on top as you work, so the underside is always the right side. To make the patterns easier to copy, the samples of these sectional laces have been worked up backwards, so that their right side, as in the photographs, will correspond with the uppermost (wrong) side while you are working. Your finished pieces, turned over, will be the other way round.

Winding bobbins

Wind one of each pair as full as possible, i.e. until the neck wound with thread is the same diameter as the handle of the bobbin. Then assess how much thread you will need for the passives of the next section and wind that on to the second bobbin of the pair. When you cut pairs off at the end of the section, unwind and throw away the thread from the nearly empty bobbin, then wind enough thread on to the empty bobbin from its full partner to work the next section.

Hanging on pairs to start the lace

You will need a lot of thread on the bobbins of the two edge pairs and the worker pair so make sure these bobbins are the full ones. The passives only need a calculable amount of thread, depending on the pattern, often only an inch or so, though you will have to wind on a little more than that or the thread will keep slipping off the bobbin. If you are working half-stitch the pairs will criss-cross from side to side and thus more thread will be needed. The diagram (Fig. 126) shows how to hang on the bobbins to ensure that the full bobbins are in the right place.

In Fig 126 the bobbins are placed to enable the workers to work to the left first, i.e. there is an edge pair on each side plus the worker pair on the right. Reverse this if the first pinhole to be worked is on the right. You must decide whether it is best to work first to left or right. This will depend partly on which pinhole is higher: normally the higher one would be worked first. It also depends on the rest of that section. If, for example, there are more holes to the right, perhaps because it is the outside of a curve, it would be better to work to the right first, unless by doing so you cause the work to slant, since the line of the worker threads should always be approximately at right angles to the direction of work. If there are more pinholes on one side, which would cause this to happen, you will have to make a back-stitch into one or more pin-holes. This is described in Pattern 4.

The gimp thread (if there is one) is laid under all the central passive pairs and on top of the two edge pairs plus the worker pair. Its bobbins are laid to the back of the work while you twist all the pairs twice and work the first row, starting with the edge pair and worker pair working WS, twist three times, then work the inner pair across all the passives in WS, then twist the workers three times followed by WS with the edge pair, twist both three times and stick a pin in front of both pairs. This pin can be stuck before the stitch if you feel it helps when drawing up the threads but the danger in doing this is that you may occasionally forget to make the stitch, and this will not show until you have finished and taken the pins out. After sticking this pin, bring down the gimp pair from the back of the work: lay them each side of the central block of passive pairs, with just the two edge pairs and the worker pair outside them. Be sure to bring the gimp *inside* the pin you have just stuck or it will make a loop. From now on these gimps pair up with the thinner thread

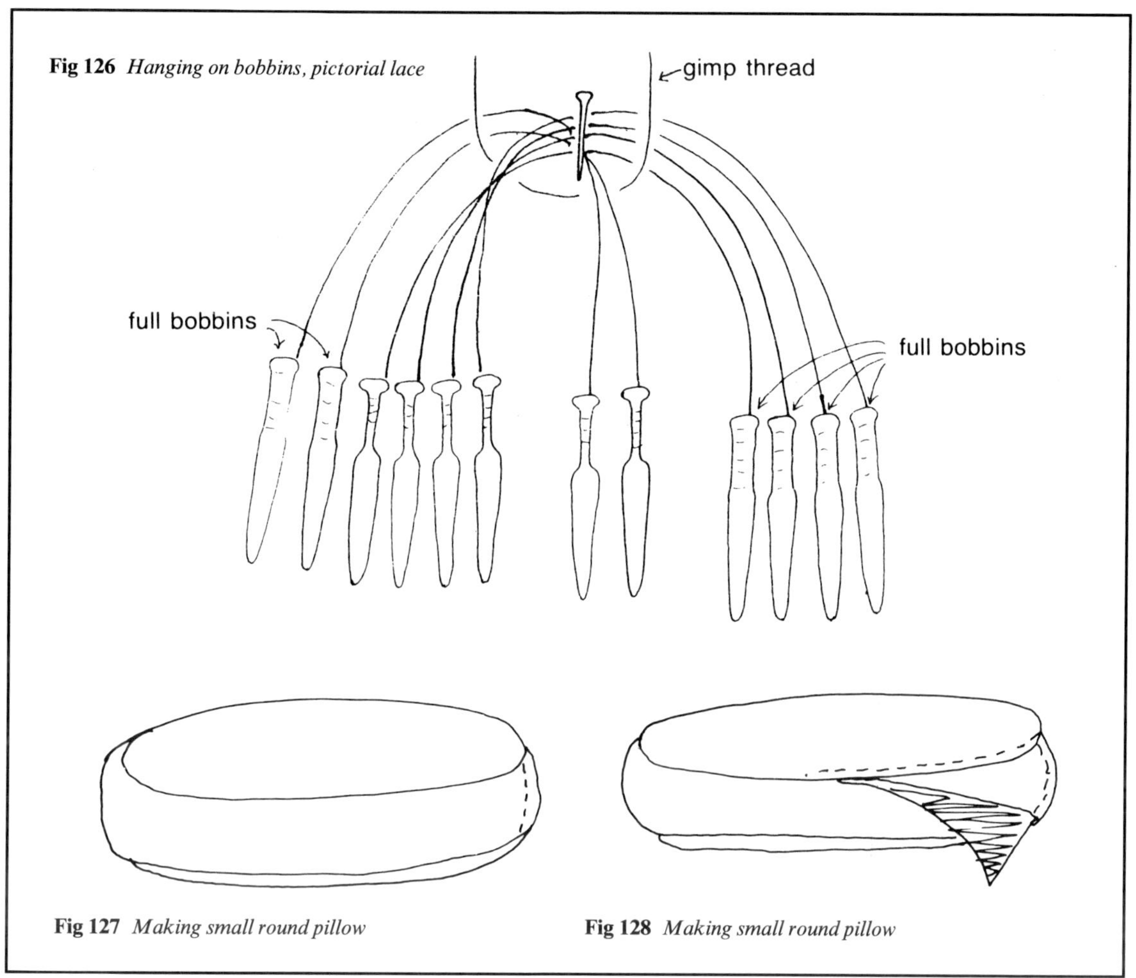

Fig 127 *Making small round pillow*

Fig 128 *Making small round pillow*

next to them and are worked through as ordinary passives.

You will need a fairly small round pillow for the sectional laces that can readily be turned round in every direction as you work your motifs. A mushroom-shaped polystyrene pillow is fine but, if you wish to make your own, see Figs 127 and 128.

Use strong calico and cut out two circles of 13in diameter plus a gusset 3in wide. Machine stitch all seams except those marked with dotted lines in Fig 128. Stuff very hard with hay or chopped straw, bang with a rolling pin or mallet and stuff again. Repeat until it is rock hard. Sew up remaining seams by hand. If you have stuffed it hard enough the edges will not meet so 'lace' them together first like shoe laces by long stitches in very tough thread. On your second attempt with strong oversewing stitches you should be able to get the edges together.

A slider is a useful tool. It is a piece of strong, clear plastic, like washed, used X-ray film, only about 3in × 2in, which you slide into position under the edge of your worker cloth in order to cover up the pin-heads so that your threads do not catch on them.

Other tools you will need to make the sewings are any or all of the following: the finest possible crochet hook, you can buy a .60 hook or you may acquire an old very fine one; a needle-pin, which is the pointed end of a no. 8 needle projecting about 1in from a handle. You can drill a small hole into a piece of $\frac{1}{4}$in dowelling and stick the needle in yourself. The final alternative is a

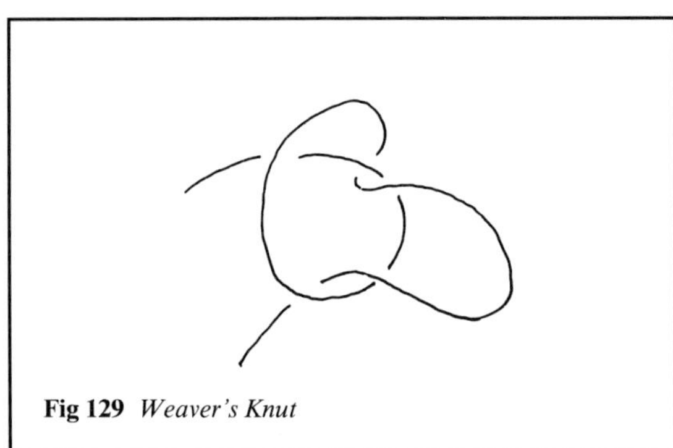

Fig 129 *Weaver's Knut*

beading needle. This can be used as it is or bent or can be inserted with the pointed end stuck into a drilled hole in a handle so that the eye end of the needle projects about $1\frac{1}{2}$in. At about halfway this should be bent to an angle of about 135 degrees whilst holding it over a candle-flame, or you can buy one ready made.

The old Honiton workers used a needle-pin exclusively but, for those of us who have not been brought up to it, a straight point seems a ridiculous tool to draw a loop up through a small pin-hole. A fine crochet hook is ideal, used carefully so that it does not snag any threads, except in very tight situations as, for example, sewing into the point where you have hung on six or eight pairs round the same pin. Here the bent beading needle on a handle comes into its own and is worth buying for this purpose and also for top sewings, which are often not very satisfactory with a crochet hook. To use the beading needle, thread its eye with the looped end of a doubled over fine thread. Take this loop downwards through the required pin-hole then unthread the needle and gently withdraw the needle from the pin-hole. Take the loop of thread which you want inserted through the pin-hole and put this well into the loop which is through the pin-hole. It is then ready for you to pass its partner thread through the loop in the normal way.

A wig-hook is not advised as it is very difficult to withdraw it through the pin-hole without catching the threads and you can get to a situation where you absolutely can't get it out.

The sectional patterns are designed to be worked through in order, so that you gradually build up your knowledge of this work. The first time a technique is encountered it is described. Thus, if you work them in a different order you will have to look back for instructions for the various techniques. The headings are printed boldly to make them easier to find. The patterns have been graduated so that you work up from coarser to finer threads. This will be helpful because otherwise you will have the frustration of frequently breaking threads until you are used to handling the very fine threads.

As you work you will need to push down the pins so that they do not get in the way. You can remove every alternate pin and then push in the others right up to their heads. Do not do this until you are about $\frac{3}{8}$in further on.

If you break a thread up close to your work you will need to make a *weaver's knot*. You must have at least $\frac{1}{4}$in to tie on to so, if there is less, undo the work until you have that amount. With the new thread from the bobbin make a loop round your finger then bring the top thread over that loop and down, then draw it in a loop upwards through that first loop. Draw the first loop fairly tight then make the second loop fairly small, lassoo it over your end of thread then draw the two ends briskly apart (trying not to flick it off the short end of thread), when you should both feel and hear a click as the knot transfers on to the short end of thread (as in tatting). Pull the newly attached bobbin and, if it does not pull away, you have succeeded. If the knot slips you will know that you did not transfer it properly, so you must try again.

GENERAL INSTRUCTIONS FOR PATTERNS 1, 2 AND 3

The braid

There are many variations in working the braid, but one of the best general-purpose braids in the early stages is as follows. Estimate the number of passives suitable for your thread and your pattern by laying threads side by side down the 'tramlines' of the pattern. It is best to trace off a small section of pattern, then pin this scrap of tracing paper directly on to your pillow and work an inch or so. Be sure to include a point so that you can see how the thread will look there as well as on the straight. In these patterns the correct number of bobbins is listed but, if you have a different thread, you will still need to decide for yourself, as also on other patterns you may acquire elsewhere or may design for yourself.

For an average braid use a worker pair, four central passive pairs and two edge pairs, plus one or two gimp pairs (see under 'Gimp Threads'). Starting with the worker pair and an edge pair hung round a pin, work WS, twist, then *take the pair next to the pin across the other four pairs in WS, then twist workers once, make a WS with the last pair, twist both pairs once and stick a pin between them. Make a WS again between the two pairs and twist each pair once*. The inner pair now works across the remaining passives, repeating from * to *. It is best to experiment to find out whether to twist once, twist twice or three times before and after the edge stitch. This will depend on the size of thread and the space available in the pattern.

It would be wise for the inexperienced lace-maker to work a practice length of the above braid to become familiar with it before including gimp threads, as described in the section headed 'Gimp Threads'.

To work a rounded curve in braid lace
Where a pinhole is shown within the body of the trail, as opposed to along the edge, this will be indicated in the first three patterns by the edge passives being outlined in that place, as in Fig 130. Where this occurs, work the workers through the pair that includes the gimp, but not through the edge pair, then stick the finest pin you have between the last two pairs worked (without any twists), then work the workers back through the pairs to the other edge. Often there will be two such holes, so you repeat for the second hole and, at the next true edge hole you take in the edge pair and work through them as usual. After about two more rows remove these fine pins. Because you did not twist the workers, because you used very fine pins and because you removed the pins quickly, the pinhole made should disappear. In the old methods of working this lace, pins were not stuck in this manner to hold the stitches in exactly the right place. Instead, a turning stitch was worked and the lace continued without a pin at this place. The result was inevitably a slight hole, as the workers tended to pull away.

To work a sharp point
Where there are sharp points the edge passive pair is again indicated by a line drawn along the

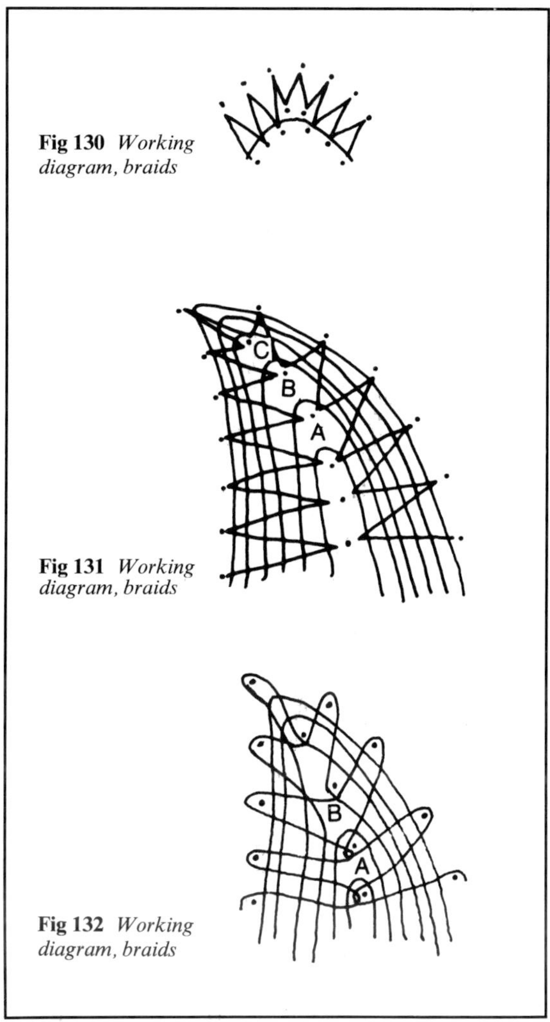

Fig 130 *Working diagram, braids*

Fig 131 *Working diagram, braids*

Fig 132 *Working diagram, braids*

inside edge of the trail each side of the point. There are usually three holes marked outside this line (A, B and C in Fig 131). In Fig 131 all the passives are drawn, not only the inside ones, as on the patterns. This illustration is a simplified diagram of the way pairs are left out at the pinholes. Fig 132 shows the exact path of each pair of threads.

Follow the zig-zag lines indicating the path of the workers, †Work through the passives plus the gimp pair as usual but leave the inside edge pair out, then place a very fine pin in the hole, but between the worker pair and the gimp pair, then work back through all the pairs with the worker pair (see Fig 132)†.

At the next and any subsequent holes, work as follows: *work the workers through the pairs up to but not including the last inner pair worked at the previous hole. Place a very fine pin *in front of both of the pairs* which worked the last stitch, then work back to the other edge with the last pair worked through (which is *not* the original worker pair). Continue through any remaining pinholes, leaving out one more pair each time. There must, however, always be at least one passive pair left (and I prefer two) as well as the edge pair.

After reaching the point, in returning down the other side from the point, work as follows: at the inner pinhole take out the pin and work through the pair you had left there. Do not replace the pin but work back to the other edge with the LH of these pairs (which is the pair that had been waiting at the pin). By doing this, the work is drawn together at the centre and a hole is avoided. Repeat at the other pinholes* except at the last of these extra pinholes where you work through the coarse pair then make a sewing into the pinhole in the lace, do not replace the pin, then work back to the other side with this worker pair. At the next pin-hole you work through the edge pair then make a sewing into the pin-hole of the lace, replace the pin, work back through the edge pair again and continue as usual, still making the usual twists of both worker and edge pair at each stitch.

Note The work at the pinhole where the gimp pair is left out is different from that at the other pinholes simply to avoid the gimp pair being used as workers. If you do not have a gimp pair down the edge in your lace you work all the pinholes as described above from * to *. If the gimp pair is in the centre, when you arrive at the pinhole where this pair should be left out, work through the pair as described above from † to †. If you have two gimp pairs (as described below in 'Gimp Threads') leave both pairs out together at the same pinhole.

Gimp threads (also called coarse threads)
Gimp threads are the thicker threads used to give the pattern definition. It is a good idea to experiment with different threads as a surprisingly thick thread can be very effective. For those who like it, a coloured thread may be used for the gimp: e.g. a brown gimp with the other threads being cream. You do not have to have a gimp at all, though most patterns are improved by it. I consider the two best ways to insert a gimp are as follows.

Either (1) Lay in one gimp thread each side of the central block of passives so that you just have the twisted edge pair outside the gimp thread on each side of the braid. Each thread is then worked as a pair with the thread next to it on the inside; this pair is then known as the gimp pair or the coarse pair even though only one thread of the pair is thick.

Or (2) Have the gimp pair as the central pair of the braid, e.g. with two passive pairs and an edge pair on each side of it. Work the twisted WS with the edge pair, work through the next two (or three or more) passive pairs in WS, then proceed as follows. (a) Working from left to right, lift the LH gimp thread and lay it to the left of the worker pair, now lift up the worker pair and lay it to the right of the RH gimp thread. Twist the gimp pair once, right over left. (b) Working from right to left, lift the worker pair and lay it over the RH gimp thread (i.e. in between the gimp threads). Lay the LH gimp thread over worker pair. Twist the gimp pair once, right over left. After either (a) or (b) work through the remaining passive pairs then work the twisted WS with the edge pair.

There are two other variations you might like to try.

(3) One was used a great deal in Victorian times and was called a 'streak'. This was a separate gimp thread being laid in each side in the same position as in (1) above. This time, however, the gimp threads are not worked as pairs with the neighbouring threads. Instead they are separated from the main body of passives by one twist of the workers and from the edge pair also by another twist. This echoes the Bucks Point gimps, which are separated from the blocks of patterns they are outlining by twists of the workers each side of the gimp thread as they pass through.

(4) Chain stitch, this is a variation on (2), using two gimp pairs side by side in the middle instead of one. Work twisted WS with the edge pair then WS with the two (or three or more) passive pairs, then proceed as follows. (a) Working from left to right, lift the worker pair and lay it over the LH gimp thread, lift the RH gimp thread and lay it

over the worker pair. Cross the gimp threads once, left over right. Work through the second gimp pair as at (2a) above.

(b) Working from right to left, work through first gimp pair as at (2b) above. Work through second gimp pair thus, lift **RH** gimp thread and lay it over worker pair. Lift worker pair and lay it to the left of **LH** gimp thread. Cross gimp pair once, left over right.

After either (a) or (b) work through the remaining passive pairs then work twisted **WS** with the edge pair.

Leg and picot

When you need to work a leg (often with one or more picots) to connect two sections, work as follows. As you arrive at the pinhole where the link is to be made work the **WS**, twist, with the edge pair and stick the pin between them in the normal way. Now using these same two pairs, continue working $\frac{1}{2}$sts until you reach the picot(s), drawing the threads up after every three stitches.

Picots (see Fig 133)

Twist the outside pair nearest the picot hole once. Pick up the bobbins in your left hand with your index finger between them and turn them over (right over left) so that the tips of your fingers point upwards. Place a pin under the RH thread and hold it up then hold that right hand still while you twist your left hand back again so that the palm is downwards, twisting the threads *under* the raised pin. Bring the pin and its loop of thread towards you and down between the bobbins, then put the point of the pin up under the LH thread to come out between the two threads, bringing a loop of thread with it. Take this loop out to left or right, wherever the pinhole is, and stick the pin in the pinhole.

Where there are two picots, one each side of the leg, work one picot as above then a $\frac{1}{2}$st between the two pairs, then a second picot the other side.

After the picots, continue working the $\frac{1}{2}$st leg. If you are working the petals of a flower you will be working to the centre hole and back. Work at this hole by sticking a pin into this central hole

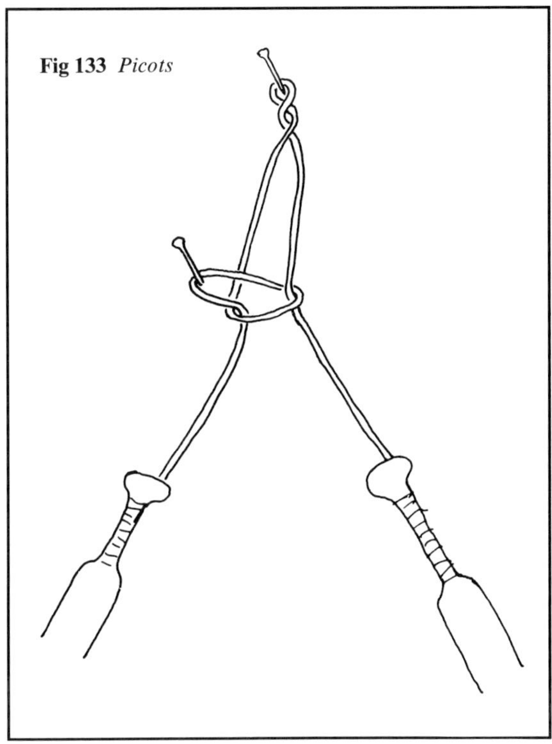

Fig 133 *Picots*

between the two pairs, give an extra twist to the pair that goes round the pin, then make a leg and, if necessary, a picot back to where you started, at which point you need to make a 'sewing' into the last edge stitch. There are further instructions on sewing, with a diagram, in Pattern 5. Follow this with a $\frac{1}{2}$st, with the edge pair then work across the passives and any gimp threads as usual.

Flowers

Each petal is worked as in the instructions above, except the last petal, where you work up to the centre then, instead of just going round the pin, as before, this time draw two of the threads of the leg through the three or four loops of previous petals and thread the remaining two threads through the loop as a sewing. If this is too difficult to achieve, then the sewing can be made with just one pair and the following series of $\frac{1}{2}$sts will be sufficient to hold all the threads in place.

PATTERN 1   RUSSIAN LACE: EDGING OR INSERTION

Materials

7 pairs of bobbins wound with
Swedish linen no. 120
and 4 gimp bobbins wound in pairs
with Swedish linen no. 40
or DMC Cordonnet no. 50
or Coton Perle no. 12

This fascinating pattern could be used to trim clothes, as an edging to a handkerchief or cloth, or as an insertion.

Make three extra pinholes across the middle of the first row, as in Fig 134 and hang on two pairs, one splayed outside the other, on the LH pin (the edge pair and the workers). Two passive pairs

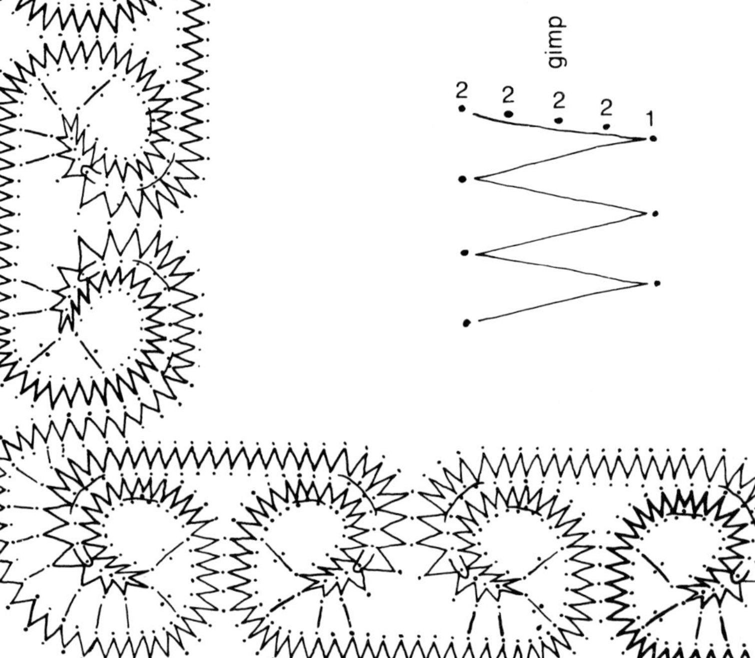

Fig 134 *Working diagram, Russian lace*

Fig 135 *Pattern*

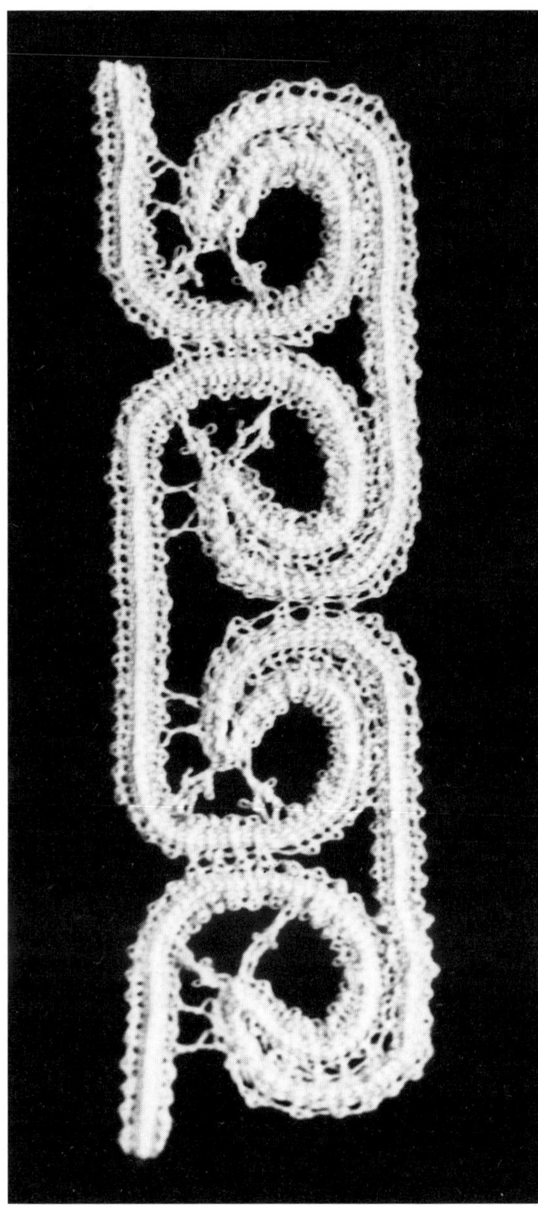

'General instructions for Patterns 1, 2 and 3', with the fourth variation of gimp threads, i.e. chain stitch.

The linking bars are always made when your work reaches the second end of the bar, so that there is a completed piece of lace to make a sewing into, then the threads return to their starting point. The legs with picots are worked as described in the 'General instructions'.

The two *bars without picots* linking the point with a flat section of braid are made like the kiss described in the Bedfordshire instructions thus. The worker pair is twisted about five times (depending on size of thread) after the pin has been stuck; it is then sewn into the pinhole indicated by the line on the pattern and released again. It then twists twice, then you do a sewing by drawing a loop from one of the threads of this pair behind the bar you have just made, threading the other bobbin of this pair through the loop and drawing it up. You then twist the pair twice more and return it to the section from where it started.

The dotted line on the pattern indicates a floating section which can be used each end of the pattern for the purpose of moving it up on the pillow without removing the pins, as described in Chapter 1.

PATTERN 2 COCK IN RUSSIAN LACE

Materials

7 pairs of bobbins wound with
DMC Cordonnet no. 50 or
equivalent
and 2 gimp threads wound as a pair
with Coton Perle no. 8 or
equivalent
26 pairs wound with the finer
thread were used for the filling

side by side on the next pin, two gimp pairs side by side on the central pin, two passive pairs side by side on the next pin and one edge pair on the final pin. After working a few rows, take out the extra three pins in the centre and gently draw up the threads so that no visible loops remain. The loops will, however, be there for you to make sewings into on completion of the work.

The braid is worked as described in the

I worked the original cock in coloured pure silk threads. The edge was in terracotta with a thicker dark brown gimp, Variation 2, the body-filling in yellow and it was mounted on a cream linen background before framing.

I started under the tail and worked first towards the legs, up the body, over the head and back, finishing with the many-feathered tail, working the link sections between the tail

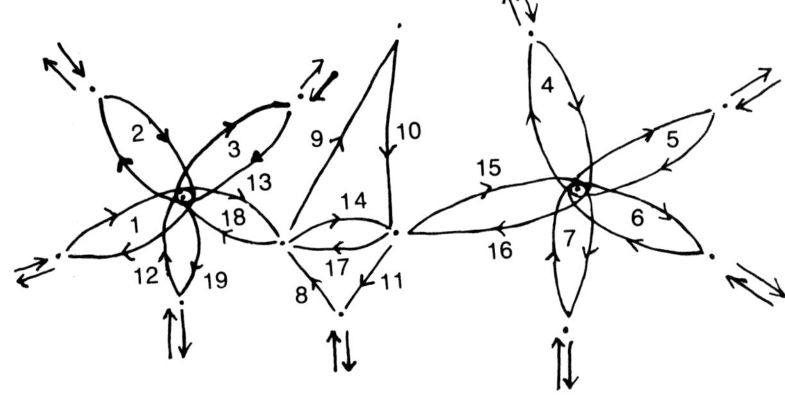

Fig 137 *Working diagram, Russian lace*

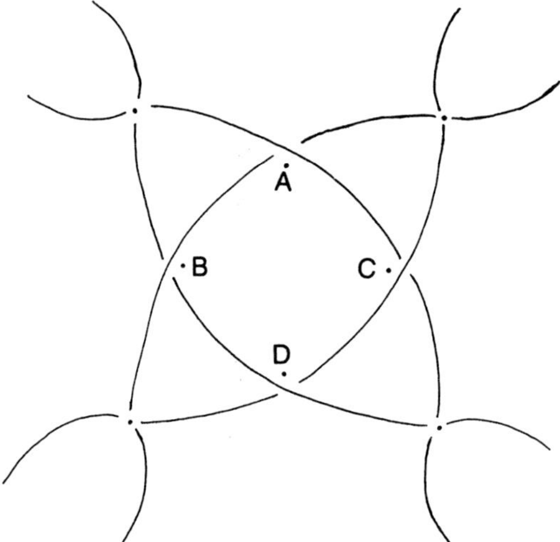

Fig 138 *Working diagram*

feathers as I came to them, in the main terracotta colour. Fig 137 shows how this can be done, working in turn through the numbers from 1 to 19. The method is described in 'General instructions' under 'Leg and picot'. The triangular link is worked a little later when you reach the third point of the triangle.

You may finish off the cock in the normal manner by sewing the finishing threads into the starting loops. However, as the finished lace is to be mounted, you may get a neater effect on the right side if you work a short extra length of braid, about four rows, then tie the thread ends close up to it, knotting them in pairs. This lies neatly behind the first braid and should not show from the front.

Before starting the body-filling it is well worth taking time working out if there are places where the pairs finished with from one diagonal can, instead of being finished off, be left in to work another section, often at a right angle to its previous direction. Remember always that it is the finished effect that matters and you can make up your own rules of the game. In other words, if it is neater to carry the threads over the back of the work to use in a nearby section instead of cutting off (with the risk of the ends showing) and starting again, then do it. What works best for you is the right way. Don't be misled by old-fashioned rules of what is right and wrong.

This filling consists of a trellis of $\frac{1}{2}$st legs alternating with more complicated squares of double criss-crossed legs. It is mainly straight-forward: a series of $\frac{1}{2}$sts with the same two pairs form the legs: draw up the threads after every three stitches to keep the tension even. At the places where one leg crosses another, work a windmill stitch: i.e. using each pair as a single bobbin, work the first two parts of a WS, stick the pin with two pairs on each side of it, then finish the WS by crossing the LH middle pair over the RH middle pair of the four. You then continue working $\frac{1}{2}$sts with the two LH pairs and then with the two RH pairs to form more legs.

At the double cross-over, where two pairs meet two more pairs, work thus (see Fig 138). At hole A lay three of the threads from the LH leg over three of the threads from the RH leg then cross the remaining LH thread over the remaining RH thread. Stick pin A with two pairs to the right; and two pairs to the left.

At holes B and C, lay three of the threads from

the RH leg over three threads from the LH leg
then lay the remaining RH thread over the
remaining LH thread. Stick pin B to the right of
both of its pairs and pin C to the left of both of its
pairs.

At hole D stick the pin before repeating the
instructions for hole A below the pin.

You will see that all the stitches are *outside*
these four pins.

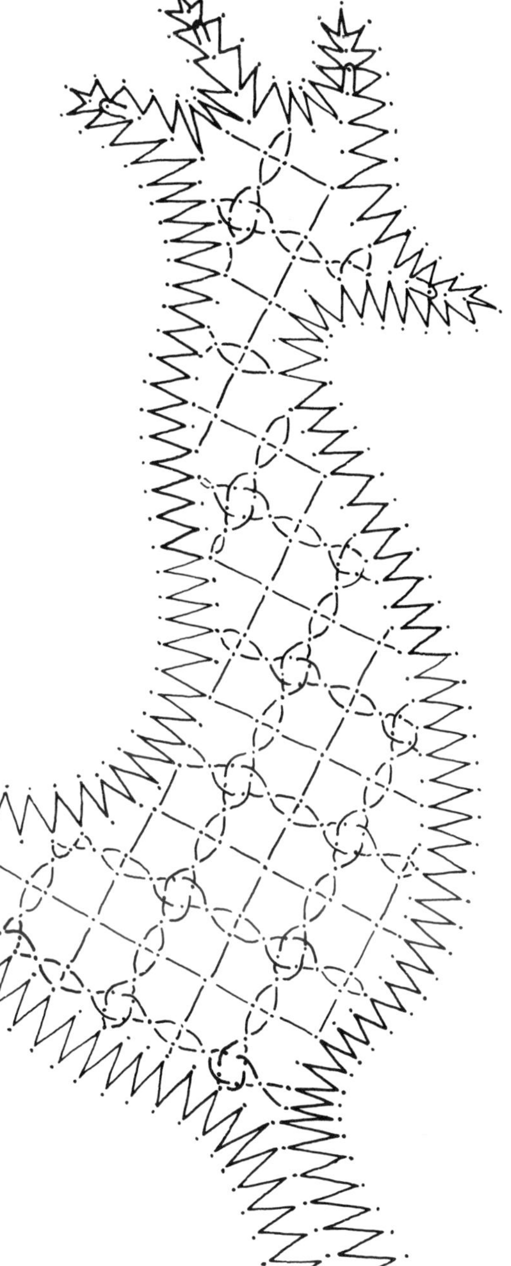

Fig 139 *Pattern*

PATTERN 3   RUSSIAN LACE CHRISTMAS TREE HANDKERCHIEF CORNER OR CORNER INSERTION

Materials

6 pairs bobbins wound with
Unity Glace cotton no. 150
or Retors d'Alsace no. 50
or Swedish linen no. 120
and 2 gimp bobbins wound with
DMC Cordonnet no. 50 or
equivalent

Note In the sample the gimps were worked as described under 'Gimp threads' in the 'General instructions' for this chapter. In this pattern it would have been effective to substitute an ordinary thread (the same as the passives) for the outer gimp thread round the edge, which would become the inner thread round the tree.

Start at A and work in the direction indicated by the arrow: hang on two pairs at A and one pair at B and three more pairs on the two holes further back which form the centre of the trunk and are in the correct vertical alignment for the

central passive pairs. These latter three pairs will have the pins removed and the loops drawn up after about six rows. Hang the two gimp threads round a pin further back again to allow enough free end of thread to sew in afterwards with a needle along the line of gimp in the section of lace worked last. Do this after the final 'sewings' have been worked and the completed lace has been removed from the pillow. Since the gimps could easily pull through, do not remove these pins until you have worked round the corner. Bring down the gimp threads with the RH thread being the fifth from the right and the LH thread the third from the left.

At C, F and G make legs and picots to the central hole of the flower and back, making an extra twist with the outside pair as you go round the pin (see note on 'Flowers').

At D and E work a leg up and back, sewing each time to the point of the scroll, with a picot to

Fig 143 *Working diagram, Christmas tree*

the side of each leg, as indicated by the pinhole. Continue right round the edge without making any other connections with the lace inside except at H, I and J, which you work like C, F and G. When you reach the equivalent place to D and E on the other side of the base of the triangle, remember to work the legs to the point of the scroll.

Continue the trail round the tree, working leg and picot connections at K and L. From M work three legs in a triangle, with picots both sides, returning to M, where you sew in before continuing with the trail. At N (the point) work a leg and picot to the centre of the flower, sewing into the three loops at the central pinhole, then returning to N and continuing (see note on 'Flowers'). At O work a similar triangle to M, except that the second side will only have a picot on the inside.

At P, Q, R and S work legs to the edge and back, each leg having one picot on the outside.

Work the second half of the tree to correspond, connecting down the middle as follows: at T and U the connection is simply the worker pair, once the pin has been stuck, twisting twice instead of once, sewing into the opposite pinhole, twisting twice and working WS, twist, again with the edge pair, then continuing as usual. V and W are worked similarly. Y is also worked similarly, whereas at X and Z, the distance being greater, legs are worked (with one picot) to the other side and back.

Finish at A and B, making sewings with each pair into the corresponding pin-hole, then darning in the threads a little way before cutting them off. Most people do this after removing the lace from the pillow but the most perfect finishing I have ever seen was achieved by doing the darning-in while the lace was still on the pillow. Cut off the gimp threads with a 3in end and, after removing the lace from the pillow, darn these through a few stitches in one direction and the starting gimp ends in the opposite direction before cutting them off.

PATTERN 4   MILANESE LACE

Materials

15 pairs bobbins wound with
Swedish linen no. 120
or Unity Glace cotton no. 150
or Retors d'Alsace no. 50

This pattern was adapted from a seventeenth-century Milanese flounce, which consisted of countless different motifs, joined together in a flowing design with brides (i.e. bars or legs). There were no gimps in this type of lace. (The numbers of pairs given in this pattern are correct when using linen no. 120.)

Section A (10 pairs)

Hang two pairs, one splayed outside the other, on each of the top five pin-holes (noting the direction arrow in the diagram [Fig 145]). Twist each pair twice.

Basic braid

Using the RH pair work WS, twist twice, *then use the inner pair to work across the next seven pairs to the left in WS. Then twist the workers twice, work WS with the extreme LH pair, twist both pairs twice and set the LH pin with both these pairs behind it to the left. Use the inner pair to work to the right through seven pairs then twist the workers twice, work WS with the RH pair, twist both pairs twice, then set the pin at the RH edge with both these pairs behind it to the right*.

Continue repeating from * to *. As the piece narrows, throw back a passive pair near each of the two edges but not including either the RH three threads or the LH three threads. The threads you throw back need not be an actual pair. Look ahead when throwing back pairs and aim to have only four or five pairs by the final pin-hole. To throw back threads, merely lay the bobbins over to the back of the work and cut them off later.

Bunching

After sticking the last pin, work through all the pairs and tie the worker pair in a reef knot, close up to the last pair it passed through. (With finer threads, as in Honiton lace, you would tie off pairs three times, but with this coarser thread two parts of a knot are bulky enough.) Similarly tie the edge pair on the other side. Lay these two tied pairs out to the left and the right. Tie the

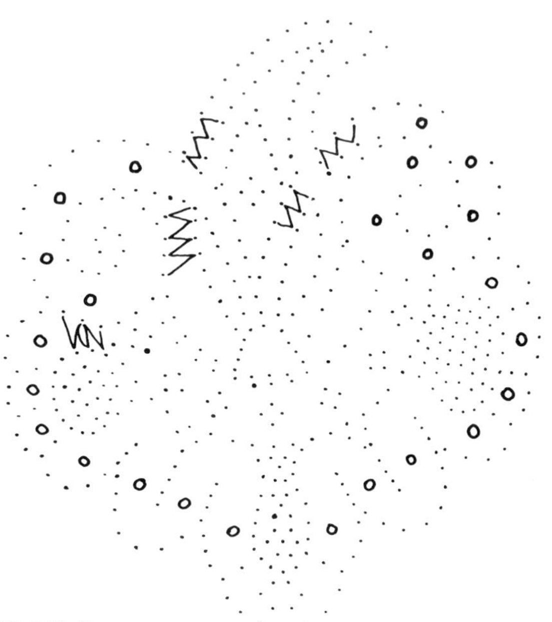

Fig 144 *Pattern*

Fig 145 *Working diagram, Milanese lace*

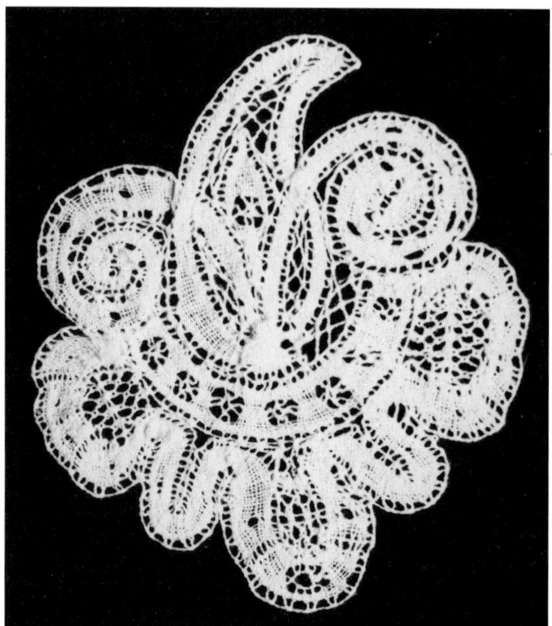

Fig 146 *Finished Milanese lace*

remaining pairs in reef knots then lift them up as a bundle, as in Fig 147. Lay the LH pair under the bundle to the right and the RH pair under the bundle to the left and lay the bundle down on top of them. Now take the back two threads of the tying pairs, A and B in Fig 148, and bring them round over the bundle and tie on top with a reef knot. Repeat with threads C and D. Press down alternate pins, taking out the ones in between. Do this whenever you finish a section or when the pins get in the way.

To tie cut-off threads back out of sight
Go to the first pair of threads left out near a pin-hole on the left or right. Open this pair out, as in Fig 149. Now lay the tied bundle back over the completed lace and between these threads. Tie these threads round the bundle firmly in a reef knot, being careful not to pull the tying threads so tightly that they distort the lace. Remember that you are working from the wrong side and your aim is to make all ends and knots invisible from the other side. By this method, you will have hidden the tassel of threads which otherwise might have shown in the gap between two sections. Now cut off all ends close to the knots. Re-wind the bobbins ready for the next section.

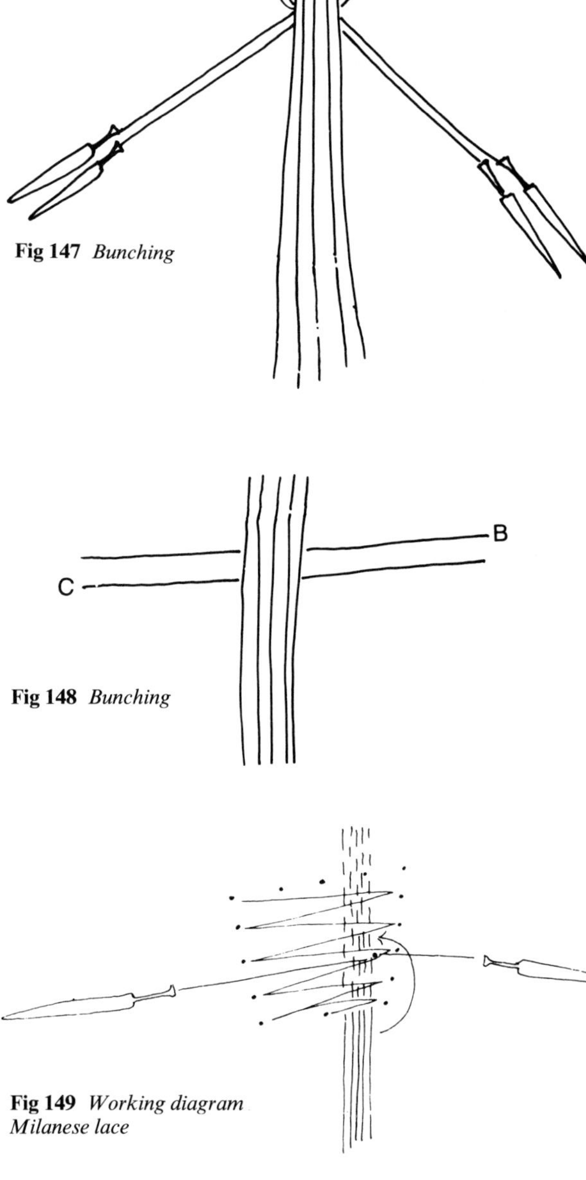

Fig 147 *Bunching*

Fig 148 *Bunching*

Fig 149 *Working diagram Milanese lace*

Fig 150 *Scroll B, working diagram*

Scroll B (10 pairs)

See Fig 150 and work alphabetically, starting at the fourth hole from the point of the scroll, hanging on eight pairs and working first towards the point. Tie the workers once after passing through the first passive pair inside the edge pair after each of the edge holes round the curve (C, E, G, etc.). Always do this on the outside of a curve to prevent the passives pulling over to the inside, thus making a gap at the edge or enlarging the edge holes. Hang on extra pairs at holes C and E, thus: **to add a new pair** always do this on the outside of a curve. At the pin-hole, twist the workers twice (three times in patterns using a finer thread) and set pin but without working the stitch with the edge pair. Slide the thread linking a pair of bobbins up the threads of the worker pair until the loop is behind the pin and lay the pair of bobbins inside the edge thread of the group of passives, so that the new pair is split, each thread making a pair with a different bobbin. Now work the edge stitch and twists and work the workers back through the passives, as usual. Whilst it is better to add and subtract pairs gradually, it is occasionally necessary to add two pairs together. In that case, slide both pairs along the threads of the worker pair, but only lay one down in place, as described above. Lay the second pair upwards over the back of the work and bring them down after one row has been worked by the worker pair.

A backstitch

This involves two (or more) visits to the same pin-hole: the first time twist the workers once instead of the normal twice or three times, with the edge pair still un-worked outside it. Stick a pin and work this same pair back through all the passives, making the usual edge stitch on the other side. On the second visit, twist the workers twice (or three times) and make an edge stitch as usual, take out the previous pin and put it back into the same hole with both pairs behind it: in other words, a normal edge. Draw up gently the edge pair on the other side to close up the previous pinhole.

At hole F, the point of the scroll, back stitch on the first visit. On the second visit omit the edge pair again and work a turning stitch with the previous pair, i.e. work a $\frac{1}{2}$st followed by a WS then use the RH pair as workers to go back to the opposite side. On the third visit work a normal edge, replacing the pin in hole F.

After hole F you will be making a sewing at each inner hole instead of an edge stitch. Undo the two twists of the inner edge pair after the pin-hole at F and let this pair hang down as an ordinary passive. When the workers arrive at this side, work them through this pair, twist twice the workers only, make a sewing into the edge hole, tie the workers once, replace the pin in the hole, twist the workers twice and continue across to the other edge.

To make a sewing

Take the pin out of the hole into which you are going to sew. Slide a crochet hook downwards through this pin-hole and draw one of the threads of the pair to be sewn up through the pin-hole in a loop. Take out the crochet hook and thread the other bobbin of the pair through this loop then draw them both up gently.

Because of the shape of the scroll, you will need to make two sewings into most inner holes to keep the work level.

Small holes in the trail

There are two methods of working these and you may like to try both then stick to your favourite.

1. Work the worker pair to one pair beyond the centre, working the turning stitch of $\frac{1}{2}$st, WS with this pair. Lay down the workers and take the last pair they worked through as the new workers back to the edge, work the edge stitch or sewing and leave them there. Go back to the next passive pair beyond the laid-down workers. Twist once this pair and its neighbouring passive pair and use it as the other worker pair to work to its nearer edge and back, leaving it in the same position as it started from. Go back to the other edge, pick up the worker pair where you left it and use it as the worker pair right across all pairs as usual.

2. Divide the passives into two halves and put a pin in the pillow at the half-way point. When the workers reach the pin twist them once and also the pair they have just passed through. Work another WS then twist these passives (but not workers) once. Work the workers to the edge and back. When they reach the pin twist them once to complete the four sides of a square of twists and continue working normally.

Of these two methods, the first works better in a very close cloth stitch and was used in the original Milanese, which is worked very closely, but it looks messy in places where the cloth stitch is thinner. The latter type can disappear altogether in a very close braid but looks tidier in a thinner cloth stitch section.

When the braid becomes separate from the scroll, with two edges, twist the edge passive pair twice and let it from now on be the edge pair as before.

To link sections where two rows of holes run closely together (as here and also between F and C on the left).

At the three inner holes before the cross-over with C, link the sections thus. As you arrive at the edge, twist the workers twice, work the WS with the edge pair then, before sticking the pin, sew the workers into the adjacent edge hole. (This is easier to do before you stick the other pin). Then work another WS with the edge pair and twist both pairs twice then stick the pin in the usual manner inside both pairs. Continue with the inner pair as workers.

Lay back one pair on the outside of the curve at each of the crossing holes with section C. Sew out into A at the finish.

Braid C (10 pairs)

Sew in eight pairs to A to start braid C and also add one pair at each of the next two holes on the outside of the curve. Drop two pairs off gradually on the outside of the curve as the braid narrows.

Crossing of braids

On arrival at the crossing of braid B, first sew in the edge pair on the right and tie twice, then the workers work another row to the left and are sewn into the next hole, as also is the LH edge pair. Tie each of these twice then, using the edge pair on each side, lay them apart and tie the bundle, as in Figs 147 and 148 above. Then sew each of these pairs into the corresponding holes on the other side of braid B, as well as the worker pair, on the RH side in order that the first row should go to the left.

Turn the sharp curve as suggested in the Introduction. Finally, sew out into A.

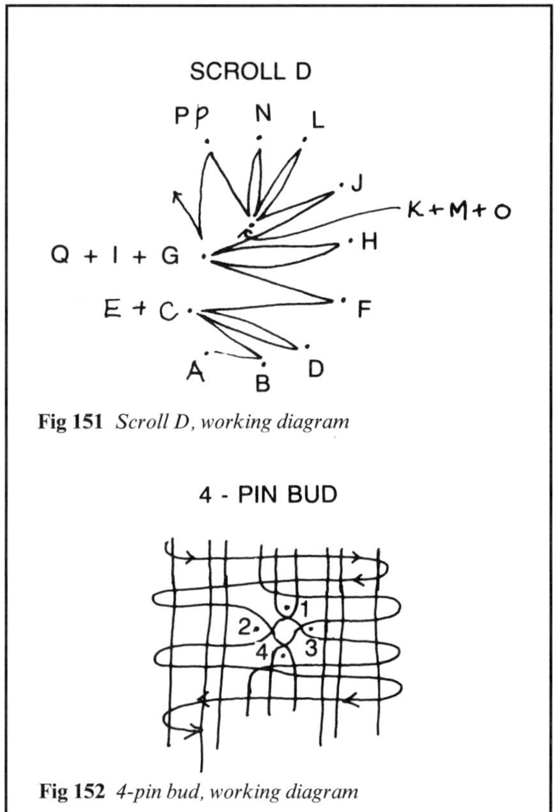

Fig 151 *Scroll D, working diagram*

Fig 152 *4-pin bud, working diagram*

Scroll D (8 pairs)

Start at A (Fig 151), hanging on eight pairs, and follow the holes alphabetically, making a back-stitch on all the inner holes, as indicated. Tie the workers once after passing through the first passive pair inside the edge pair after each of the edge holes round the curve (B, D, F, etc.), as you did in scroll B. Work this scroll much as scroll B, except you can keep the same number of pairs throughout. Work the braid crossing as in the previous instructions, except that the lefts and rights will not necessarily correspond, but the direction of working has been marked on the pattern to assist you.

Section E (10 pairs)

Start at the point with six pairs. Add two extra pairs on each side gradually. The four central holes indicate a four-pin bud (Fig 152). (Virtually any shaped section in pillow lace is known as a bud.)

Four-pin bud and six-pin bud
When working with finer thread substitute three twists for the two twists given in these instructions. Using the ten pairs, work through five more pairs after the edge pair. This worker pair plus the three last pairs it has worked through form the centre four pairs which make the bud. The last pair the workers passed through is the other worker pair. Work it now through the other two pairs of the central four pairs. Now the two pairs it has just passed through must be twisted twice and pin 1 stuck between them, then it is enclosed with a WS and two twists. *Now the two workers (immediately outside these two centre pairs) must be worked, each to the nearer edge, and back to the same position. Twist each pair twice and make a WS and twist both pairs twice with the nearer of the two centre pairs then stick pin 2 to the left of the two LH pairs and pin 3 to the right of the two RH pairs (so that all four pairs are between the pins)*.

If you are working a six-pin bud, repeat from * to * for pins 4 and 5.

To complete the bud take each worker pair out to its edge and back to the same position. With the two centre pairs work WS, twist both pairs twice, put the final pin between them. Work one of the two worker pairs through the other three centre pairs then work the other back through the other two centre pairs, followed by the remaining passives on that side and the edge pair then continue the braid as before.

Sew out the edge pairs as the edge joins sections B and D. Start sewing the workers into the pin-holes each side from now on as the section narrows and throw back pairs at each side until only six pairs remain. To finish, sew out, bunch and tie as usual.

Filling (for section between E and the pointed part of C)
Turn the pillow until the point of E is towards you, see Fig 153. Hang on two pairs at the top of this section, one at A and one at B. Twist each three times and work WS, twist three times. Sew in RH pair to pin-hole on right and LH pair to pin-hole on left and continue with three twists then WS, then three twists. Continue down RH narrow section, sewing into alternate holes. Wait where this section opens out and becomes wider.

Hang on another two pairs at the top of the

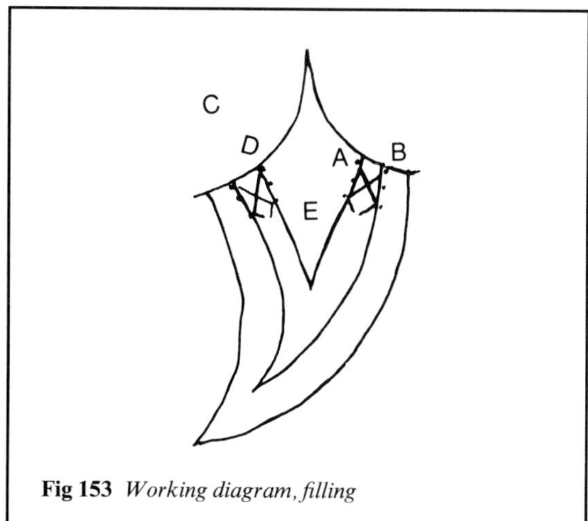

Fig 153 *Working diagram, filling*

LH section at C and D and work the LH section, similarly sewing into alternate holes again.

When the two sets of two pairs of bobbins meet near the point of E, the LH pair is sewn out and one row of stitches made across the space, using the three pairs of bobbins, twisting three times between the WS and sewing into appropriate holes. Continue the diamond mesh down the space and sew out the pairs when the space is filled.

Work the fillings for the two long, narrow spaces between B and C, and C and D the same as each other; place the pillow with the motif right way up and hang a pair on each of the top two pin-holes. *Twist the pairs three times, work a WS and twist three times again. Sew the pairs into the next pin-hole but one to those where the pairs were sewn in. Tie one knot in each pair after the sewings to make them secure*. Repeat from * to * twice more, but the second time you will have to sew into the next hole instead of the next but one.

Section F (12 pairs)
Start on the left by hanging in ten pairs to the four pin-holes of scroll B. Add a pair each side at the next two pin-holes. For the first half of this section you will be linking sections where two rows of holes run closely together, on the RH side, as described under scroll B. For the four-pin buds follow the directions under section E but, as you have two extra pairs, work through six more pairs after the edge pair. Finally, sew out into

scroll D then, after knotting all the pairs, tie them into *two* bunches so that there is no obvious gathering-in from the right side.

Before going on to section G, make the filling between C and F on the RH side in the same way as the previous fillings; turn the pillow and start at the junction of F and A. Use three pairs altogether. Mostly two twists will be enough, but twist 3 times where the section is at its widest.

Section G (10 pairs)

You start at the left and work the convoluted braid, leaving the three spaces to be filled in afterwards. Hang six pairs on the three holes of F and at first link the LH edge with scroll B. The direction of working is indicated on Fig 145. On the second visit to the middle of the holes of scroll B add two pairs. At the third hole of scroll B add an edge pair and add the tenth pair at the next outside hole. Work holes wherever they are indicated. Where the lines are marked work windows.

Windows

Work WS, twist, across the row (you would need three twists if you were using a finer thread). Work the edge as usual. On the next row do not twist the passives but twist the worker pair once after every stitch (three times in finer thread) to complete the little grid of twists.

Sewing the braid to itself (where it doubles back)
There are two methods and in this situation I prefer the latter.
1. When you arrive at the joint holes which are common to both braids, untwist the twists in the edge pair and work it as an ordinary passive. When the worker pair has passed through, it is sewn into the pin-hole without any twists.
2. When you arrive at the joint holes which are common to both braids, twist the worker pair as usual before working with the edge pair, work a WS with the edge pair but no twists, then sew into the pin-hole, work another WS with the edge pair, twist both pairs the usual number of times (two in this pattern) and continue across the passives.

To work the rounded curves

As you go round the tight curves, particularly those on the inside linked to F, the expedient of

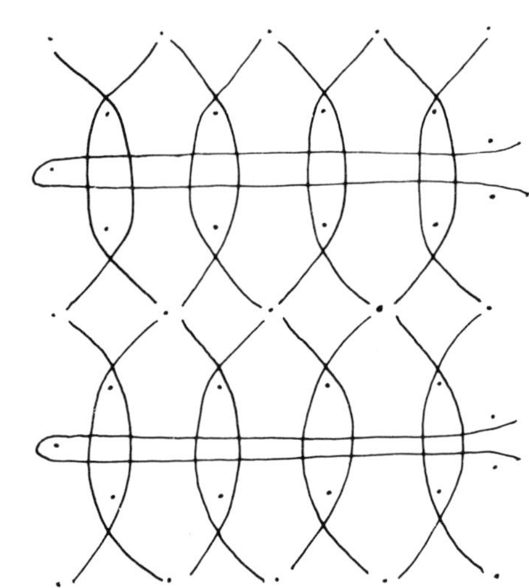

Fig 154 *Working diagram, filling*

Fig 155 *Milanese filling, pattern*

alternating back stitches with turning stitches, as described at hole F in scroll B, will not be sufficient. You will have to make several turning stitches in succession, i.e. work a half stitch followed by a WS then use the inner pair as workers to go back to the other side. If you find a hole appearing as the work gets pulled away, you can insert a fine pin for these two pairs to go round, but do remove it as soon as possible.

On the centre scallop there is a typical Milanese six-pin bud, for which directions are given under section E.

Sew out the edge pair as you meet scroll D and sew the workers to the scroll D holes from now on, throwing back pairs at each hole. Finally, sew out into F, tie off and bunch as usual.

Your final job is to fill the spaces in the section G braid. I have chosen a typical Milanese filling.

Milanese filling (maximum 14 pairs in this pattern) See fig 154 and 155.

I suggest you try this as a block first on a spare pillow or at the side of this pillow. When you are familiar with it you can easily fit it into the spaces available. Just pin the threads down at the edge of the block where they would normally be sewn into an existing framework.

Hang eight pairs on four pin-holes. Twist all pairs three times. *Work $\frac{1}{2}$st, pin, $\frac{1}{2}$st, twist twice with first two pairs on left. Lay aside*. Repeat from * to * with next two pairs (three times). †Work $\frac{1}{2}$st, pin, $\frac{1}{2}$st, twist twice with second and third pairs from left. Lay aside†. Repeat from † to † with fourth and fifth pairs then with sixth and seventh. ‡Work $\frac{1}{2}$st, pin, then cross two over three to complete a WS, but missing the twists of a second $\frac{1}{2}$st. Lay aside‡. Repeat from ‡ to ‡ with next two pairs (three times).

Hang on a pair on the right slightly below the last line of stitches. Twist three times. §Work WS through two pairs then twist this worker pair three times§. Repeat from § to § three more times. Sew into LH edge and bring the pair back in a similar manner then sew it out and tie it off at the RH side. This is one complete repeat of the pattern starting at *. You may like to experiment with working this pattern without pins or with pins only in the net row and not where the pair passes through and back in WS. Because of 300 years of washing and wearing, it is difficult to see if the original workers used pins or not, but I suspect not.

PATTERN 5   HONITON FLOWER

Materials

14 pairs of bobbins wound with
cotton no. 120
and 2 gimp bobbins wound as a pair
with no. 50 sewing cotton

In Honiton lace there are normally gimp threads running down inside the edge at each side of the passives. Each is paired up with the neighbouring thinner thread and the pair is treated as a normal pair except in $\frac{1}{2}$st sections, as described later.

Start by hanging on five pairs at the end of the stem (A) and work in *rib* towards the flower. There is no gimp thread in rib (which is also known as *stem stitch* or *ten stick*, because you usually use ten bobbins). The line of holes in rib, is always on the *outside* of the curve. To make the rib, after twisting the pairs twice (see 'Hanging on' in the introduction to this chapter) make a WS between the two RH pairs then twist them both three times. *Work the inner pair through the other three pairs to the plain side. Now work a backwards $\frac{1}{2}$st between the last two pairs worked, i.e. twist both pairs right over left then cross the two centre bobbins left over right. Next take the inner of the two pairs back across the passives but not including the edge pair. Now twist this worker pair three times, work WS with the edge pair and twist both pairs three times then stick a pin inside both pairs*. Continue the rib by repeating the instructions from * to *.

At the start of the petal B twist the LH pair three times to become the LH edge pair and *hang on a gimp pair* by weaving the thread which is between the two bobbins over and under the central passive pairs and laying the bobbins to the back of the pillow. Hang on a new pair at the next pin-holes on both sides and continue to do this until you have enough. After the next row, bring down the gimps into their correct position at the outside of the central block of passives, with only the two edge pairs and the worker pair outside them. Continue increasing as the petal widens then, as it narrows, lay the pairs back, not more than one pair on each row. At first, just lay the bobbins to the back of the pillow. Cut off the ends later. One normally lays back the two threads inside the gimp thread but other threads, not necessarily a pair, may be chosen if, for example, they are running out of thread.

Towards the top of B, where section E starts, there are three pin-holes indicated in the diagram. As you arrive at each hole hang on two pairs at each and lay all six pairs aside in order, to be used later when you start E.

At the junction between the tip of the petal and the rounded strip C it is a good idea to cross the gimp threads over each other, which will help to draw the threads in and make a point to the petal. (This was not done on the sample.) Work the strip C then again cross the gimps and work down petal D, increasing the number of pairs as required then decreasing again as the petal narrows. Sew out, bunch and cut off the threads.

Start E with the six pairs already hung on. As there are more pin-holes on the outside of the curve, work first in that direction, so that the two inner pairs will be edge pair and worker and the outer pair will be an edge pair. Take the gimp pair (newly wound with no joins) and weave it over and under the three central passive pairs then lay it back. Start by working WS, twist three times, with the two RH pairs then work WS through the three central pairs, twist the workers three times, stick the pin, add a new pair, work WS, twist (both pairs) three times with the edge pair, then bring down the gimps into position, inside the pin just stuck, with two pairs to the left of one thread and one pair to the right of the other thread. Continue this section of braid in WS but, on reaching the outside edge in future, *picots* will be made thus. Twist three times and work WS with the edge pair then twist the worker pair seven times, place a pin under the outside thread with its point towards the lace, bring its point towards you over the thread and down, into its pin-hole. Take the second thread of the pair and wind it round the pin from the outside inwards, then lay it down *outside* the other pair. Lay the other pair over this pair (crossed left over right on the right, twisted right over left on the left) so that the first pair to have twisted round the pin ends up on the outside.

Now work WS with the edge pair, twist both three times and continue as before, adding extra pairs when required (about nine pairs in all).

Adding pairs inside a picot edge
Do this in the same way as when adding into a WS section, i.e. before the edge stitch, but lay the pair backwards over the pillow until after the picot and following edge stitch, when you bring the pair forward into its correct place.

Towards the end of the first scallop, indicated by a central dot in the pattern (which is not used as a pin-hole), calculate your holes to ensure that your workers are at the outside edge for the hole which is level with the central dot. (This is not absolutely vital but ensures a firmer edge.) Now *cross your gimps* to divide the two sections by taking the outside gimp and weaving it over and under alternate threads right across the passives until it reaches the other gimp thread. Take it over and round and back under this gimp, then bring it back, again weaving alternately, which will mean that you are now passing *under* threads you previously passed *over* and vice versa. When

the gimp is back in its original place, draw it up gently against the pull of the other gimp to hold the width between the two edges, not to make a waist of it.

The next section is in *half stitch*. The edges are worked as usual, the gimp pairs are also worked in WS, otherwise the gimp threads would start going across instead of staying down each side. So, after working the edge pair proceed as follows. *Work WS with the gimp pair, twist the worker pair once and work half stitch through all the remaining passives except the last (gimp) pair. Work WS through this pair, twist the workers three times and work the edge as usual*. Continue repeating from * to *.

Adding pairs in a half stitch section
You will probably have added all the pairs you need by the time you reach this section, but I will describe here how to do it for future reference. Please refer also to the instructions in Pattern 4 for how to add a pair in WS braid.

When you reach the edge twist the workers three times and stick the edge pin in front of them. Lay the central loop of a pair of bobbins under the worker bobbins and slip the loop right up to the pin. Draw the new bobbins and threads downwards between the pin you have just stuck and the one next to it, so that the new bobbins hang level with the rest. Lay these bobbins as before just inside the edge gimp thread but immediately twist the second pair in from the edge, right over left, so that the pair is ready to go straight into half stitch. Now make up the edge stitch, stick the pin and continue normally.

The two top central sections are worked in WS and each has a four-pin bud in the centre (instructions in Pattern 4).

Sew out into D when the scalloped section is finished.

Sew in three or four pairs for the zig-zag *purl-pin bars* on to two pin-holes at F. (The instructions are the same for either number and three pairs may be preferable in this rather small space.) Take one of the edge pairs, work it in WS through the other pairs, twist it once and leave it.

Work back in WS through the other pairs with the last pair worked through, twist it once and leave it and use the last pair worked through to work back again. Repeat from * to * for the bar. Make double picots, as described above, at

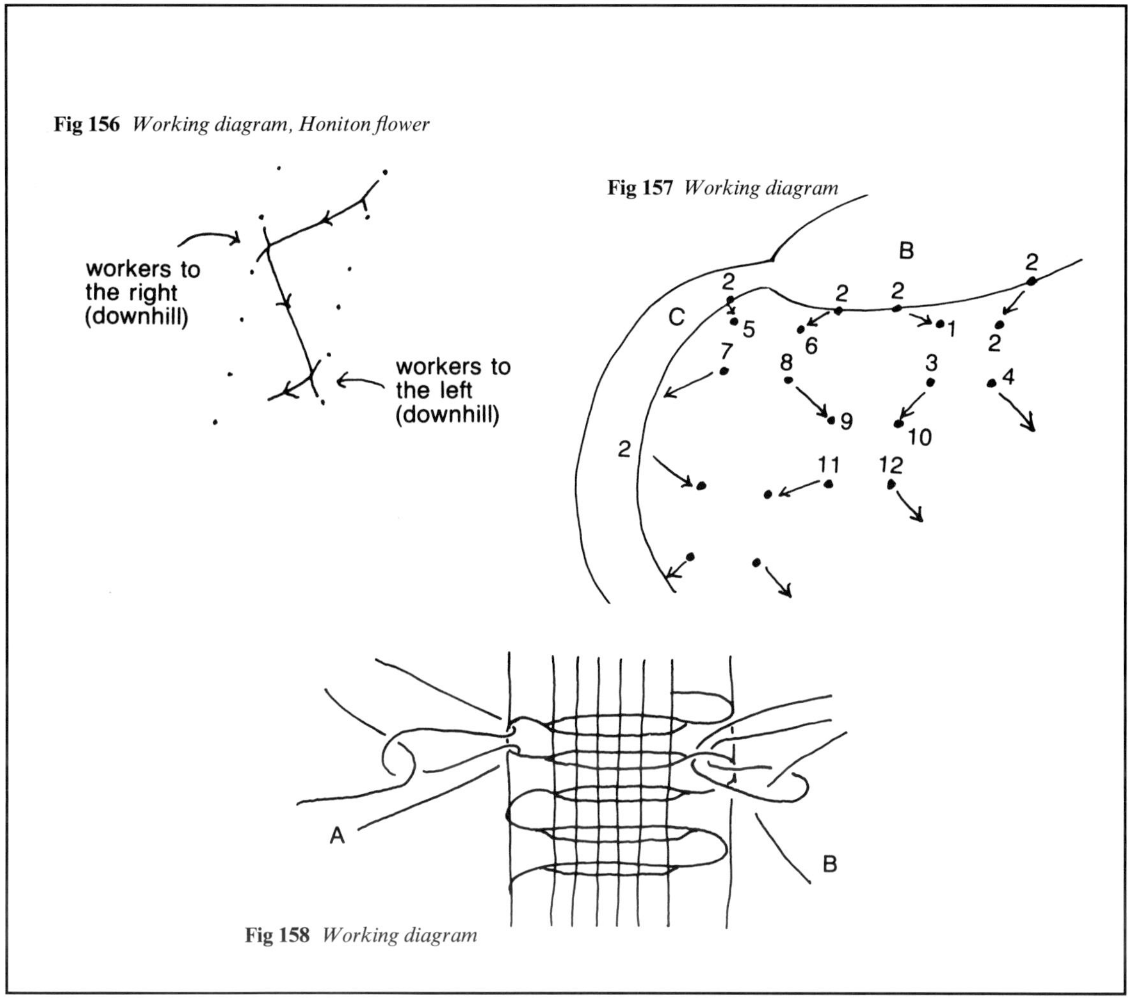

the two pin-holes on each bar (only one on the first and last). When you reach the edge there will be two holes to sew into. If you only used one, the work would tend to distort the pin-hole. Work it so that the workers finish on the downhill side of the group of passives; they will be to the right when your sewing is on the LH side and to the left when your sewing is on the RH side (see Fig 156). Sew the worker pair first into the top (further back) pin-hole of the two, then work the next pair to it through the worker pair and then use this second pair (not the workers) to sew into the second hole. Tie this pair once and use it as the worker pair from now on to continue the bar and picots (purls).

The four-pin filling

At G this is worked as follows (see Fig 157). Sew in two pairs to B section above and to the side of each of the holes marked 1 and 2. *With the two LH pairs work WS, twist three times, and stick pin 1 between them. With the two RH pairs work WS, twist three times, and stick pin 2 between them. With the two centre pairs work WS, twist three times but do not stick a pin*.

Repeat from * to * at holes 3 and 4. This completes one section of the filling. Lay aside these pairs for the moment and sew in two pairs from C section for hole 5 and two from B for hole 6. Always hang on pairs in the same diagonal as the line of working. *If there is not a hole in exactly the right place*, sew into the nearest and ease the

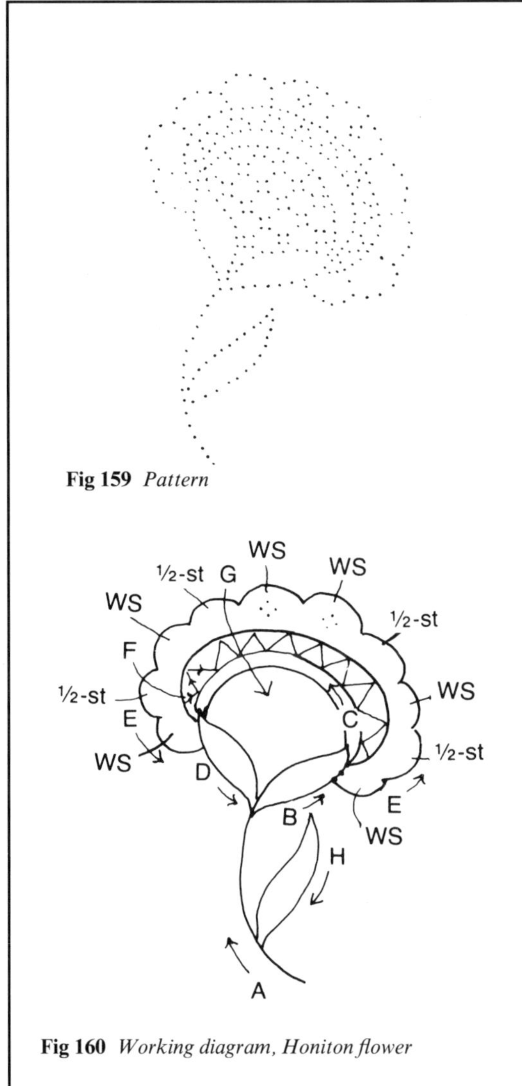

Fig 159 *Pattern*

Fig 160 *Working diagram, Honiton flower*

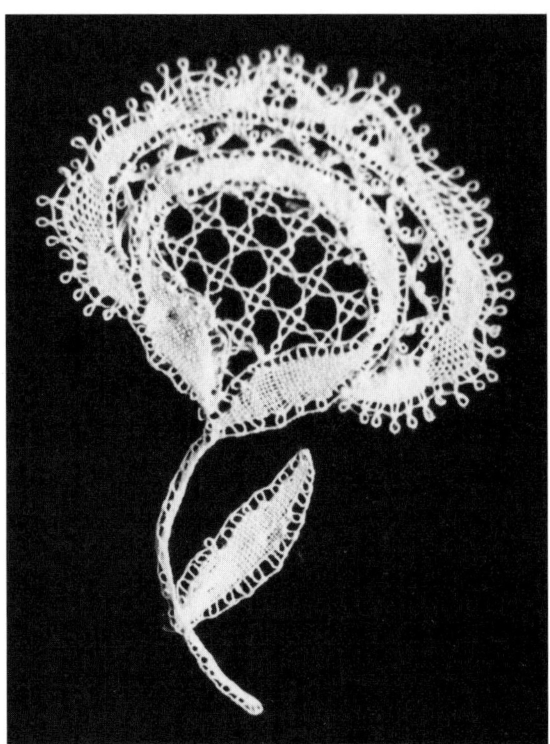

Fig 161 *Finished lace, Honiton flower*

threads into the correct position as you tie a single knot, which should hold them in that place. It is a good idea to tie a single knot when sewing in pairs in any case.

Repeat from * to * twice at holes 5, 6, 7 and 8. The two LH pairs are then sewn out into C while the two RH pairs go to work hole 9. The two LH pairs from holes 3 and 4 work hole 10 and both these latter sets link in the centre, before completing holes 11 and 12 and the following centre link, still repeating from * to *.

Continue thus throughout the filling, adding on and taking out pairs at the edges, as required.

At H, start a leaf with six pairs and add more pairs as required. *Note*: always work inwards from the tip towards a solid section so that the ends, when sewn out and cut off, will be hidden by a solid part of completed lace. When you sew out this leaf, a slightly unusual thing will happen, as your leaf comes up to the 'blind' side of the rib, where there are no pin-holes. You therefore have to do *top sewings* into the two pin-holes in the pattern. For a top sewing you insert your chosen tool, e.g. beading needle (see introduction to this chapter), into the pin-hole but bring it out under the side bar as opposed to the edge cord. Then take the loop through and continue as a normal sewing. Fig 158 shows both types of sewings. (The top sewing is B.)

If your eyes are like mine, you may not be able to see the difference on your actual lace and, in that case, you will need a magnifying glass. The most convenient forms (leaving both hands free) are either the one on a headband like eye-surgeons use or ones that clip on to your spectacles or, best of all, the fluorescent lamp that has a magnifying glass as its centre, which makes this fine work easy.

PATTERN 6   HONITON FUCHSIA

Material

12 pairs (approximately) of
bobbins wound with no. 140 to
180 Brok cotton
and 2 gimp bobbins wound as a pair
with no. 50 sewing cotton

This pattern is designed to be inset into a brush-back or as a bookmark. Brushes of the correct type for mounting lace and clear plastic book-mark covers can be obtained from lace suppliers.

Hang six pairs and a gimp pair on at A and work first to the left. Hang in extra pairs at the second, third, fourth and fifth LH pinholes. Tie the worker pair once after passing through the gimp pair after pins 3 and 4 on the left. Always do this on a bend or curve to keep the passives out into place. Otherwise they will pull in and cause an ugly, enlarged pin-hole. Work the leaf up the LH side (as the work faces you) in WS. When you approach the point of the leaf drop off one or two pairs as the leaf narrows then make a back stitch into the last vein hole. Work the top hole of the leaf, tie the workers once after coming back through the gimp pair inside the edge, then work back up to but not including the inner gimp pair. Take the last passive pair worked through as the new workers out to the edge and back then through the gimp pair and make a stitch with the inner edge pair. Replace the top vein pin and use the inner pair as workers out to the edge as normal. Very gently draw up the inner passives and gimp to make them lie smoothly round the sharp bend. Before the workers return, untwist the three twists in the inner edge pair and weave the gimp thread over and under the threads of this pair so that it hangs down the vein-edge of the passives. You now work in $\frac{1}{2}$st except with the gimp pairs and the edge pair. From now on you do not twist the workers when they arrive at the vein. Merely make a sewing into the appropriate vein hole (twice into one hole if necessary to keep the work straight) then back through the passives to the outside edge.

Work the tiny leaf at B, always working from the tip towards a completed piece of work, so that there is something solid to sew into (and hide the cut-off ends).

Raised work

Work a rib at C, with the holes on the outside of the curve. Continue down the calyx. At the third hole from the end of the calyx add a pair and lay it aside, tying it once to prevent slipping. Do the same at the second hole from the end. Then lay the next passive pair alongside the other two pairs and work to the top hole.

Turn the pillow the other way round and work back towards yourself in $\frac{1}{2}$st over the rib (which will then be raised on the other side). Twist the edge pair on the outside three times and work a normal edge there. Tie the worker pair once when they have worked through the first passive pair inside the edge pair (which is worked in WS). This will hold the work out to the pin and avoid an enlarged pin-hole.

On the inside, work the worker pair through the passive pair which was laid aside and the second pair which was hung on (at the second from top hole). Using the last passive pair worked through as workers, tie these new workers once and work through to the edge and back, this time through the first pair that was laid aside at the third hole from the top. Tie this pair once after being worked through and use it as the new workers to work through to the edge. When it returns and every subsequent time you work through to the rib side, you must make top sewings (instructions in Pattern 5).

Add pairs as the calyx widens and drop them off as it narrows. The narrow section is worked in WS. To add pairs in half stitch see the instructions in Pattern 5. Leave out a pair at the third hole from last and the second hole from last. At the end of the calyx tie the pairs and bunch as usual then use these two pairs to tie back the bunch over the calyx so that no ends show from the right side. Instructions for this are detailed in Pattern 4.

Refer now to Fig 162. The petals D, E, F and G are quite straightforward. For H you will need to increase to 11 pairs at the widest part, where you work the central hole by dividing the passives and using the middle pair as workers to the other edge once the original workers have passed

Fig 162 *Enlarged flower diagram*

Fig 163 *Pattern*

Fig 164 *Working diagram, Honiton fuchsia*

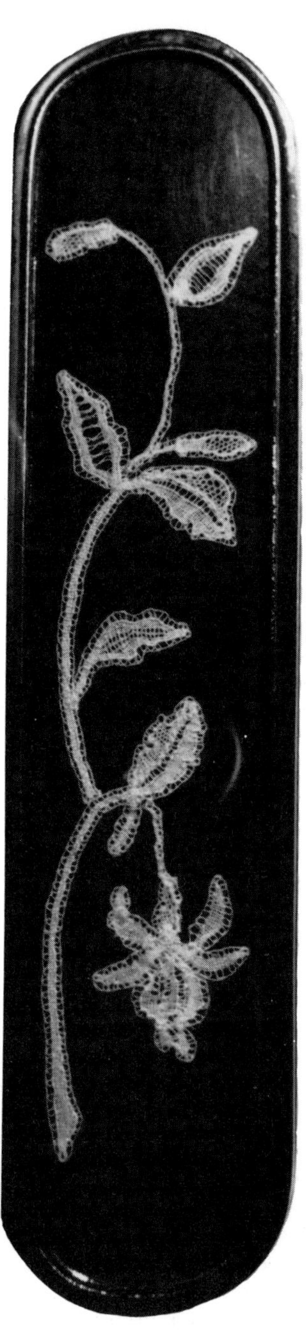

Fig 165 *Lace set into a clothes brush*

144

through them in WS, twist, pin between, WS, at the top hole. Immediately after this top hole work each worker pair through the next passive pair, then twist both pairs on each side to form an edge before working its worker pair to its outside edge. Thus you work an edge both outside and at this central hole, unlike the holes you will come to in the rose in Pattern 7, which are normal snatch-pin holes, without inside edge pairs.

Continue working the sections alphabetically.

Leaf L is a divided leaf, like A.

Leaf M has a *central vein*, made thus. Increase the number of bobbins from the narrow tip. At the top of the vein there should be an edge pair, gimp pair and one passive pair on each side, then an extra passive pair down the centre and the worker pair. You will increase the passives as the leaf widens. Twist the workers once before the central passive pair then work WS with the pair, twist both pairs once and continue through the other pairs as normal.

Leaf N has a *mittens* (or *ladder*) vein, made thus. Work the workers to the middle, twist three times and leave. Take the next pair of passives and work them through to the other side and back, twist them three times. *Work WS with these two worker pairs in the middle and twist both pairs three times. Then the LH pair works out to the LH edge and back and the RH pair works out to the RH edge and back. Twist both pairs three times*.

Repeat from * to *, adding extra pairs as the leaf widens. Towards the base of the leaf, drop one worker pair off in the centre to become a passive pair and continue with the other worker.

O is a rib and a raised bud. Work it like section C, with again the narrow section in WS. When you turn round from the rib and start the $\frac{1}{2}$st, add a gimp thread on the outside and a thin thread to even up the numbers.

P is a bud without raised work but you can make it raised if you wish.

Q is a leaf with a vein made by twisting the workers in the centre, first once then twice then three times from then on until it narrows near the base, when you twist it twice then once, then not at all for the final rows.

PATTERN 7 VALENCIENNES MOSS ROSE

Materials

16 pairs of bobbins wound with no. 180 Brok cotton or finer if you can obtain it

This enchanting rose is adapted from a nineteenth-century Valenciennes pattern. It is not generally realised that old Valenciennes was not a trolly lace but the sectional motifs were linked by a bobbin-made diamond mesh, worked afterwards. Valenciennes lace is very flat, with no gimps, no raised work and the solid parts are all in WS. It is characterised also by the tiny holes all around every motif. The reason for this is that the linking net was much coarser and only sewed into some of the pin-holes, missing many in between. 'True Valenciennes', made only in that town, was sold at a premium and was often considered the most superb of all bobbin laces. It was extremely fine.

Work alphabetically from A to W. You will realise from this that you are going to have to re-wind your bobbins 23 times and do the fiddly sewing out 23 times. This is therefore not a pattern for the faint-hearted.

Hang on seven pairs at the tip of the stem at A. Add one more pair a little later. Finish off where the leaf joins and bend the bunch of threads back, tying it out at the two previous pins (as described in Pattern 4).

Join three pairs on at the pointed base of leaf-stem B then another three pairs at the next hole where the two stems join. Separate the two edge pairs by three twists in the usual way. Work up one side of the leaf, round the tip and down the other side, where the pairs are finished off. The side veins are worked as *windows*, i.e. work to the chosen spot then twist the workers and the pair they have just passed through three times each. Work another stitch then twist that passive three times. On the next row twist the workers only in the same position as before, between the two pairs that were twisted in the previous row. These two rows complete a window.

For the side veins the position of these windows is moved outwards by one pair on each alternate row.

Side leaves (C and D): hang on six pairs,

Fig 166 *Pattern*

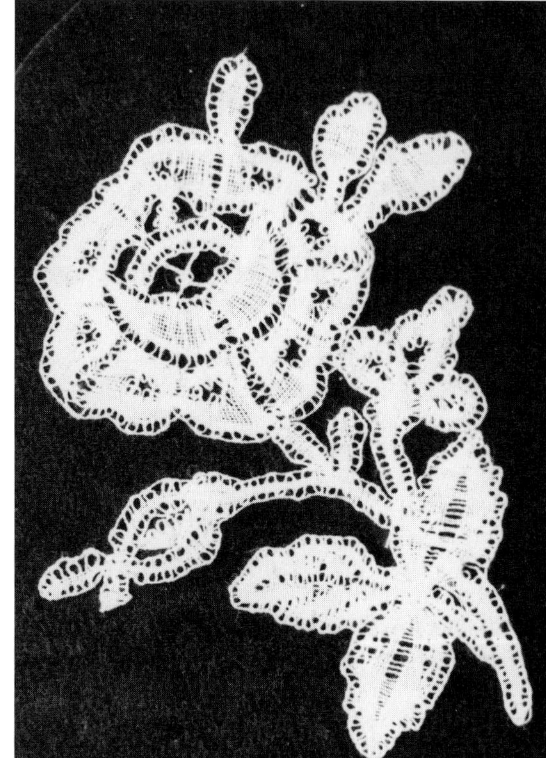

Fig 167 *Finished lace, Valenciennes Moss Rose*

adding new pairs at the fourth, fifth, sixth and seventh holes. Start a centre vein by twisting the workers once at first, then twice, then subsequently three times at the centre of each row. Add more pairs gradually until you have 13 pairs altogether. Decrease as the leaf narrows and finish the vein off by a row of two twists then a row of one twist then several rows of no twists.

Calyx of closed flower bud (E). Hang on eight pairs. Decrease the number when the stem is reached. Hang on five pairs at tip of each side of bud. The crossover is described in Pattern 4. Sew in the five pairs for the centre section so that it is attached at each end. This section does not have edge pairs, the same workers going round each pin and back (see next section). Although not done in the sample, it would give a more mossy effect if the inside edges of the sections F and G which face towards the centre section (H) were also worked with snatch-pins and no edge pair.

Open flower bud. Work the calyx (I) first, then the three circles, one at a time, following the alphabetical order, working the inside of the circles without an edge pair, just a snatch pin, i.e. the worker pair is twisted three times, the pin stuck inside it, then the same worker pair continues back through the passives: five pairs for each of the three circles, then eight pairs for the small top piece.

Work the thorn, N, with five pairs, then leave the stem, T, to work after the rose.

The rose

Start at the tip of the inner LH petal, O, with six pairs, then add a pair at most of the next pinholes until the number seems right. (I used 13 pairs at the widest part.) At the link between the two petals, check that all threads other than the two edge pairs and the worker pair are divisible by four. If not, leave out the odd pair on the previous row. Now twist all these pairs once, then work $\frac{1}{2}$st, pin, $\frac{1}{2}$st between each group of two

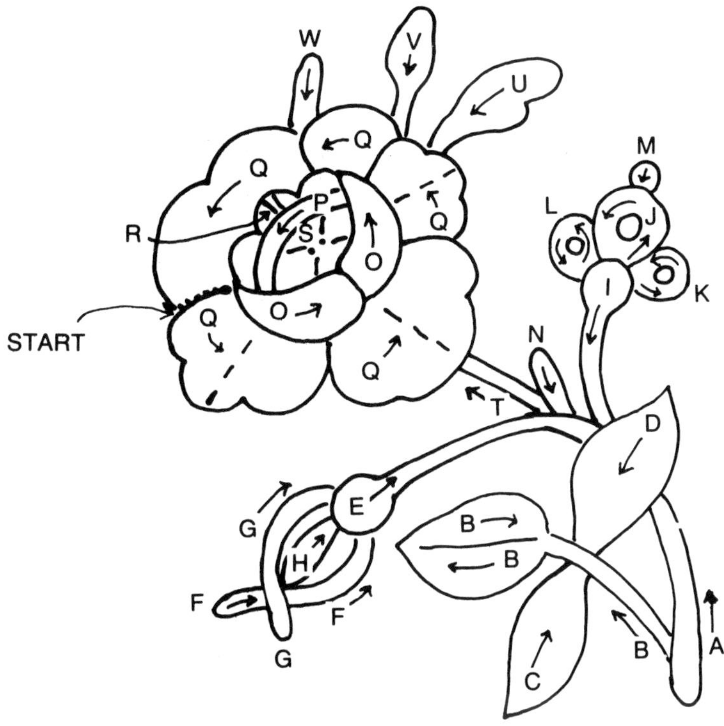

Fig 168 *Working diagram, Valenciennes Moss Rose*

pairs across the row, then continue as before. As the petal narrows, leave out pairs and leave out a pair at each of the two penultimate holes on the right, ready to tie the bunch back after finishing (as in Pattern 4, 'To tie cut-off threads back out of sight').

Work the centre braid P.

The main part of the rose (Q)
Hang two pairs, one splayed outside the other, on each pin across the row at Q and twist each pair twice. Work WS, twist, at each hole. Sew the worker pair into the nearby pin-hole in the inner petal. Add more pairs, as required, until there are about 16 pairs.

The first hole in the petal is a 5-pin hole. First, here are instructions for working a *6-pin hole*. Count the central passives and stick a pin between them to mark the centre. Work the workers towards the centre; if there is an odd extra pair, work through these too. Use the workers and the last pair worked through to

work twist, WS, twist, pin between, WS, twist at the top pin-hole. After this each pair works out to the nearer edge and back three times. On the first two returns the worker pair is twisted three times and a pin stuck inside it, then it returns to the edge. This is known as a *snatch-pin* or *winkie-pin*, the latter from a Dutch word meaning quick. On the third return each worker pair works twist, WS, twist, pin, WS, twist, and then the LH one works out to the edge and becomes the worker pair while the other one remains in the centre as a passive.

Five-pin hole
Where the outside edge is much longer than the inside edge, as in this first petal, omit one inner row to the edge and back so, by working one less pin-hole in the central hole, you work extra rows on the outside, which will give a flat, neat finish.

At the double line of holes, leave the worker pair at the edge then, starting at the inside, *take two pairs, twist each three times, stick a pin between them, then work WS and twist each three times. Stick a pin between them*. Repeat from * to * across the row. Start the next row with the inside passive pair as workers, working across the row in WS to the edge.

At the junctions of petals, indicated by a dot, twist all the passives three times before working the next row.

Work the link bar R with snatch-pins and no edge pairs.

Work the Valenciennes bar and winkie-pin filling at S as follows. Sew in two pairs each side of the centre space, diagonally above the two pin-holes, as indicated in Fig 168. Make a leg consisting of about four half-stitches with each set of two pairs. Stop slightly above the pin-holes. With the second pair from the right work WS to the left through two pairs, twist the workers five times, stick the pin and work back through the other three pairs. Twist the workers five times, stick the other pin and work back through two pairs. Now make legs of the two LH pairs and the two RH pairs and sew them out in a position equivalent to where they were sewn in.

Work the stem T and finally, buds U, V and W.

PATTERN 8   SWALLOW-TAIL BUTTERFLY

Materials

28 pairs (maximum) of bobbins
wound with no. 180 cotton thread
or finest available
and 2 gimp pairs wound with no. 50
sewing cotton

Hang on six pairs at tip of left antenna (A). Work down it in 'ten-stick' rib, with the pin-holes on the outside (left). Work the hole where it joins the body and leave workers there. Hang on six pairs at tip of right antenna (B). Work in rib down it with the pin-holes on the outside (right). Work down to the hole where it joins the body and leave the edge pair and workers to the right of this pin. Work WS, twist three times, with the two middle passive pairs and stick pin between them at C. Bring LH workers through to the centre and leave them there as passives. Leaving out one pair on the left and two pairs on the right, lay the gimp thread over and under alternately through the remaining pairs. Lay back the gimp

threads while you work a row to the left with the workers from the right. Work a normal edge and stick the LH pin then bring down the gimp threads to lie fifth from left (inside this pin) and third from right.

Add pairs each side as the body widens. I used 16 pairs and the gimp pair. **Note** The number of pairs suggested throughout the pattern is only approximate and depends on the size of thread used. Decrease as body narrows then, as it widens again before dividing, add a pair at every pin-hole. Make back stitches at S and T (in Fig 169) or there will be a gap in the centre. After the second visit to S work to the top centre pin-hole (D) through exactly half of the passives (or one less if there is an odd number). Add a gimp pair and an ordinary pair, laying them diagonally (gimp on the right) across the pillow from right back to left front, laying this front pair down the pillow to the right of the passive pair which lies to the right of the laid-down worker pair from S. Work this LH pair of gimp and ordinary passive through first the passive pair to its left and then the worker pair. Temporarily lay the gimp pair to the back of the pillow. Make a WS between the passive and worker pairs and stick centre pin (D) between them. Wind two pairs of bobbins and lay them side by side across pillow from back right to front left, with the RH front pair falling to the right of the two centre pairs which have just worked the stitch. Work this pair in WS through the first pair, twist it three times, then through the second pair and lay it temporarily to the back of the pillow. Work WS between the two centre pairs which did the stitch round the pin. Twist both three times and leave. These will be the edge pairs. The two last pairs added (now laid to the back of the pillow to left and right) will be the workers to pins U and T (to make up the back stitch). Continue as normal with these two worker pairs, twisting them three times and bringing down the new gimp threads into position. Work a little way down on the LH side and leave it. Pin the bobbins down firmly under a cloth so that they are out of the way. Continue now with the RH side.

Decrease as the braid narrows (I went down to eight pairs including the gimp) then rapidly increase again to 13 pairs and the gimp pair. Leave a round hole at M in Fig 170 by using a centre passive as a worker out to the edge of the

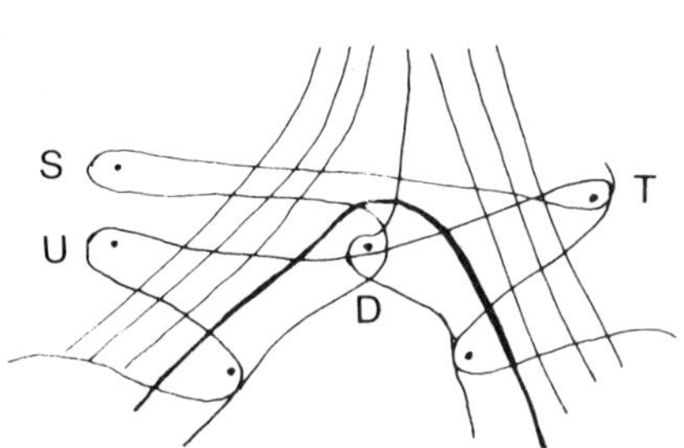

Fig 169 *Working diagram, Swallow-tail Butterfly*

second side after working the top stitch of the circle thus. Worker through passive, twist both pairs twice, pin between, WS again, twist both pairs once, then each continues as a worker pair to its nearer edge and back. For these circle holes use the finest pins possible and twist worker pair only once round the pin, to aim for as clean a line as possible round the circle.

The next hole is a 6-pin bud with only one pin between the first and last pins on the inside and three pins between them on the outside. This will help to turn the corner neatly. To start, find the centre four pairs by counting off from the edges when the workers are about half-way across and

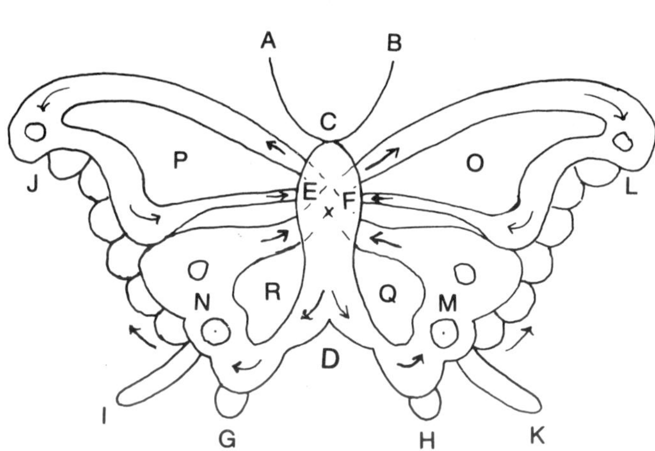

Fig 170 *Working diagram*

Fig 171 *Pattern*

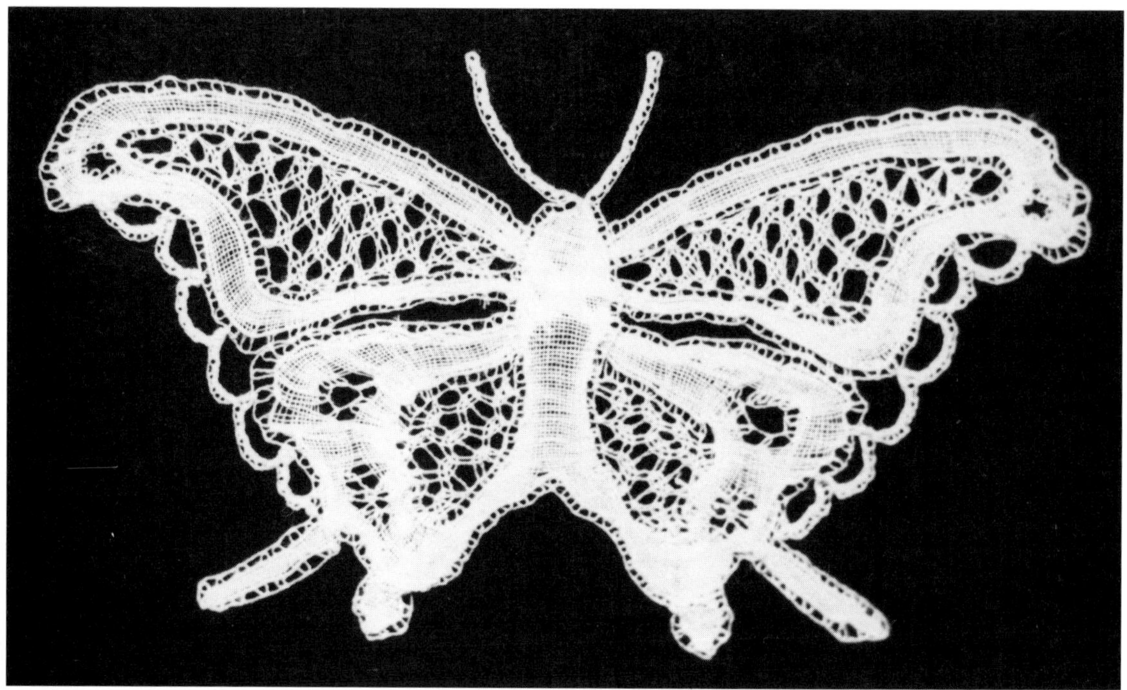

Fig 172 *Finished lace, Swallow-tail Butterfly*

continue, following the instructions in Pattern 4.

When you reach the body, having finished the lower wing, sew in the two edge pairs and the worker pair, cross, bundle and tie, then cross the bunch diagonally to start the upper braid of the upper wing on the other side, (This is at a better angle than the lower braid of the upper wing.) Sew in the two edge pairs and the worker pair to the relevant holes in the body and continue the braid. There are rather too many pairs, so cut off one or two where they cross the body, first tying them three times and leave out one or two pairs near the beginning of the braid. I found eight pairs and the gimp pair were about right.

After working about ½in, leave the pairs fixed down and return to the second half of the body and finish the second lower wing, crossing its pairs similarly over the body to start the other upper wing.

On the upper wings there is a 6-pin bud on the outer point, which again has only one pin between the first and last pins on the inside and three pins between them on the outside.

Sew each side into the body at E and F, having thrown out several pairs at this final length of braid and having added pairs near the point to go round the 6-pin bud. The braid should not be 'starved' as it goes round this bud.

Work the knobs at the bottom, G and H, starting with six pairs and a gimp pair and increasing to nine pairs and a gimp pair. Sew into the braid to finish it off.

Start the first tail at I with five pairs and gimp pair. Add pairs at the next two holes to make seven pairs and the gimp pair. When you reach the body the workers should be on the right. Sew out the workers and edge pair on the right and lay them aside to work the scalloped edge to J. Sew in, tie, bunch and cut off the remaining pairs.

Rolled work

Now turn to the *scalloped edge*. Sew in another pair to the same hole as the two pairs left in, then sew in another three pairs to the next hole (six pairs altogether). Work ten-stick rib with the holes on the outside. At W in Fig 173 take the workers from the edge to the inside, sew them into W and tie twice. Turn the pillow round through 180 degrees and lift the bunch of threads so that the bobbins are towards you.

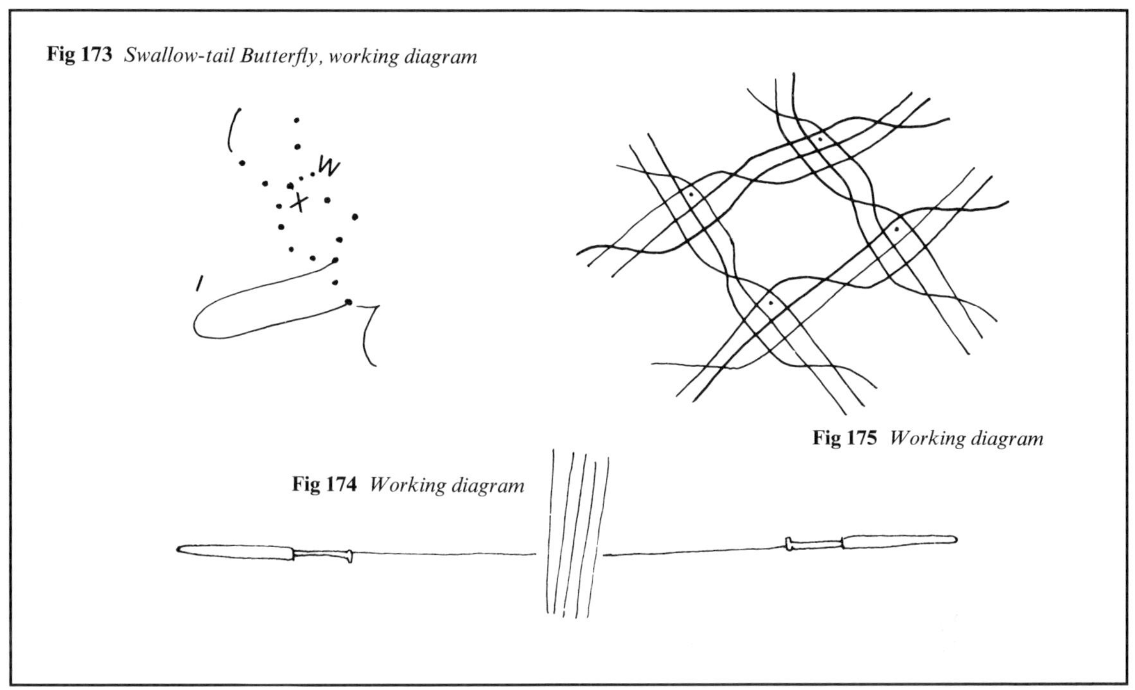

Fig 173 *Swallow-tail Butterfly, working diagram*

Fig 174 *Working diagram*

Fig 175 *Working diagram*

The worker pair should still be on the left of the bunch. Slide the RH thread of this pair under all the other threads so that the bunch is between the two worker threads, as in Fig 174. Tie the workers twice round the bunch then take the LH tied thread under the bunch to lie inside its partner on the right of the bunch. Holding the pair together, roll it round the bunch, over to the left, under to the right, three times, then sew in this pair to the next hole but one, at X in Fig 173 with the bunch of threads to the left. Tie these workers twice, straighten out the threads in the bunch and continue as before with the sewn pair as workers, first untwisting the three twists in the edge pair on the right of the bunch, then work a WS with it, twist both pairs three times and continue across with the workers as usual. Continue the scalloped edge to J, where you sew out, tie and bunch and cut off as usual.

Work the second tail K and the scalloped edge to L to correspond. You will need to reverse the instructions for the rolled work as you are going in the opposite direction.

The butterfly is now complete apart from fillings for the larger holes that you have left. You may choose your own fillings if you wish but the two main fillings that I have chosen are revivals of fillings used in the exquisitely fine and beautiful Flemish lace of the seventeenth century. For the little round holes near the tail I found the simple torchon spider the most effective filling.

Holes M and N, 8-legged spider. Hang on one pair at each of the top four pin-holes. Twist the legs three times then work WS with the centre pairs, the LH pairs, the RH pairs, then the centre pairs. Stick a pin between them, then repeat the above four stitches. Twist the legs three times and sew them out into the remaining four pin-holes.

Chain-mail filling (see Fig 175)
Fifteen pairs maximum. Start with RH point of RH top wing. Turn it to the top of the pillow and hang three pairs on the right and three pairs on the left. Twist all pairs once and work pattern thus:
Take LH pair through two pairs to the right in WS, twist.
Take RH pair through two pairs to the left in WS, twist.
Take third pair from the right through three

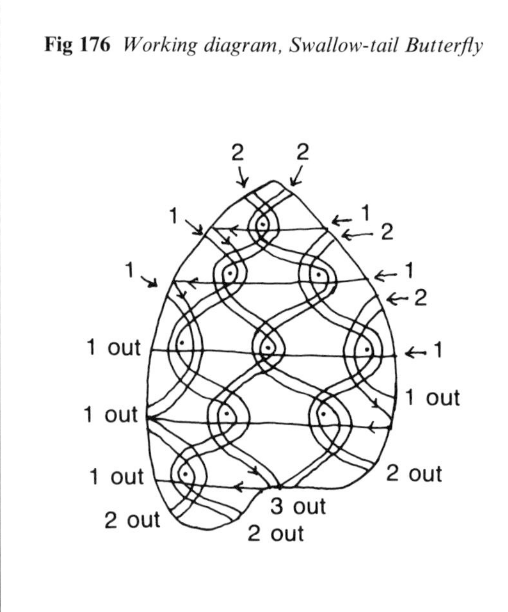

Fig 176 *Working diagram, Swallow-tail Butterfly*

pairs to the left in WS, twist.

Place finest available pin with three pairs to the right and three pairs to left.

Take second pair from right through three pairs to the left in WS, twist.

Take RH pair through three pairs to the left in WS, twist.

Take third pair from left through two pairs to the left in WS, twist.

Take third pair from right through two pairs to the right in WS, twist.

This forms one repeat of the pattern and, following it, the three RH pairs follow the diagonal line marked and are sewn into the edge and then return and the three LH pairs are sewn into the LH edge and then return. As the wing broadens out you will get into a rhythm of taking three pairs to the right and three pairs to the left to the pinholes diagonally below on the right and the left. You will also, of course, sew out pairs as they arrive at the side, bringing them back on the other diagonal.

When you finally sew out pairs ready to cut them off, it is best to do a top sewing instead of the normal one, because then the cut off ends lie over (and eventually *under* when the work is turned over) the solid parts of lace so that they do not show. In a normal sewing, the cut off ends tend to show through the open-work edge of the braid.

Brabant spider filling (see Fig 176)
Thirteen pairs maximum. Start at top LH point of RH lower wing by hanging on two pairs to the left and two pairs to the right, then one pair at the next hole to the right, as in Fig 175. Twist all five pairs twice and work the spider thus:
WS, twist, with centre pairs.
WS, twist, with LH pairs.
WS, twist, with RH pairs.
WS (no twist) with centre pairs and stick a fine pin between.
Draw pairs up gently.
Bring a single pair from either side through the pairs thus:
WS, twist, with first pair.
WS with second pair.
WS with third pair then twist the worker pair once.
WS, twist, with fourth pair.
The single pair is then either sewn out, as here, or it continues to the next spider, as in the next row. Where there are two or more spiders alongside each other, twist the travelling pair about four times in the space before working with the travelling pair to the edge.
Continue the spider with the remaining four pairs thus:
WS, twist, with centre pairs.
WS, twist, with LH pairs.
WS, twist, with RH pairs.
WS, twist, with centre pairs.
Twist all pairs once more.

Figure 176 shows exactly the path of all the pairs and where pairs are added in and taken out or where they are sewn into the edge then return immediately into the work.

Again finish off with top sewings and your butterfly is complete.

Take out the pins very carefully.

Note I guess that the original Flemish lace-makers worked these fillings free-hand without pin-holes or markings. However, I have marked both the holes and the lines to help achieve a more perfect result than could otherwise be obtained without a great deal of practice. I like to remove the pins as soon as possible so that the pin-holes in the work do not show.

Further Reading

Atkinson, Judith, *Pattern Design for Torchon Lace*, B. T. Batsford

Collier, Ann, *Creative Design in Bobbin Lace*, B.T. Batsford

Collier, Ann, *New Designs in Bobbin Lace*, B.T. Batsford

Cook, Bridget, *Introduction to Bobbin Lace Patterns*, B.T. Batsford

Cook, Bridget, and Stott, Geraldine, *Introduction to Bobbin Lace Stitches*, B. T. Batsford

Dye, Gilian, *Beginning Bobbin Lace*, Dryad Press

Dye, Gilian, *Bobbin Lace Braid*, B. T. Batsford

Earnshaw, Pat, *Bobbin and Needle Laces: Identification and Care*, B. T. Batsford

Hardeman, Henk, *Bucks Point Lace Patterns*, B. T. Batsford

Hardeman, Henk, *Torchon Lace Patterns*, B. T. Batsford

Harris, Valerie, *The Lavendon Collection of Bobbin Lace Patterns*, Dryad Press

Lewis, Robin, *101 Torchon Patterns*, Dryad Press, 1987

Maidment, Margaret, *Manual of Handmade Bobbin Lacework*, B. T. Batsford

Nottingham, Pamela, *Batsford Lace Pattern Pack: Bucks Point*, B. T. Batsford

Nottingham, Pamela, *Bobbin Lace Making*, B. T. Batsford

Nottingham, Pamela, *Bucks Point Lace Making*, B. T. Batsford

Nottingham, *Technique of Bobbin Lace*, B. T. Batsford

Nottingham, *Technique of Bucks Point Lace*, B. T. Batsford

Nottingham, *Technique of Torchon Lace*, B. T. Batsford

Stillwell, Alexandra, *Drafting Torchon Lace Patterns*, Dryad Press

Stott, Geraldine, and Cook, Bridget, *100 Traditional Bobbin Lace Patterns*, B. T. Batsford

Stott, Geraldine, and Cook, Bridget, *Book of Bobbin Lace Stitches*, B. T. Batsford

Stott, Geraldine, *Visual Introduction to Bucks Point Lace*, B. T. Batsford

Sutton, Edna, *Bruges Flower Lace*, Dryad Press

Sutton, Edna, *Designing for Bruges Flower Lace*, Dryad Press, 1987

Voysey, Cynthia, *Bobbin Lace in Photographs*, B. T. Batsford

Withers, Jean, *Mounting and Using Lace*, Dryad Press

Zwaal-Lint, Tiny, *Bobbin Lace Patterns*, B. T. Batsford

Zwaal-Lint, *New Bobbin Lace Patterns*, B. T. Batsford

Suppliers

U. K.

Alby Lace Centre
Cromer Road
Alby
Norwich
Norfolk

T. Brown
Woodside
Greenlands Lane
Prestwood
Great Mussenden
Bucks

The English Lace School
Honiton Court
Rockbeare
Nr Exeter
Devon

John and Jennifer Ford
5 Squirrels Hollow
Boney Way
Walsall

Frank Herring and Sons
27 High West Street
Dorchester
Dorset DT1 1UP

Honiton Lace Shop
44 High Street
Honiton
Devon

D. J. Hornsby
149 High Street
Burton Latimer
Kettering
Northants

Capt. J. R. Howell
19 Summerwood Lane
Halsall
Nr. Ormskirk
Lancs L39 8RG

The Lace Guild
c/o The Hollies
53 Audnam
Stourbridge
West Midlands
DY8 4AE

Mace and Nairn
89 Crane Street
Salisbury
Wilts SP1 2PY

Newham Lace Equipment
15 Marlow Close
Basingstoke
Hants

B. Phillips
Pantglas
Cellan
Lampeter
Dyfed

Sebalace
Waterloo Mill
Howden Road
Silsden
Nr Keighley
W. Yorks BD20 0HA

A. Sells
Lane Cove
49 Pedley Lane
Clifton
Shefford
Beds

D. H. Shaw
47 Zamor Crescent
Thurscroft
Rotherham
South Yorks

Shireburn Lace
Finkle Court
Finkle
Sherburn in Elmet
Shropshire

C. and D. Springett
21 Hillmorton Road
Rugby
Warwicks CV22 5BE

Enid Taylor
Valley House Craft Studio
Ruston
Scarborough
N. Yorks YO13 9QE

George White
Delaheys Cottage
Thistle Hill
Knaresborough
N. Yorks

U S A

Frederick J. Fawcett
Glimakra Looms 'n' Yarns
1304 Scott Street
Petaluma
CA 94952

Happy Hands
3007 S. W. Marshall
Pendleton
OR 97108

Lace Place de Belgique
800 S.W. 17th Street
Booa Raton
FL 33432

Lacis
2990 Adeline Street
Berkeley
CA 94703

Robin & Russ Handweavers
533 N. Adams Street
McMinnville
OR 97128

Robin's Bobbins
RT. 7. Box 1736
Mineral Bluff
GA 30559

Van Scriver Bobbin Lace Supply
310 Aurora Street
Ithica
NY 14850

The World in Stitches
82 South Street
Milford
NH 03055